A Just Cause

A JUST CAUSE

The
Impeachment
and Removal of
Governor
Rod Blagojevich

Bernard H. Sieracki
Foreword by Jim Edgar

Southern Illinois University Press
Carbondale

19 18 17 16   4 3 2 1

Jacket illustration: Governor Rod Blagojevich. Photo by Jay Barnard.
Courtesy of the Illinois Senate Republican Caucus.

Library of Congress Cataloging-in-Publication Data
Sieracki, Bernard H.
A just cause : the impeachment and removal of Governor Rod
Blagojevich / Bernard H. Sieracki ; foreword by Jim Edgar.
 pages cm
Includes bibliographical references and index.
ISBN 978-0-8093-3463-6 (cloth : alk. paper) — ISBN 0-8093-3463-
1 (cloth : alk. paper) — ISBN 978-0-8093-3464-3 (e-book) — ISBN
0-8093-3464-X (e-book) 1. Blagojevich, Rod R., 1956– Trials, litigation,
etc. 2. Illinois—Politics and government—1951– 3. Governors—
Illinois—Biography. 4. Political corruption—Illinois. I. Title.
F546.4.B55S55 2015
977.3'044092—dc23
[B]   2015013989

Printed on recycled paper. ♻

The paper used in this publication meets the minimum requirements of
American National Standard for Information Sciences—Permanence of
Paper for Printed Library Materials, ANSI Z39.48-1992. ∞

To Mary Alice, whose support makes everything possible

Contents

Foreword

Jim Edgar

Even in a state stained through the years by corruption at every level of government, this profound moment claimed a special place in the annals of wrongdoing. Three governors had been imprisoned soon after leaving office, two for misdeeds while serving as Illinois' chief executive. But none had been impeached until the General Assembly, like a team of surgeons removing a cancer, urgently but methodically excised Rod Blagojevich, the state's fortieth governor.

The unanimous votes by the Illinois senate on January 29, 2009, to uphold abuse-of-power charges brought by the house and to bar Blagojevich from ever again holding elective office came less than eight weeks after Illinoisans were jolted by news bulletins that FBI agents had arrested, handcuffed, and booked their governor. There had been rumors of wrongdoing almost from the time he took his oath in January 2003. Various media and government watchdogs had uncovered suspicious activity by Blagojevich and his cronies even before he won reelection in 2006 by a comfortable margin. But the drama of his arrest in the predawn hours of December 9, 2008, both shocked and focused the Illinois political establishment, especially the leadership of the legislature.

In a real sense, that most shameful day in Illinois political history led to some of the most heartening activity we had seen from the General

Assembly in recent years. The arrest brought to a head the turbulent six years of Blagojevich's erratic and arrogant stewardship. It became obvious that the legislature, criticized for avoiding the tough decisions necessary to right the state's fiscal course, needed to act quickly to begin rebuilding public trust in state government as well as the state government itself. From a political standpoint, Democratic legislative leaders had the most at stake; Blagojevich shared their party label, and almost all of them had backed him for reelection. However, after years of partisan wrangling, leaders of both parties largely cooperated to ensure that the impeachment was handled responsibly, resolutely, and expeditiously, working through the Christmas holidays to get the job done. In doing so, they reaffirmed that public officials must exercise their power with restraint and integrity.

What captured the most attention from the public and the majority of reporters was Blagojevich's unethical and ultimately illegal maneuvering to benefit personally and politically from his power to appoint a US senator from Illinois to succeed the newly elected president Obama. However, lawmakers also appropriately held Blagojevich accountable for defying state and federal laws while issuing state contracts and spending hundreds of millions of tax dollars without General Assembly authorization.

In this important book, Bernard H. Sieracki painstakingly documents the fashioning of the charges against Blagojevich and the strategy for pressing them. Readers of *A Just Cause: The Impeachment and Removal of Governor Rod Blagojevich* will benefit from the numerous interviews he conducted with those intimately involved in the process, including the legislative leaders and the chief prosecutor, David Ellis, who is now an appellate court judge. As a professor and lobbyist, Bernie brought academic rigor, as well as state house savvy and access, to this endeavor.

In addition to his interviews, Bernie reviewed countless newspaper reports and public records. His solid research reassures us that his observations and analysis are fact based and worthy of consideration by the readers of today and historians of tomorrow.

Governors in the fifty states have rarely been impeached. It happened— and only once—in Illinois. That makes this impressive effort by Bernie Sieracki especially meaningful.

A Just Cause

Prologue

On Tuesday, December 9, 2008, a gray dawn arrived over Illinois, bringing an intermittent rain and a chill in the air. It was one of those damp, early winter days when the struggle between fall and winter seems finally resolved, and people go on with a sense of acceptance. There was nothing special about the dawning of this day, but that would rapidly change. In the early morning hours an FBI arrest team arrived at the Chicago home of Governor Rod Blagojevich and took him quickly into custody. The arrest was conducted like a raid. The governor was not given advance warning or the courtesy of being able to turn himself in; rather, he was snatched in the night like a common criminal. Wearing a jogging suit and handcuffs, the stunned governor was photographed being led away by federal agents. Word of the governor's arrest quickly spread throughout the state and began a political crisis that would grip Illinois for the next seven weeks and three days.

Prologue

With helicopters hovering overhead, broadcasting events on live television, news crews followed the caravan of police and federal vehicles transporting the governor through the streets of Chicago, first to a federal lockup facility on the city's near west side and then downtown to federal court. People were mesmerized by the chaotic scene playing out before them. Veteran reporters who rushed to cover the story could not believe what was happening.

The six years of the Blagojevich administration resulted in a steady stream of indictments and convictions of those close to the governor, exposed mismanagement and possible criminal activity within his administration, and fueled rumors of corruption and abuse by the governor. The Blagojevich administration was in constant conflict with the legislature, which frustrated the legislators and greatly dissatisfied the public. The governor's poor relationship with the legislators began when he first took office in 2003, the first Democrat to take the oath of office of Illinois governor since Dan Walker in 1973. In 2003 the Democrats had won the majority in both the state house and senate, and many anticipated being able to control the policy agenda. Instead, it marked the beginning of a political civil war.

The Blagojevich administration descended on Springfield with the promise of change from his predecessor, George Ryan. Ryan, who was under indictment, was tried in 2005 and found guilty of racketeering, conspiracy, and fraud. He was sentenced to six and a half years in prison. Under the Blagojevich administration, governance certainly *did* change, but not the way most anticipated. Blagojevich quickly sought to consolidate his power by controlling the hiring of staff and consultants and engineering decisions regarding state contracts in agencies under the executive branch. He consolidated facilities management, internal auditing, legal functions, and leasing decisions under the Department of Central Management Services (CMS), where his office could oversee who would be chosen to receive leases for state facilities and contracts.[1]

Blagojevich delegated the power to appoint people to state jobs and positions on state boards to people outside of state government—his political confidants and fund-raisers. There are few secrets in Springfield, and the obtrusive methods and audacity of the governor's intimates in raising campaign cash and kickbacks for themselves did not go unnoticed. Audits conducted by the state auditor general, released in 2005 and 2006, uncovered gross incompetence and possible pay-to-play activity. In late 2003, the *first* year of the Blagojevich administration, the FBI and the US attorney began investigating those around the new governor.[2] The office of governor is an integral part of state government, and for practitioners of the political process, lobbyists, those with special interests, legislators, and legislative staff, government is a business. Those who engaged in the political machinations of Illinois government took note, but like the citizens of Pompeii, they chose to go on with their daily affairs, ignoring the ominous rumblings of Vesuvius.

In retrospect, the six years of the Blagojevich administration defined a time of moral disengagement. Initially, some legislators naïvely facilitated Blagojevich's administrative antics, but by 2007, the first year into his second term, the governor's relationships with most members of the legislature had deteriorated significantly. His remarks concerning the legislators became increasingly hostile, referring to the legislators as "drunken sailors" and taunting the house Speaker, Michael Madigan.

By the end of the 2007 session, the governor had failed to reach an agreement with the legislature concerning the state's budget. That summer marked the nadir of the relationship between the governor and the legislature. The Illinois Constitution authorizes the governor to call special sessions without pre-specified conditions by issuing a proclamation and stating the purpose of the session.[3] Throughout July and August 2007, Blagojevich issued proclamation after proclamation, repeatedly calling the legislature back into special sessions. Negotiations on budget matters between legislative leaders and the governor stalled, and consequently there were no policy proposals to debate and act on. The legislators could do nothing but travel to Springfield, commence the special session, and then adjourn. As soon as the legislature adjourned, the governor called another special session. It became a schoolyard game of one-upmanship, and the legislators were furious. They were away from their families, wasting their time, forced to cancel district events or vacation plans, and it was costing taxpayers thousands of dollars a day to have them in Springfield. Blagojevich enjoyed it. He stayed at his Chicago home, went jogging or to his campaign office, and rarely ventured to Springfield. During that frustrating summer, serious discussions took place among the legislators as they considered their options to solve the never-ending problems created by the governor. "We had to do something about this," State Representative John Fritchey recalled.[4]

Impeachment and a trial to remove Blagojevich were made problematic by the nebulous criteria for impeachment and removal contained in the 1970 Illinois Constitution: "the existence of cause for impeachment."[5]

Definite criteria for impeachment and removal had not been a major concern of the delegates who drafted the Constitution. The Illinois legislature had not employed the provision for 137 years, and there had been little discussion. John Marshall Law School professors Ron Smith, a delegate to the 1970 Constitutional Convention, and Ann Lousin, who served as a staff lawyer to the convention, both recalled that impeachment was not addressed as a major subject.[6] It also had not been an important topic for the delegates to the 1869–70 convention or the 1862 convention (which was never ratified) or during the deliberations of the 1847 convention.[7]

It is important to put Illinois' absence of an extended debate concerning impeachment into a historical context. The subject of impeachment was a central concern to the federal delegates who met in Philadelphia in 1787. They were men acting in their own time, who sought to reject England's heritage of monarchy and to establish a republican system of government that ensured a separation of powers as well as a balance of powers. They were well aware of potential abuses by the executive, but they also were very concerned with the actions of factions and the passions of majorities.[8]

The development of Illinois' constitutions did not follow the national narrative. The state did not have the kind of agonizing debates over impeachment and removal of the chief executive that took place during the drafting of the federal constitution. Illinois' constitutions were developed under different circumstances. The authors of its first constitution in 1818 were primarily concerned with Illinois becoming a state and drafting a constitution that would be approved by Congress. They spent little time struggling with republican ideals. Illinois became a Jacksonian state and was populated by men on the make. The communication revolution had begun, and the three subsequent constitutions drafted in the nineteenth century were undertaken in response to evolving economic, political, and technological events.[9] The subject of impeachment became less and less a concern, and in 1970 impeachment and removal became a prerogative of the legislature.

Despite the absence of definitions or standards, impeachment is a path that has been seldom traveled in Illinois; the legislature has shown great restraint in calling for impeachment. Before Blagojevich, the Illinois house held impeachment investigations only twice: in 1833, when Supreme Court justice Theophilus Smith was accused of selling public offices and other misconducts, and in 1997, when another Supreme Court justice, James D. Heiple, was investigated by the house for misconduct associated with traffic stops and disregarding police instructions on multiple occasions. Smith was impeached by the house and tried by the senate. His defense team included future Illinois governor Thomas Ford, future US senator and Supreme Court justice Sidney Breese, and future US senator Richard Young. The trial was held at downstate Vandalia in January, and several senate members failed to attend the trial. The majority of those present voted to convict on most of the charges, but they failed to reach the constitutional majority of two-thirds. Smith stayed on the bench until 1842.[10] Heiple was not impeached and left office when his term expired, having agreed not to seek reelection.

The arrest of Rod Blagojevich in 2008 and the criminal allegations that followed ignited a series of events that resulted in the most consequential action the state legislature has ever taken. For the first time in Illinois history, the legislature, exercising its constitutional authority, impeached, tried, and removed a governor from office. The story of the impeachment and removal of Rod Blagojevich is a story of the workings of the legislative process, but it is also the story of the people involved, the legislators and legislative staff and their decisions and experiences. Not one of these people awoke on the morning of December 9 with any idea that their actions in the coming weeks would earn a place of significance in Illinois history. They are now a part of that history.

Chapter 1

The Crisis
Erupts

For the Chicago media, the news of the arrest was like a fire bell in the night. Reporters rushed to find out what was happening, where the governor was, and where he was going. Was he being processed at a federal facility? When was he going to be taken to federal court? What did the arrest warrant allege? What was going on at the State of Illinois Building? The questions were endless. Most radio and television station newsrooms had heard of the arrest by monitoring the police radios. They scrambled resources and were soon broadcasting live from the field.

Many reporters had not yet arrived at work. Paul Meincke, a seasoned political reporter for Chicago television station WLS, was in the shower when his wife called out that the governor had been arrested. He quickly finished getting ready and rushed downtown. Meincke believed that the federal agents arrested Blagojevich the way they did to shock him and perhaps prompt him to start talking.[1] Andrew Porte, managing editor for WLS news, was not surprised that the governor had been arrested. In the days leading up to the arrest, there had been a steady drumbeat of revelations concerning a federal investigation and wiretapping of Blagojevich's phones. But Porte was surprised at the way the governor had been arrested—whisked from his home in the early morning hours, with no advance notice and no time to prepare.[2]

Chuck Goudie, also a veteran reporter for WLS television, rushed to federal court and was waiting when the governor arrived. Although the governor was escorted by deputy US marshals, "he might as well have been in the company of political handlers, because he immediately began working the room, glad-handing with court staff, waving to spectators as he would at a rally," Goudie recalled. "It might have been the first time a criminal defendant ever used such an occasion as a campaign stop." Goudie asked himself, "Is he already looking for jury votes?" For Goudie the scene was paradoxical, with this man who thought he should be president of the United States standing under the American eagle inscribed on the wall overlooking the judge's bench.[3] Julie Unruh, a reporter for WGN television, was also in the federal courtroom, and her reaction was similar to Goudie's. Here was Blagojevich, as cocky as ever, smiling, shaking hands, seemingly oblivious to the seriousness of what was happening to him. For Unruh, a veteran reporter of political events, the scene was dreamlike, and she felt almost detached from the reality being played out before her.[4]

For members of the legislature and legislative staff, the startling news of the governor's arrest remains a frozen moment. Jim Durkin, a Republican state representative from a district that includes the western suburbs of Chicago, was just waking up. "I was groggy, just getting the cobwebs out," he recalled. His wife, Celeste, called out from another room, "Come in here—you have to see this!" As the ten-year veteran of the Illinois house watched the scene unfolding on Chicago television, it seemed surreal. The events of that Tuesday morning were unforgettable, and for Durkin the incident seemed comparable to the death of Chicago mayor Richard J. Daley, the explosion of the Challenger, or the terrorist attack on September 11, 2001. "I was watching the governor of Illinois being led out of the federal lockup in a blue jumpsuit, in handcuffs," he expressed with amazement. "This was the governor."[5] But the coming eight weeks would prove to be even more amazing.

Raised in a family of eight boys in Chicago and its western suburbs, the forty-six-year-old Durkin had followed a career trajectory that was familiar to many from the city's ethnic Irish community. His father was an accountant whose clients included Chicago-area labor unions. Many of his relatives were Chicago police officers, and he was especially influenced by his uncle, Jim Keating, who was chief of detectives for the Chicago Police Department. Durkin wanted to be a police officer and majored in criminology at Illinois State University. But after graduating, he was influenced by his brothers Tom and Kevin, both attorneys and county prosecutors, to go on to law school. After law school, he worked for the state's attorney general and later as a prosecutor in the narcotics and felony trial units of the Cook County State's Attorney's Office.

The Durkin family, many of whom were Chicago police officers or had ties to labor unions, were Democrats. But national events in the late 1980s, the hostage crises, and dissatisfaction with President Jimmy Carter prompted Jim Durkin to become aligned with the Republican Party. In 1995 Judy Baar Topinka, the Republican senator from the Twenty-Second Senate District, was elected state treasurer. Tom Walsh, the state representative from the house 44th District, encompassed by the Twenty-Second Senate District, was moved to the Illinois senate. Jim Durkin was chosen by local Republicans to fill the house vacancy created by Walsh's transition. Durkin left the house in 2002, but after an unsuccessful run for the US Senate, he returned in 2006. One of his earliest conversations the morning of the governor's arrest was with Republican leader Tom Cross. For Durkin there was no other option but an impeachment investigation. "We have to do something about this," he thought.[6]

In Marengo, a small city northwest of Chicago and just a few miles from the Wisconsin border, Jack Franks was working in his home office. A Democrat from a rock-ribbed Republican county, Franks had served in the Illinois house since 1998. Franks was informed of politics for much of his life and was active in McHenry County Democratic organizations. After receiving a bachelor's degree from the University of Wisconsin and a general studies degree from the London School of Economics, he had gone on to earn a law degree from American University. Franks also studied abroad, first in Brazil, where he learned Portuguese, and while in law school he attended Beijing University for a semester. After his studies, he returned to Marengo and practiced law. In 1998, disenchanted with single-party dominance in McHenry County, he decided to run for state representative. In a year when Republican George Ryan won the race for governor, carrying 76 percent of the vote in McHenry County, the popular Jack Franks defeated his Republican opponent. Now married and the father of two sons, Franks lived on the family farm where he was raised.

The morning of the arrest Franks was anticipating a busy day, with a new staff person scheduled to start work and a fund-raiser that evening in Chicago, when he received a call from his friend Steve Kling, who told him to turn on the television. Franks had a personal interest in what was displayed on his screen, and he was not surprised. He was intimately aware of the administrative antics of the Blagojevich administration. Franks was the chairman of the house State Government Administration Committee and over the years had held hearings on several questionable actions by the administration. In 2007 the committee, in response to an audit conducted by the Illinois auditor general, held hearings concerning the administration's purchase of flu vaccines and prescription drugs from a foreign country (the latter through the governor's I-SaveRx program). It is illegal to import drugs from a foreign country. Franks was an outspoken critic of the governor and had been urging the Speaker to form a committee to investigate impeaching Blagojevich for almost a year. The house leadership demurred; impeachment was an unprecedented step. With the governor's arrest, Franks's request had been justified. He did not hide his emotions; "I was happy he was arrested," he said. Now impeachment could go forward. He called Speaker Michael Madigan and told him that only the formation of an investigative committee would satisfy him.[7]

Like many legislators that morning, John Fritchey also received a telephone call informing him of the arrest. Fritchey represented the same legislative district that Rod Blagojevich represented when he had served in the Illinois house. An attorney, Fritchey came to politics by a different route than most Chicago politicians. He was born of modest means on a military base in Louisiana. His father was an enlisted man in the US Air Force, and his mother was a Moroccan immigrant. Moving to Chicago, Fritchey saw a chance for advancement. With the help of scholarships, he attended college and law school. Fritchey had a keen interest in government and became involved in Chicago ward politics. He was able to network with the power brokers of the city's north wards, and when Rod Blagojevich decided to move from the Illinois house to congress, Fritchey told Thirty-Third Ward alderman Dick Mell that he wanted to run for the Illinois house. He received the backing of Mell and the committeemen and found himself sharing a campaign office with congressional candidate Rod Blagojevich. At first Fritchey and Blagojevich were friends, but the amity did not last, although the two tolerated each other. Fritchey felt that Blagojevich resented him and was unnerved by his rise in Chicago politics, from humble beginnings to the Illinois state house. "He thought I was taking something away from him," Fritchey said.[8]

The two men had little contact when Blagojevich served in congress, and by the time Blagojevich became governor, the resentment had given way to open hostility. Blagojevich had a few allies in the legislature, and Fritchey was certainly not among them. He chose instead to side with the Speaker and became a vocal critic of the governor. When he was informed of Blagojevich's arrest, Fritchey began calling legislative allies and drafted a letter calling for the removal of the governor. To show broad-based geographical support for the governor's removal, he strategically asked three other house Democrats, each from a different section of the state, to sign the letter: Thomas Holbrook, who represented a downstate district; David Miller, who was African American and represented a Chicago south suburban district; and Jim Brosnahan, who represented southwest Chicago and the southwest suburbs. Fritchey insisted that he be appointed to the investigative committee being contemplated by the Speaker.[9]

News of the arrest spread quickly through the state capitol building in Springfield. The arrest was a surprise, but to those who had experienced the legislative turbulence of the past six years, it did not come as a shock. Those working in the capitol building felt a special sense of involvement, as if they had a front-row seat to the drama now unfolding. Legislative assistants answered the many phone calls from legislators and constituents and made calls of their own. People gathered in groups. Many were smiling. Everyone was "in a twitter," remarked a senate staffer. The governor's office on the second floor was quiet, and there was a sense of foreboding as staffers passed by and took note of the empty outer reception area.

Andy Manar, deputy chief of staff for outgoing senate president Emil Jones and the newly appointed chief of staff for the incoming senate Democrats, had just settled into his office and had much to do—make new staff appointments, assign offices, and start thinking about the upcoming legislative agenda. His most immediate task was to plan the inauguration ceremony, just weeks away. Manar had worked for the senate Democrats for a decade and had acquired the insights of a veteran of state politics. His home was the small town of Bunker Hill. While in high school, he had met the influential senator Vince Demuzio from downstate Carlinville. Demuzio was teaching a course at a local community college, and Manar, wanting to get a jump on college courses, enrolled. Manar was already interested in politics and US history, and his acquaintance with Demuzio prompted him to join the Macoupin County Democratic Organization. After graduating from Southern Illinois University with a degree in political science, he went to work for the Democratic senate, first as an intern, then on Demuzio's staff. He later was promoted to staff budget director and then deputy chief of staff. In November John Cullerton, the choice of the majority Democrats to be senate president, asked Manar to be chief of staff. Manar was surprised, but his budget acumen and staff experience, and the fact that he came from downstate and would balance the influence of Chicago, had led Cullerton to believe that Manar would be a perfect fit.

When Manar was informed of Blagojevich's arrest, his first reaction was one of disbelief. "That can't be true," he thought. Although rumors of investigations concerning the governor had been going around for years, and the rumors and newspaper stories had become more frequent during the past few weeks, this seemed incredible. After he verified the arrest, however, he began to realize that it had been inevitable.[10]

Clayton Harris, the governor's deputy chief of staff, was on his way to the State of Illinois Building in downtown Chicago. It was time for the regular morning meeting with the chief of staff, John Harris. John Harris liked to schedule morning meetings with his deputy early, to plan and go over the day's events. "Before the chaos," John Harris would say. As Clayton Harris was driving into the parking lot, he received a text message asking, "Is it true?" Another text a few moments later informed him, "They have arrested your boss." He was stunned, but as he pulled into the parking lot, his phone went dead. He noticed an ominous sign: John Harris's car was not there. The chief of staff always arrived early. He quickly made his way to the back elevator and to his office on the sixteenth floor. As he got off the elevator, he was greeted by a state trooper, who just shook his head. He was soon informed that both the governor and John Harris had been arrested. The former county prosecutor was greeted by a swarm of federal agents who demanded to know who he was. The agents showed him a search warrant and started taking files from offices. Clayton Harris described the scene with the word so many have used: *surreal*. He turned on a television. His cell phone was working again, and his first phone call was from former Speaker of the US House of Representatives Denny Hastert, a friend with whom he had worked on the Illinois Works Coalition. Denny Hastert was calling to see if his friend was all right. The second call was from his mother. She was worried about her son and, like so many that day, wanted to know what was going on. He told her he did too.[11]

Clayton Harris had joined the governor's staff in August 2008, after serving as chief of staff for the Illinois Transportation Department. He majored in aerospace technology at Middle Tennessee State University and then worked for an engineering firm at the Pentagon. He decided to go on to law school and graduated from Howard University in 1999. His work in government started after he moved to Chicago. He first worked as an assistant state's attorney and later for the city of Chicago. Although a seasoned government professional, Clayton Harris was not part of the governor's inner circle, had never contributed to the governor, and had never worked on his campaigns.[12]

Now, with the top of the organizational structure lopped off, confusion set in. Some people who should have come to work that day did not. People began to come into the deputy chief of staff's office asking what was going on. Some were crying. Harris instructed everyone to meet in a conference room on the fifteenth floor. "Someone had to step up," he later said. He told those present to calm down and carry on as if it were a normal workday. And he asked those who were crying to please stop. "I can take everything but crying," he said. He officially became the acting chief of staff one week later.[13]

For Illinois' longtime Speaker of the House Michael Madigan, the day started in an ordinary way, with a visit to his chiropractor. Madigan was contemplating an out-of-town trip and felt relaxed, and his doctor later remarked that he had seemed particularly happy that morning. He then returned to his home on Chicago's Southwest Side, oblivious to what was happening. He found that his wife, Shirley, had been trying to contact him and was somewhat agitated. She had been fielding calls from seemingly everyone. The methodical and controlled Speaker began returning the calls and made some of his own. Madigan spoke to his chief of staff, Tim Mapes; chief counsel David Ellis; and soon-to-be senate president John Cullerton. He decided to go to his political headquarters, the Thirteenth Ward office, on South Pulaski Road. The ward office was a familiar and comfortable place, out of the public spotlight, where the most powerful politician in Illinois could surround himself with trusted confidants, digest incoming information, and discuss and plan the reaction of the legislature.[14]

Michael Madigan is sometimes referred to as a master chess player, because he thinks several moves ahead. The arrest was a surprise, but the Speaker was prepared. For years the Chicago papers had been reporting on the corruption occurring within the Blagojevich administration. Some of the governor's confidants had been convicted, and several more were under indictment. The reportage of the *Chicago Tribune* was particularly withering. On September 29 the paper had run an editorial titled "Indict or Impeach." Indeed, the possibility of removing the governor was being discussed as a real option. In June 2008 Republican senator Larry Bomke had written a letter to Michael Madigan urging him to begin an impeachment investigation, and the Speaker's staff had begun to compile evidence of the governor's indiscretions and maladministration.[15]

With his arrest, there were few options to consider. Blagojevich had to be quickly removed from office. The governor had been arrested and booked on suspicion of several criminal acts and was facing certain indictment and a trial. There was some hope that in the coming days, Blagojevich would consider his situation and resign from office. Another option, presented in the Illinois Constitution, was that the governor could temporarily step aside, and his duties would be assumed by the lieutenant governor.[16] The third option was that the Illinois house of representatives could immediately hold an impeachment investigation and pass an impeachment resolution. The senate would hold a trial to decide whether to remove the governor from office.

Madigan was hesitant to act immediately that Tuesday morning, conscious of the political repercussions of acting too soon. Lisa Madigan, Illinois' attorney general, was the Speaker's daughter, and there was talk of her possible aspirations to the governor's office. The following Monday, the delegates to the Electoral College would meet in Springfield and officially cast their votes to elect Barack Obama president of the United States. Madigan decided to give Blagojevich six days to resign or step aside. If the governor did not remove himself from office, the Speaker would announce an impeachment investigation on Monday after the Electoral College met.[17]

Madigan was managing events instinctively, thinking of moves three steps ahead of the current situation. His instincts and political skills were honed by years of involvement in old-fashioned Chicago ward politics. His family was involved in city politics and had an early association with Richard J. Daley, when the future mayor worked in the Cook County Clerk's Office. Madigan's political career had followed a charted course. He went to Chicago's St. Ignatius College Prep, a Catholic preparatory high school; attended college at Notre Dame University; and then earned his law degree from Loyola University. The young attorney was chosen by the Democratic organization to be a delegate to the 1970 Constitutional Convention. A year later he was elected to the Illinois house of representatives. He rose rapidly in the house, and when the Democrats gained control in 1983, he was elected Speaker. Madigan served in this capacity until 1995, when the Democrats lost the majority in the first midterm election of the Clinton presidency. The Republicans held the house for only two years, and in 1997 Madigan again became Speaker. In 1998 he was elected chairman of the Illinois Democratic Party and still held that position in 2008.

The removal of the governor was a decision the Speaker did not take lightly. Madigan has a sense of history, and colleagues say that he has an almost religious respect for the legislative process.[18] Despite calls from both parties for an impeachment investigation during the year leading to the arrest, Madigan remained cautious. He knew that impeachment and removal from office would be an unprecedented action by the Illinois legislature. Never before in the state had the sovereign will of the people, as expressed through the ballot, been nullified—an executive office holder had never been removed by the legislative branch.

In December 2008 the legislature was completing the two-year cycle of general assemblies. The Ninety-Fifth General Assembly would end when the legislature adjourned in January, and the Ninety-Sixth would be sworn in. In November John Cullerton, a senator from Chicago's North Side, had been elected by the majority Democrat caucus to be the new senate president. Cullerton, a veteran legislator who came to the Illinois house in 1979, had served in the senate since 1992. Achieving the position of senate president had become the personal goal of the former public defender from Cook County. When he moved to the senate after an unsuccessful run for Congress, he set his sights on the senate presidency. Surprisingly, Emil Jones, the senate president since 2003, chose to leave the senate, and John Cullerton had his chance. Several senators vied for the spot. Jones worked against Cullerton, but Cullerton prevailed. After the November election, the Democrats again held a firm majority in the senate and elected Cullerton their candidate for senate president, a move tantamount to being elected by the full senate.

Cullerton was having breakfast in downtown Chicago when he heard of the arrest. He talked by phone with the Speaker. Emil Jones was still senate president, but Madigan did not want to talk to Jones; he dealt with Cullerton instead.[19] Both Cullerton and Madigan agreed that Blagojevich had to be removed quickly. The idea of Blagojevich remaining as governor while he went on trial, an event that could have been years away, was totally unacceptable. Cullerton understood Madigan's three options: the governor could resign, temporarily give up the office, or be impeached. On the morning of the arrest, planning an exact schedule of events leading to removal was impossible, but the two men agreed that an impeachment investigation would begin in six days. If Blagojevich could be persuaded to resign or step aside, the legislature could avoid taking action and the state could avoid the trauma of impeachment and a senate trial. The last thing John Cullerton had on his mind as he sat down for breakfast that morning was commencing a trial to remove the governor as his first legislative act as senate president.[20]

The arrest of Rod Blagojevich occurred against a backdrop of partisan and personal hostilities that had played out in Illinois state government during the preceding sixteen years. In 1993 the Republicans had gained control of the senate, and James "Pate" Philip, from the solidly Republican DuPage County, was elected senate president. A veteran legislator, Philip had first been elected to the Illinois house in 1967 and moved to the senate in 1975. Philip was well liked, known to most as a regular guy, and accessible to rank-and-file senators from both parties. A former marine who in his early days sported a crew cut, he was unpretentious but could be rough and short with those who disagreed with him. He was staunchly conservative by the standards of the 1960s and 1970s and a rock-solid supporter of the business community. Upon becoming senate president, he had the audacity to offer committee chairmanships to two Democrats. Newly elected senate minority leader Emil Jones interpreted the move as an attempt to undermine his authority. The two Democrat senators declined the chairmanships, but the games had begun.

Emil Jones, in contrast, was a product of Chicago politics. He came to his position in a fashion well known among the city's legislators. Jones grew up in Morgan Park, a neighborhood on Chicago's far South Side. He worked as a newspaper carrier and then held a series of public jobs, first at the US Postal Service and then as a sanitary engineer for the city's South District Water Filtration Plant. He paid his dues, as did many public job holders in the 1960s and 1970s, doing political work in Chicago's Thirty-Fourth Ward. His work for the ward organization and his loyalty and political skills caught the attention of the Thirty-Fourth Ward committeeman and alderman, Wilson Frost, who appointed him ward executive secretary. In 1972 Frost picked Jones to be the candidate for state representative. Jones won and served in the house for ten years before moving to the senate in 1983. After an intraparty struggle, he was elected by the Democrats to be minority leader in 1993.

The Crisis Erupts

When Pate Philip became senate president, the Democrats had controlled the Illinois senate for eighteen years. Philip set out to change the
way the senate operated and to consolidate control by adopting new rules
and procedures that diminished the minority party's role in policy-mak-
ing. The clash between Philip and Jones was immediate. The men knew
each other from a decade of serving together in the senate, and there was a
mutual dislike. Philip dismissed Jones and rarely consulted him on policy
matters. During one yearly budget meeting, negotiations that occur at the
end of each legislative session and are attended by the four legislative leaders
and the governor, Philip suggested to Madigan that the senate Democratic
leader be excluded, but Madigan insisted that Jones be included.[21] Jones was
resentful and felt that Philip did not give him the proper respect. Mindful
of his self-image, Jones informed his staff to call him Leader Jones.

The mutual dislike between Philip and Jones was manifest in all their
dealings. Both men had prosaic personalities but diverged in their backgrounds and political views. They both approached politics as a personal
enterprise to be manipulated and managed. They each shared a high concern for their individual self-esteem, and they both treated the political
craft as a complex interaction guided by the constant influences of paranoia,
struggle, and intrigue. Both men approached political leadership as a military battle. Jones often said that his personal heroes were Sun Tzu, author
of *The Art of War*, and Machiavelli, author of *The Prince*. He would listen
to a books-on-tape version of *The Prince* while driving from Chicago to
legislative sessions in Springfield and often quoted passages from the book.
Both Philip and Jones were directed by their own moral compasses. Their
histories and their deeply rooted, distinct cultures proved to be barriers
to understanding each other. Given their similar personalities but their
differences in cultures and experiences, tension was predictable.

For ten years under two Republican governors, the Democrats remained
the senate minority party. In 2003, when Rod Blagojevich was sworn in as
governor, the Democrats gained the majority in the senate and Emil Jones
attained the office he had long sought, that of senate president. In addition
to his perceived mistreatment by Philip, Jones chafed at the authority and
influence of House Speaker Michael Madigan. With the election of Rod
Blagojevich and his own ascent to senate president, Jones felt that there
were now three important—and most significantly, equal—Democrats in
Springfield. An alliance with Blagojevich was a way, Jones believed, to check
the power of Madigan.[22] With Pate Philip now retired, Jones directed his

built-up animosities toward Madigan and the newly elected senate minority leader, Frank Watson.

Watson could not have been more different from Jones or Philip. A pharmacist from downstate Greenville, he was rooted in small-town America. His family had owned Watson's Drug Store for generations, a symbol of permanency on the Greenville town square. Before holding public office, Watson had been involved in local civic organizations. Soft-spoken, he was popular among members of both parties. Initially, Jones was cordial to Watson and would call him on session days and offer the courtesy of going over the legislative calendar. By the spring of 2004, however, budget contentions had forced legislative alliances, and Jones and Blagojevich were allied against Watson and Madigan. Having Watson allied with his old nemesis, Madigan, irritated Jones. According to Watson, one particular incident that vexed Jones occurred during a budget meeting of the four legislative leaders and the governor. Blagojevich opened the meeting by asking the Speaker, "Well, what do we do now?" Jones apparently became upset that the question had not been asked of him. The relationship between Jones and Watson rapidly deteriorated. Watson made an effort to cooperate: "I told Jones I was not Pate that I wanted to work together," he recalled, "but it did no good." He characterized Jones as "a very vindictive man." When Watson suffered a stroke in the fall of 2008, the Speaker called several times to offer support and encouragement, but Jones never called him.[23]

After 2004 the relationships between the governor and the members of the legislature also declined. Blagojevich shunned Springfield and most legislators. He refused to live in the governor's mansion, preferring to commute by state plane from Chicago to Springfield. On session days the governor was frequently absent. When the legislature was not in session, he seldom went to Springfield. He became disengaged from the legislative process and had little interest in policy details or even policy subjects. He was "a big-picture guy," Frank Watson recalled. Blagojevich seemed to have no interest in governance. Watson became exasperated when the governor walked out of meetings several times. After one particular meeting, when the waiting press asked what they had been discussing, the frustrated Watson replied that the governor had discussed whether the Chicago Cubs or the St. Louis Cardinals had the best third baseman in past decades. But on occasion, Watson said, Blagojevich could be an "engaging guy." He would have "heart-to-heart talks" with the senate Republican leader concerning personal matters: Blagojevich's disagreements with his father-in-law, Chicago alderman Dick

Mell, or matters involving the governor's wife, Patty. The governor's staff, surprisingly, informed Watson that Blagojevich was just trying to win him over in an attempt to get him to support Jones and oppose Madigan. Although Watson was aware of the governor's motives, he found the governor's behavior intriguing and, he admitted, "somewhat captivating."[24]

The Speaker tolerated Blagojevich as a Democratic member of the house and as a congressman, but the relationship was never amicable. Outside of being the son-in-law of a powerful Chicago alderman, Blagojevich, as the saying in Springfield goes, brought nothing to the table. He took little interest in legislation, his attention span was short, and he had no time for the details of governance. His relationship with the Speaker had steadily deteriorated since he had taken the office of governor. The two men could not have been more different. Blagojevich was a master at political gamesmanship, a tinseled circus ringmaster, driven by his ambitions and the desire for personal gain. He was obsessed with his appearance and spent an extravagant amount on expensive clothing. To him, politics was personal combat and public office merely a stepping-stone to the next higher office. "He was beyond egotistical," Clayton Harris recalled; "he was egocentric."[25] He traveled with a large entourage and a state police escort, and he governed by crisis, confrontation, and threats.[26] Some legislators who had worked with Blagojevich described him as bizarre; others characterized him as reckless and mean.[27]

Blagojevich alienated Michael Madigan, who, by contrast, was private, reserved, and thoughtful. He possessed a sense of history and, colleagues report, a respect for the legislative process. Madigan was unpretentious in both mannerisms and style. He lived modestly, preferred a small circle of confidants, and seldom mingled with legislators and lobbyists. He frequented a few familiar restaurants, ate restrictively, and traveled without an entourage or an escort. Michael Madigan could appear remote, and for many, he remains an enigma. But Madigan personified the leadership and trench values honed in the Chicago wards during the 1950s and 1960s. His leadership style was reminiscent of that of a ward committeeman. The ward committeeman was a powerful position in the city's Democratic machine, and to preserve political power, he remained inaccessible and skeptical. One had to keep the barons at bay. A strong work ethic, pragmatism, modesty, and loyalty were attributes ascribed to the culture of second-generation ethnics who populated Chicago's working-class neighborhoods at midcentury. Madigan's personal ethics and style paralleled those values.

Chapter 2

Cause for Impeachment

On the morning of December 9 David Ellis, chief counsel to the Speaker of the Illinois house of representatives, was at his Springfield home with his children when he received a call from his sister-in-law in Iowa. "Turn on the TV," she told him. "What channel?" he asked. "Any channel," she replied. Ellis saw the reports of the arrest of Rod Blagojevich and called the house Democrats' chief of staff, Tim Mapes, and later spoke with the house Speaker. They discussed their options, and for the rest of the day a flurry of calls were made among house and senate Democratic leaders and their staffs. The arrest of Rod Blagojevich was an embarrassment to Illinois Democrats; they had tolerated his misconduct, but after the arrest everyone agreed that Blagojevich had to leave office. Ellis and his staff had been accumulating evidence of malfeasance by the governor for months. But the question remained whether he would resign. Madigan told Ellis that they were going to give Blagojevich six days to resign before starting a house impeachment investigation. Ellis asked Madigan if he should get ready for an impeachment investigation, and Madigan replied in a restrained tone, "That's a good idea." Madigan's instruction began what seemed like a stream of unending days and nights for the meticulous attorney, who authored fiction novels in his spare time. He had six days to develop causality and prepare evidence for impeaching the governor.[1]

There was little doubt once the investigation proceedings began that Rod Blagojevich would be impeached. The governor had few friends among house Democrats, and though the house Republican leader Tom Cross, from west suburban Plainfield, had a personal relationship with Blagojevich, the Republicans would hardly support the governor. The Illinois Constitution states the need "to determine the existence of cause for impeachment."[2] Solid charges were required for the senate to remove Blagojevich from office. Legislators also weighed the possible repercussions of ousting a governor who remained popular in some sections of the state and excelled at public relations. Partisan politics complicated the situation. The governor was a Democrat, Speaker Madigan was chairman of the Illinois Democratic Party, and attempting to display party unity, both Madigan and Jones had served as official co-chairmen of Blagojevich's reelection campaign two years earlier.

But the governor's mismanagement and the corrupt practices of his advisors and staff members during his first term had become well known. Several aides and associates had been indicted and some convicted. A steady torrent of negative newspaper coverage in the weeks prior to the arrest, including the *Chicago Tribune*'s demand for an impeachment investigation, had created a major embarrassment for the Democrats. Now, with the arrest, it became clear: Blagojevich had to leave office.

The house Republicans recognized a political advantage and immediately reacted to the Blagojevich arrest. House Republican leader Tom Cross was playing golf with a group of lobbyists at the exclusive Isleworth Country Club, near Orlando, Florida, when he was informed of the arrest. "We were getting ready to tee off when everyone's phone began to go off," one lobbyist recalled. The Republicans wasted no time and filed a resolution that same day calling for the formation of a special investigative committee to determine if there was cause to impeach the governor. The resolution was modeled after the impeachment resolution used to hold hearings on Supreme Court justice James D. Heiple in 1997. It was filed with the clerk of the house and became House Resolution (HR) 1644, with Tom Cross listed as the chief sponsor. HR 1644, a political statement by the house Republicans, called for equal representation of both parties and proposed a committee of ten members, five Democrats and five Republicans. The Speaker and the minority leader would each appoint one member to serve as co-chairperson, and both parties would have equal control of the committee proceedings. But the house was firmly under the control of Michael Madigan, and few, if any, expected the Democratic Speaker to give equal control of impeaching a Democratic governor to the Republicans.

On December 15, six days after the governor's arrest, Madigan filed his own resolution calling for the formation of a special investigative committee, HR 1650. This Democratic version proposed a twenty-one-member committee made up of twelve Democrats and nine Republicans to investigate allegations of "misfeasance, malfeasance, nonfeasance and other misconduct of Governor Rod Blagojevich." The resolution stated that the purpose of the investigation was "to determine the existence of cause for impeachment." The Speaker would appoint one individual as chairperson. The Republicans would appoint one person to serve as minority spokesman. Accepting the inevitable, as Democrats outnumbered Republicans in the House, Minority Leader Cross joined as a co-sponsor of HR 1650.

Both resolutions were sent to the Rules Committee on December 15. The Rules Committee, by majority vote, can assign a legislative initiative to a substantive committee for review or can advance the initiative directly to the full house. On that same day the Rules Committee quickly passed and sent HR 1650 to the full house. The vote was four in favor and zero against. HR 1644, the Republican version, never was presented for a vote and remained in the Rules Committee.[3]

The full house met on December 15, and after some obligatory political jousting, Republican efforts to have HR 1644 discharged from the Rules Committee and considered by the full house failed. The house took up the Democrats' HR 1650 and approved it by a vote of 113 to 0.[4] Soon after HR 1650 was passed, Madigan held a press conference announcing the formation of an investigative committee. The Speaker appointed a trusted ally, Barbara Currie, the house majority leader, as committee chairperson. Though not an attorney, Currie was skilled at running a committee, and she was unflappable. She also had chaired the impeachment committee investigating Heiple in 1997. Most important, Currie would not deviate from the Speaker's script. James Durkin, the former prosecuting attorney from Cook County, was named Republican spokesman.

December 15 was also the day that the delegates elected to the Electoral College in November met in Springfield to cast their votes for either Barack

Obama or John McCain for president. Barbara Currie was one of these delegates. After she cast her vote, she attended the Illinois Speaker's press conference. Currie had served in the Illinois house since 1979. Her district included the University of Chicago, and early in her legislative career, she was considered by some to be a "Hyde Park liberal." Her skills soon became apparent, and among legislators, staff, and lobbyists, she was respected for her intelligence, fortitude, and refined comportment. A slight woman, Currie was a trusted and capable legislative manager and a confidant of the Speaker. She was fiercely loyal to Madigan, and it was safe to assume that when she spoke, Speaker Madigan was in agreement.

To Currie, it seemed strange attending the press conference just moments after standing in Illinois' Old State Capitol building to cast her vote for Barack Obama as president of the United States. Now she was attending an event a few blocks away in the capitol's Blue Room to announce the beginning of an investigation of Rod Blagojevich for possible impeachment. The incongruity of events aroused conflicting emotions. She had felt pride voting for Barack Obama, a friend who had been the state senator from her legislative district, a US senator from Illinois, and the first black man to attain the highest elected office in the United States, and then experienced utter dejection and revulsion at the press conference to begin the impeachment of the governor of Illinois.[5]

During the previous six days, Ellis had begun to prepare the case for impeachment. He considered using the criminal complaint filed by the federal government as part of the cause for impeachment, but the governor had not yet been found guilty of anything or indicted on any of the allegations pertaining to the arrest, and if he was indicted, a criminal trial would be months, perhaps years, away. In developing the evidence to justify the existence of cause, Ellis had to include conduct that constituted a pattern of maladministration and malfeasance. He had to show that the governor had used his office in an illegal manner, had used his position at times contrary to the law, and had failed to perform his official duties.[6] But Ellis had only six days, not enough time to investigate and assemble new evidence. He had to rely on existing data developed by the legislature and state agencies in past administrative investigations. Fortunately, he had plenty of material to choose from.

Ellis found one instance that had occurred halfway into Blagojevich's first term particularly intriguing. In October 2004 the US Food and Drug Administration (FDA) announced that half of the US flu vaccine supply for the 2004–5 flu season was unsafe. Illinois, like many other states and municipalities, began searching for replacement vaccines. The Blagojevich administration immediately began negotiating the purchase of flu vaccines from Ecosse Hospital Products, a European company based in the United Kingdom, and on October 22, 2004, the state of Illinois' special advocate for prescription drugs, Scott McKibbin, agreed to purchase thirty thousand doses of the vaccine from Ecosse. Aware that it was a violation of federal law to import drugs from a foreign country, the governor's office announced that the agreement was subject to FDA approval.[7] Deputy Governor Bradley Tusk increased the order the following day by two hundred thousand doses and again on November 1 by an additional thirty thousand doses.[8] The Blagojevich administration had developed a plan to obtain vaccines not only for Illinois but also for other states and out-of-state municipal governments. The total cost for the vaccines ordered from Ecosse was $8.2 million.[9] FDA approval was never granted. Although the flu vaccine program was promoted by the governor's office with much fanfare, by the end of 2004 the state of Illinois and Ecosse still had not entered into a contract specifying the terms of purchase or delivery. And the US Centers for Disease Control (CDC) announced that it had located sufficient vaccines to serve Illinois' priority population: people over age sixty-five, pregnant women, and other vulnerable citizens. In January 2005 the CDC announced that an additional two hundred thousand doses were available for Illinois. By late December 2004 McKibbin was already aware that the vaccines from Ecosse would not be allowed to legally enter the United States and that an adequate supply of vaccines was available. He sent an e-mail alerting administration staff, "We probably will never take delivery of these doses so we will need to find a way to pay [Ecosse] for the service they performed."[10] Saying "service" instead of "product" or "drugs" obfuscated just what the state had been planning to purchase. On January 11, 2005, Ecosse submitted a bill for $2.6 million. Even though Illinois did not need the vaccines, importing drugs from a foreign country was a violation of federal law, and the administration was aware that the drugs would never be delivered, two days after receiving the Ecosse bill, Deputy Chief of Staff for Social Services Louanner Peters signed a contract for the vaccines.[11] The drugs were never shipped, and at the time of the governor's arrest, Ecosse was still seeking payment of $2.6 million through the Illinois Court of Claims.

Another incident involving the importation of drugs from foreign countries also took place in October 2004. The governor announced the I-SaveRx program, which would enable state employees and state retirees to obtain prescriptions from foreign pharmacies—another violation of federal law.[12] The governor knew that it was illegal to import drugs from a foreign country—the FDA had written a letter warning Blagojevich that the program, "if implemented, would be in direct conflict with federal and state law." The governor appealed to the FDA to allow Illinois to establish this pilot program, but the FDA denied the request. Nevertheless, Blagojevich launched the I-SaveRx program with another high-profile media campaign.[13] He continued promoting the program and encouraged state employees and state retirees to illegally purchase drugs from foreign countries.

The Blagojevich administration's mismanagement of the flu vaccine purchase, the Ecosse claim for $2.6 million, and the I-SaveRx program did not go unnoticed by the legislature. In the spring session of 2005 Representative Jack Franks, chairman of the house State Government Administration Committee, was aware of the flu vaccine fiasco and the governor's flagrant disregard of the FDA warning. Franks's committee was responsible for administrative oversight and held hearings in March 2005 concerning both the flu vaccine and I-SaveRx drug procurement. The committee found several instances where both federal and Illinois law and state procurement procedures were not followed. Franks summoned the director of the Illinois Department of Central Management Services to appear before the committee. Instead, a department lawyer appeared. Franks was outraged. "I went ballistic," he later said. Franks told the lawyer that the director should appear the next day and that he would be sworn in and would testify under oath. The director resigned that night, rather than appear and testify under oath before Franks's committee. "I knew we were on to something," Franks said.[14]

After the hearings, Franks filed and the house passed identical House Resolution 394 and House Joint Resolution 040, instructing the state auditor general to audit and determine what roles the governor's office and the special advocate for prescription drugs played in the flu vaccine procurement, what agencies were responsible for the I-SaveRx program, and whether the "entities involved in these programs followed all applicable laws, regulations, policies, and procedures."[15] Senate President Emil Jones was an ally of the governor, and the senate never considered the house joint resolution. But HR 394 was sufficient for the auditor general to take action.

The auditor general's office began the mandated audit and released its findings sixteen months later, in September 2006, just a few weeks before the general election in early November. Blagojevich was up for reelection, and the audit was highly critical of the administration's actions. The governor's office was furious. John Harris, a former aide to Chicago mayor Richard M. Daley and then Rod Blagojevich's deputy governor, called Bill Holland, the state auditor general, and complained about the timing of the report release and the negative effect it could have on Blagojevich's chances of winning reelection. Normally, the auditor general's office can complete an audit in about a year, but the flu vaccine and I-SaveRx audit took an additional four months. As a routine practice, in election years, Holland generally did not release audits between Labor Day and the election, but this audit was different. Holland told Harris that the report was delayed through no fault of the auditor general's but because of the administration's refusal to cooperate. The audit was delayed because the governor's staff was not able or willing to give "simple answers to simple questions." He went on to say that "the governor was going to win and he would be around for four more years." Holland also reminded Harris that his term as auditor general ran for six more years. The message was clear: "learn to work with us."[16]

In the week prior to the release of the audit, the governor's office, aware of the report's contents, began the unprecedented action of attacking sections of the report. After the report was published, Holland took the equally unprecedented step of holding his own press conference in Springfield to answer the comments made by the governor's office. An audit is usually viewed as a management tool, a constructive element designed to ensure the legal and efficient operation of government. Holland spent more than an hour in the capitol press room answering reporters' questions concerning the report's methodology, legal imperatives, and the audit's conclusions. A few days after Holland's press conference, the governor's office stopped attacking the audit.[17]

The audit found that the governor's office decision to purchase flu vaccines violated federal law and state procurement procedures, that the administration did not present documentation or methodology to illustrate how it determined the number of vaccines needed, that the governor's office was not timely in contract procurement, and that it had failed to secure contracts from other states and local governments for additional vaccines, creating a potential state liability of $8.2 million. The section of the report concerning the I-SaveRx program was also damning. The audit found that the program violated federal law and that pharmacies participating in the program might be in violation of the Illinois Pharmacy Practice Act. The audit also found that oversight of safety was lacking: the

Department of Financial and Professional Regulation had not completely filled out 40 percent of the forms for pharmacies it had inspected, and the state had not monitored whether only approved pharmacies were filling prescriptions. Expenses for the program were also suspect: Illinois had spent nearly $750,000 for assistance, travel, and promotion of the illegal I-SaveRx program, and much of this amount had been awarded to outside contractual services.[18]

Jack Franks was highly critical of the governor, but legislative leaders elected to take no action. Franks received a tip that someone would be visiting him to discuss his disparaging remarks about the governor. A lobbyist subsequently paid him a visit and urged him to abandon his investigation for the "good of the Democrat Party." Franks said, "I didn't know how high up this went and who was involved." The situation unnerved the usually assured Jack Franks. A lawyer himself, he immediately sought the advice of a lawyer friend.[19]

The audit reports regarding the flu vaccine and I-SaveRx provided David Ellis with clear documentation of serious mismanagement within the Blagojevich administration, but another audit—a routine financial and compliance audit of the Department of Central Management Services (CMS) conducted for 2003–4 and published in 2005— was a treasure trove of examples of maladministration and possibly corruption. The CMS audit, also conducted by the state auditor general, examined the activities of the governor's "efficiency initiatives." Passed as part of the Illinois Budget Implementation Act of 2004, the efficiency initiatives gave CMS the authority to implement a consolidation of services for departments under the governor's control. Simply, as passed by the legislature, the consolidation of resources by state agencies would result in more efficacious and economical operation. CMS, by statute, was authorized to identify efficient restructuring and procurement within each agency or department. Each entity would be billed for its individual portion of the consolidation, rather than paying directly for the service, and each would benefit from a reduction in service costs. Each reduction in cost would be associated with a specific line item of the agency's or department's budget.

However, the audit found that CMS was not complying with the statute and that the Governor's Office of Management and Budget (GOMB) was interfering with the administration of the efficiency initiatives.[20] Illinois statute requires that CMS identify specific line-item efficiencies, but the audit found that GOMB dictated the amounts to be billed from the agencies.

CMS would select the agencies where initiatives service costs would be charged, print the amounts on CMS letterhead, and then return them to GOMB for final selection.[21] The governor's office, not CMS, was involved in deciding what agencies were to be billed for efficiency initiatives.[22] CMS did not identify specific line items, and the agencies or departments simply paid the amounts established by GOMB where they could find the money. Franks later described the practice as an elaborate "money laundering scheme," billing agencies and departments to create an amount of money for discretionary use by the governor's office, money taken from line-item appropriations passed by the legislature.[23]

The CMS audit of April 2005 also uncovered evidence that the governor's office was often part of the selection process for contracts associated with the efficiency initiatives program and was sometimes part of the team that developed requests for proposals (RFPs), which established qualifications and performance specifications for services put out for bid.[24] The audit also found that in some cases, vendors participated in the development of RFPs, writing their own specifications and vendor requirements. The entire RFP process and selection of applicants was questionable. In one instance, the audit uncovered evidence that a contract had been granted to a company, Illinois Property Asset Management (IPAM), that did not exist prior to the granting of the contract. IPAM was given the opportunity to change its proposal during the selection process, an opportunity given to no other proposed vendor, and in the course of its service, IPAM charged the state for many questionable expenses, including basketball tickets, limousines, and a victory dinner for everyone who helped IPAM receive the contract.[25]

A section of the CMS audit that caused many to speculate about the motives of the governor, and that became the topic of conversation in many Springfield bars frequented by legislators and lobbyists, concerned the processing of state contracts. The Illinois Procurement Code requires that "whenever . . . a contract liability . . . exceeding $10,000 is incurred by any State agency, a copy of the contract . . . shall be filed with the comptroller within 15 days thereafter."[26] Work performed for the state cannot be paid until the comptroller receives a signed contract. Since Blagojevich had taken office in 2003, contract delivery to the comptroller for processing began to be delayed; some contracts took as long as 248 days to reach the comptroller.[27] Performing work for the state without a contract in place has negative consequences for both the vendor and the state, but the bottom line for the vendor is that it would receive no compensation until a contract was forwarded to the comptroller. Departments responded that the delays were the result of paperwork and working out contract details with vendors, but veterans of Springfield's politics suspected that the contracts were being held up for political reasons. Contracting a vendor to perform a service or work and then wait to make payment seemingly resulted in leverage for the Blagojevich administration. Some speculated that a donation to the governor's campaign fund or participating in a fund-raising event could speed up the payment process.

Campaign donations have always been a major component of doing business in Illinois. A political donation purchases access to decision makers and inclusion in the policy dialog, and it may influence officials who determine contract awards, but as early as 2003 people spoke of the overt fund-raising approach of the new administration. At the Sangamo Club, a members-only restaurant and bar about two blocks from the capitol, where lobbyists hold court after each session day to entertain legislators or provide an introduction for their clients and their causes and claims, a common rumor circulated: the price of appointments to a directorship or senior staff position within the Blagojevich administration was $50,000, and appointments required the approval and direction of Blagojevich's key advisors. The actions of the Blagojevich administration were conspicuous: nothing, not even price, was hidden. The pledges of Rod Blagojevich during his first campaign to clean up Springfield government "seemed to last about three minutes after taking office," Auditor General Bill Holland later remarked.[28]

The evidence uncovered in the two audits constituted tangible maladministration and malfeasance. Ellis called Bill Holland and asked if he wanted to be a witness before the Special Investigative Committee. Holland, a career state employee, had begun working with the legislature as an intern for house Democrats in 1974, moved to the senate, and eventually became chief of staff to senate president Phil Rock. When Rock retired from the senate, Holland was named state auditor general and had been serving in that position since 1992. Holland had a reputation as a capable, steady, no-nonsense bureaucrat. He answered that he certainly did not want to be a witness—being part of an impeachment process was not something the conscientious career bureaucrat would relish—but, he told Ellis, he would.[29]

Although the events presented in the two auditor general reports had occurred years before, during Blagojevich's first term, legislative leaders had taken no action. Ellis, however, took note. He had a mere six days to prepare a case. The CMS audit showed a pattern that was suspicious, but investigating the contract delays would take time, and anything of tangible substance would require an investigative staff to uncover. But the content in the available auditor general's reports concerning the flu vaccines and the I-SaveRx program provided ready grist for establishing a cause for impeachment.

Another administrative incident that Ellis could quickly draw on concerned an ongoing conflict between the governor's office and the legislature over the authority of the Joint Committee on Administrative Rules (JCAR) to review, approve, change, or prohibit administrative rules developed by state agencies under control of the governor. Administrative rules interpret and implement the provisions of statutes passed by the legislative branch of government. In 1977, through an amendment to the 1975 Illinois Administrative Procedure Act, Illinois required that all rules proposed by state agencies be submitted to JCAR for review and approval. JCAR is made up of twelve members, equally divided among the two parties and the two houses, and is supported by a staff of specialists. The committee, established as a service agency of the General Assembly, presents the opportunity for public and private entities to participate in the process of rule development through written comments or by an appearance before the committee.[30] JCAR can issue a formal objection to a proposed rule if the rule is determined not to be in the public interest, safety, or general welfare, or if it would violate existing law. By a two-thirds majority vote, the committee can reject a rule. The purpose of the JCAR review is to ensure a balance between the executive and legislative branches of government.[31]

The controversy between JCAR and the governor began in 2007, when the Department of Healthcare and Family Services (HFS), the state agency responsible for state health care programs, refused to comply with a decision by JCAR. The federal government had assisted in a state program, FamilyCare, which provided health care coverage for children and the adult relatives responsible for the children enrolled in the program. In 2007 federal assistance with the adult coverage expired, and an estimated fifteen to twenty thousand Illinois adult participants would lose health care coverage unless the state made up the federal shortfall. The state statute that created the adult participation was tied to the federal contribution and set an income limit for the adult program participants of 185 percent of the federal poverty level. At the end of 2007 HFS responded with an emergency rule before JCAR to continue the adult coverage.[32] But the emergency rule expanded the coverage income limit to 400 percent of the federal poverty

level. The adjustment in income level would add thousands of new participants to the program without legislative approval or appropriation. JCAR
rejected the emergency rule and urged HFS to resubmit the rule using
185 percent of the federal poverty level, the established income level. HFS
ignored JCAR's action, however, and continued to enroll participants at
400 percent of the federal poverty level.

The actions of HFS became the subject of a citizen suit. Richard Caro, a
lawyer from Riverside, filed suit to prevent the governor from unilaterally
imposing unfunded programs that were not authorized by the General
Assembly—a violation, Caro claimed, of the prerogative of the General
Assembly and the Illinois Constitution. The lawsuit was filed two weeks
after JCAR rejected the emergency rule.

The JCAR controversy provided a solid case for charging Blagojevich
with misfeasance, the unlawful execution of a lawful act. Once the investigative committee was announced, Barbara Currie asked two professors
from the highly respected University of Illinois Institute of Government
and Public Affairs, Robert Rich, the institute's director, and Andrew Morriss, a professor of law and business, to appear before the committee and
present a "comprehensive" explanation of the JCAR experience with HFS.[33]
Currie and Ellis wanted the investigative committee—and perhaps more
important, the public—to be presented with the history, purpose, and legal
authority of JCAR's regulatory review. They were well aware that a possible defense for Blagojevich might be that the legislature had been acting
for political reasons and he might portray himself as a governor who was
interested only in helping people. It was important for the committee to
establish that the state statutes and the administrative system guarantee a
balance between the executive and legislative branches, that the administrative system allows for transparency and input from the public, and that the
constitution and the administrative system were being violated because the
governor refused to comply with the JCAR decision. The concept of legitimacy was a foremost concern of the Democratic house leadership. Having
constitutional sanction, expressed by professors at the respected University of Illinois' Institute of Government and Public Affairs, would serve
to show institutional support for the impeachment effort. The professors
were requested to appear before the committee in two days. Morriss and
Rich immediately began to collaborate and prepare their presentations.[34]

The governor's handling of contracts and leases provided house inves-
tigators with another intriguing area for review. Almost immediately after

Blagojevich assumed office, the procedures associated with the procurement of both material and rented space for state offices were greatly altered. In 2003 the state ceased all lease renewal activities. Leases that expired fell into a category known as holdover leases. Lease activity resumed in 2007 after some leases began to reach the ten-year limit prescribed under the Illinois Procurement Code. Prior to the Blagojevich administration, the number of holdover leases was negligible, but by the end of 2003 the number had risen to 93 and by 2005 it had ballooned to 172. A lease that went into the status of holdover became problematic for the state and gave advantage to the lessors. Lessors were no longer required to make necessary repairs, and the state could not modify occupancy space and would lose all leverage in negotiating a continued stay.[35]

Franks noticed the dramatic increase in holdover leases and speculated that the reason leases were not renewed was to grant advantage to lessors in exchange for campaign contributions. Staff of the Procurement Policy Board (PPB), the agency responsible for reviewing and making recommendations to state agencies engaged in the procurement process, became concerned over the holdover situation. Created in 1998 as part of Illinois' newly adopted Procurement Code to ensure that state agencies operated under the guidelines established by law, the PPB was made up of five members: a chairman and four members appointed by the legislature. From the very beginning, the PPB clashed with the Blagojevich administration. Matt Brown, the PPB's executive director since its establishment in 1998, discussed the holdover situation with staff and members of the agency and kept legislators apprised.[36]

Brown expressed his reservations and frustration after Blagojevich in 2003 signed Executive Order No. 2003-10, which consolidated facilities management, internal auditing, and legal functions for all agencies that reported to the governor, turning control over to CMS. The governor's office unveiled the executive order with much fanfare, billing it as a cost-saving move. But what the order gave the governor was priceless: control of all facilities management and legal review under one agency that he could more easily direct and oversee. After one particularly acrimonious meeting, Brown was told to leave the CMS offices because he "was not a team player."[37] From that point on, Brown and the PPB remained at odds with CMS. Brown did his best to brief legislative members on the problems that PPB faced with CMS and with the procurement of leases and the selection of vendors. The legislature eventually became aware that PPB was at the forefront of administrative clashes with Blagojevich and knew the details. Still, Brown recalled, it took several weeks for Franks to work with him. "He thought I was part of the Blagojevich problem," said Brown.[38] In a formal letter, Barbara Currie requested that Matt Brown appear before the committee. She asked him to describe the PPB's relationship with the Blagojevich administration as compared with previous administrations and to report on the administration's handling of leases and space requirements. Brown started to prepare.

Chapter 3

The House
Investigation

The First Day

The house wasted no time in commencing the impeachment investigation. On Tuesday, December 16, one week after the governor was arrested, the leadership of both parties had designated the members of the Special Investigative Committee, and the committee held its first meeting. Speaker Madigan was acutely aware of potential political ramifications imposed by the house action. Propriety required political inclusiveness; the investigative committee process had to be transparent, be sanctioned by Illinois' Constitution, and follow the rule of law. The committee could not exhibit the slightest hint of political motivation and needed to display broad support across the state for impeaching Blagojevich. Committee members were chosen to reflect gender and geographic and racial diversity.[1] The Democrats supplied a required number of African Americans, Hispanics, and women. The Republican committee members consisted of men and women from districts in both northern and downstate Illinois. Anticipating the legal discussions that would be generated by the impeachment action, both parties provided a number of accomplished attorneys.

Expecting a large public attendance at the hearings, the committee met in the largest house committee room in the capitol, room 114. On session days, when committee meetings are scheduled, one or two security guards are stationed outside the doors of room 114. Ordinarily, people walk in and out as committee business proceeds, and small groups gather in the marble hall to discuss the various bills that are being considered. People come and go as they see fit, as their curiosity is satisfied or their business is finished. But on the first day of the hearings, security at room 114 was noticeably heightened. A special security screening was set up outside the public entrance. Seats in the audience were on a first-come basis, and standing in the room was not allowed. The public was informed that if spectators left for any reason, they risked losing their seats. A special section was designated for legislators who were not members of the committee. To accommodate the press coverage for what would be a major media event, an adjoining room was set up with a video stream.

When the committee was called to order, it became immediately clear that no investigative business would take place that day. No witnesses would be called, and the governor was not present or officially represented. The purpose of the meeting was to formally open the investigation. The schedule and contents of the hearings were still uncertain. What would be investigated, what witnesses would be called, what evidence would be presented, and what rules would guide the investigation were not yet fully developed.

After officially opening the hearing and taking the roll call, the committee chairperson, Barbara Currie, asked whether a representative of the governor was present. Aware of future legal challenges to its actions and the importance of public opinion, the committee demonstrated its effort to be fair by offering the governor every opportunity to participate in the investigation. Currie's question was met with silence. Currie then formally introduced the committee members to the public and took note that Speaker Madigan was present in the audience. David Ellis was formally named committee counsel, and Jim Durkin was designated as minority spokesman. Matt O'Shea, the Republican chief of staff, was named minority legal counsel.

Currie's opening remarks established the public narrative for the investigative committee. She justified the action of passing HR 1650, described the circumstances of the arrest and the content of the criminal complaint as distressing, and stated that the legislature had given the governor a full week to resign. She sought to establish the legitimacy of the committee by citing the Illinois Constitution as the authority for the house to undertake an investigation of the governor. Currie pledged that the committee would be fair and the investigation would be conducted within the guidelines established by law, noting that the 1970 Constitution provided an "orderly and lawful means" to address circumstances of this nature. Cognizant of possible negative political and public perceptions of the house investigation, Currie cautioned against a "rush to judgment" and stressed that due process and the rule of law would guide deliberations. Once the investigative committee was announced, however, there was no doubt that Rod Blagojevich would have to resign or be impeached and tried in the senate. The investigative committee had not been formed to conduct a prolonged investigation, but to review the evidence accumulated by Ellis and his staff, justify cause, and pass an impeachment resolution. The investigative committee was part of the process to remove Blagojevich from office, but it had to provide the governor the right to participate, refute the charges, and argue his case. Currie emphasized that the committee did not want to interfere with the federal investigation of the criminal complaint that was being conducted by the US Attorney's Office.[2]

For the record, Jim Durkin also stressed the importance that committee members put aside any preconceived notions and feelings about the governor and advised them not to prejudge. "This has to be a fair and deliberative process," he said. The former state and county prosecutor likened the committee to a grand jury and said it must afford the governor due process, which was "paramount to our system." Partisan politics had predominated in the Illinois house for several years, and a degree of partisanship continued in the investigative committee. The Republican Party was relegated to the back bench, a situation that was not lost on Durkin. He wanted the committee to function in a bipartisan manner, and he cautioned that if the Republican members of the committee felt that the Democrats were infringing on their rights, they would hear about it.[3]

With no witnesses or agenda yet identified, Currie recognized each committee member for brief opening remarks. Members presented their obligatory statements, holding to a theme of fairness and due process. A few, anticipating the extensive press coverage, used the time to express outrage and shame. Without committee rules or a substantive agenda, the meeting was short. Currie announced that the committee would meet the next day, and the proceedings were adjourned.

Criminal Charges

The following day, Wednesday, December 17, the committee began the work of developing a cause to impeach Rod Blagojevich. The governor was facing two distinct legal challenges: the criminal charges that were certain to be forthcoming from the US Attorney's Office, which would follow predictable court procedures, and the impeachment proceedings taking place in the Illinois General Assembly, which were not subject to court precedent.

Barbara Currie opened the second day of investigative hearings by recognizing Ed Genson as the governor's counsel. On December 10, the day after his arrest, Blagojevich had contacted this well-known criminal defense attorney to represent him in the house hearings. The skillful and colorful Genson was a high-profile Chicago attorney whose past clients included Conrad Black, the former chairman of Hollinger International, and R&B singer R. Kelly. Both cases had been well covered by the Chicago press. Now, his entry into the hearing room caused a noticeable stir from the audience. The sixty-seven-year-old Genson, using a motorized scooter, passed down the committee room aisle like a celebrity, shaking hands with well-wishers and stopping occasionally to exchange greetings with friends. Genson was at home in Chicago's federal and Cook County courts, but now, dealing with the Illinois house, he was entering new territory. The investigative committee was not a court of law, and though there were some commonalities, it did not function strictly as a grand jury. The rules of evidence and the extent of due process were at the committee's discretion, and the rules regarding the conduct of the impeachment investigation were developed by the investigative committee. Genson was given little notice of the administrative matters that would be presented to the investigative committee and was prepared only to respond to the criminal complaint that had led to the governor's arrest.[4] He was assisted by Chicago attorney Sam Adam Jr.

Currie reiterated her remarks of the day before that the committee "was not a court of law" and "not quite a grand jury." She reminded everyone that the committee was not subject to the rules of evidence or any procedures that might apply in a court of law. She then introduced David Ellis to present the rules that the committee would follow during its investigation (48).[5]

Ellis and his staff had been working on the committee rules for the past week. The Republicans were not consulted or given an opportunity to provide suggestions and had received the rules from the Democratic staff the evening before.[6] It was clear that the rules gave the Speaker full control over the hearings, and Republican members were not pleased. Jim Durkin's response to the committee rules was predictable but measured. He and Matt O'Shea had gone over the rules with Currie the night before, and he was particularly concerned that subpoena power was granted only to Currie and the Speaker. Rules governing the 1997 impeachment investigation of James D. Heiple established a committee co-chaired by a Democrat and a Republican. The members of the 1997 committee were evenly divided between the two parties, and subpoena authority was jointly shared. Heiple was a Republican, and in 1997 the Illinois house had been controlled by the Democrats. Giving the Republicans equal control of the Heiple investigation helped the majority Democrats erase notions that he was being investigated for political reasons. Now the house was once again controlled by the Democrats, but Blagojevich also was a Democrat. Blagojevich's governing antics had been widely reported, and granting the Republicans equal control of the investigation could result in the investigation probing into areas that might be politically embarrassing for the majority party. The Speaker needed to ensure that he would maintain control of the proceedings, so the minority party was relegated to the back bench.

Ellis quickly outlined the twenty committee rules. The rules established that any committee action would require eleven votes. The majority Democrats had twelve members on the committee. The rules provided that the committee chairperson would "attempt" to provide twenty-four hours' notice of any meetings and, most important, that any requests for subpoenas would have to be delivered to the chairperson. Currie would then turn the subpoena requests over to the Speaker, and he would make the decision to issue subpoenas in the name of the committee. Madigan later recalled saying to Republican leader Cross, "He's our guy, and we'll take care of it."[7] The governor or his counsel would be limited to asking only "clarifying questions" of witnesses; they could not cross-examine them. Blagojevich or his counsel could call witnesses subject to "reasonableness" and the consent of the chairperson. Currie also maintained authority to determine admissibility of any evidence.[8]

While maintaining tight control over the committee may have been motivated partly by partisan politics, it was also prompted by a concern that Blagojevich might turn the hearings into a public relations circus. Initially, in conjunction with his arrest and the complaint of attempting to sell the senate seat vacated by Barack Obama, the governor asked that newly designated White House chief of staff Rahm Emanuel and the president-elect be called as witnesses. As the hearings progressed, Blagojevich demanded that other national political figures be called, including US senators Harry Reid, Richard Durbin, and Edward Kennedy.

Ed Genson asked to make a comment on the rules, and Currie recognized him, but not before informing Genson that his "interest" had nothing to do with the committee rules. "Our rules are very different from what happens in the places, the venues where you ordinarily ply your trade," she said (61). Her condescending tone was not lost on Genson or the audience. The legislative committee was not dealing with routine policy matters—it was considering a criminal complaint brought by the US Attorney's Office, administrative indiscretions, and possible malfeasance. Genson was a criminal defense attorney. He was not acting to inform public policy, but as an attorney appearing before the committee to address the criminal complaint brought against the governor of Illinois. Currie's attitude toward Genson might also have been a defensive maneuver. She was aware of the wily Genson's reputation. He was one of the best, always probing, sometimes with indignation, sometimes feigning a confused and befuddled manner to throw his opponents off guard. Currie was not going to allow courtroom theatrics. She made it clear from the start—she was going to run the hearings.

Taken aback, Genson replied indignantly, "I ply my trade in many places" (61). The experienced courtroom lawyer quickly regained his comportment and questioned why there was nothing in the rules that addressed the vagueness of the Illinois Constitution in regard to "standard of proof" or the "basis for impeachment." Currie was not about to debate the adequacy of the Constitution or let Genson control the discussion; either would have been problematic. She informed Genson that the Constitution was clear: "Impeachment is appropriate if there is cause for impeachment" (62). The exchange between Currie and Genson was followed by a short but restrained partisan debate regarding the committee makeup and the power to subpoena witnesses that was provided in the committee's rules. Predictably, the rules were adopted by a straight-line party vote, all twelve Democrats voting yes and all nine Republicans voting no (68–72).

Genson earlier had filed a motion with the committee to request that it appoint counsel for the governor. By appointing counsel, the state would then be responsible for attorney fees, thereby relieving Blagojevich of having to incur personal legal fees. The request was a long shot, but Genson tried. When describing the committee's exhibits, Currie addressed Genson's motion. She informed Genson that the motion was inappropriate and that the committee would not take it up. The proper place to request the motion, she told Genson, was with the state Attorney General's Office. Genson replied that he had already filed a motion with the attorney general (72).

Currie informed the audience that the day would be devoted to considering the criminal complaint submitted by the US attorney. But before the criminal complaint could be presented, Genson interrupted and asked that committee members Jill Tracy, Jack Franks, and William Black be precluded from participating in the hearing. He said that those three members, in remarks they had made the day before, had "made it perfectly clear that they already made up their mind in this case" regarding the governor's guilt or innocence (75). He stressed that in the previous day's discussions, the attitude echoed by several members of the committee was that due process should prevail, and if due process was to prevail, committee members should approach their task with an open mind. In a court of law Genson's argument would have had merit, but this was a hearing in the Illinois legislature, a procedure not subject to any provisions of the law. Currie responded that the extent of due process was the committee's prerogative, and she rejected Genson's proposal.

The experienced defense attorney had one more motion, this one pertaining to procedural substance. He pointed out that he had received just a one-day notification of the hearing, that he had received "no list of witnesses," and that he had not had the time to identify and subpoena witnesses. He asked that the hearing be adjourned to give him "appropriate time to prepare" (77). The audience followed Genson's performance with fascination. The decisions of the chairperson were predetermined—everyone knew that—and there was no question that the outcome of the hearings would be a recommendation to impeach. But Genson's blend of strategy, theater, and knowledge of the law provided an intriguing spectacle. Most in the audience knew of Ed Genson's reputation; his past clients had received much attention in the press. Now, as they observed the drama unfolding before them, they seemed both amused and captivated.

Currie again rejected Genson's motion and repeated that the subject of the day's hearing would be the criminal complaint. She reminded Genson that he was Blagojevich's attorney and said she assumed that he had read the complaint, in particular the sections dealing with Blagojevich fund-raisers Ali Ata and Joe Cari.[9] She reminded Genson that he did not have subpoena power and said she doubted that the committee would give it to him. Currie stated again, "We are not subject to the kinds of rules that might apply in a courtroom" (77). It was important that the committee proceed with the inquiry, she said. Genson quickly countered that accepting the criminal complaint as a basis for the committee's inquiry was a violation of the US criminal code, and he read a portion of the code supporting his position. He claimed that he had not been presented with the tapes or documents, so there was no way they could test the material at this point to consider whether the criminal complaint was illegal (79). Without addressing the substance of Genson's claim, Currie simply informed him again that the committee was not a court and asked Ellis to present the criminal complaint.

Taking a position at the witness table, Ellis began to summarize the seventy-six-page criminal complaint filed by the US attorney that had prompted Blagojevich's arrest. According to the criminal complaint, the US government had been investigating the Blagojevich administration since 2003 and Rod Blagojevich had attempted to gain financial benefits for appointments to state boards and commissions, state employment, and state contracts; had attempted to access state funds; had threatened to withhold Illinois Financial Authority (IFA) assistance from the Tribune Company with regard to the sale of Wrigley Field unless the company fired members of the editorial board of its newspaper, the *Chicago Tribune*; and—the most damning charge—had attempted to trade the appointment of the US Senate seat vacated by Barack Obama.[10] Ellis took note of House Bill (HB) 824, legislation banning large contributions from state contractors who received contracts worth $50,000 or more to the state officeholders who awarded the contract.[11] He explained that the bill would become law on January 1, 2009, and that Blagojevich had "accelerated his efforts to get as much money as he could" before the law went into effect. "On the basis of that information, the government obtained court approval to intercept oral communications in certain locations of the offices of Friends of Blagojevich," Ellis said. (Friends of Blagojevich was the name of the account used for expenses and donations to the governor for political activities.) It was during the monitoring of communications regarding efforts to accumulate contributions before that date that the government uncovered "three different areas of criminal conduct": the attempts to obtain campaign contributions for official acts, to extort the Tribune Company, and to trade the appointment to the US Senate seat in return for something of personal value (85).

Methodically, Ellis summarized the criminal complaint, taking care to cover each specific incident with as much detail as he could glean from the document. Ellis and the committee had access to only a small portion of the FBI's taped conversations that appeared in the criminal complaint, but what he had was powerful. He started with the Tribune Company, which owned the Chicago Cubs but sought to sell the baseball team to pay down debt when the company began to experience financial difficulty. In conjunction with these efforts, the company explored the possibility of receiving funds from the IFA.[12] But the *Chicago Tribune* had been negatively reporting on Blagojevich for years and had recently endorsed Speaker Madigan for reelection, suggesting that he form an inquiry committee to study the possibility of removing Blagojevich from office. Editorials in the paper questioned the governor's previous moves to bypass the legislature. Obtaining funds from the IFA did not require legislative approval. The governor could grant funds at his discretion—precisely what the *Chicago Tribune* had argued against in its Op-Ed pages. Blagojevich saw the irony of the situation and a chance to remove his nemeses from the *Tribune*. He instructed Deputy Governor John Harris to convey to the Tribune Company management that it needed to fire those people responsible for the negative editorials. Ellis went on in detail to describe taped conversations between Blagojevich and Harris and between Harris and a contact person representing the Tribune.

Throughout the investigative hearings, Representatives Lou Lang and John Fritchey, both attorneys, functioned as designated committee monitors, making sure that evidence or statements presented were clarified to establish facts and concepts previously determined by house leaders. Lang coached witnesses and channeled the questioning to establish the arguments necessary to justify impeachment. Lang asked Ellis to clarify the relationship between the IFA and the Illinois government both for the record and for the benefit of the audience. Ellis answered but Lang elaborated further, establishing that the IFA is not a state agency under the governor's control but instead a governing board, and that even though the governor appoints the members, he should have no control over their actions, to which Ellis agreed (97). John Fritchey asked the committee's counsel to clarify that the role of the committee was not to determine criminal conduct but to determine whether Blagojevich's conduct was "appropriate for the governor of the State of Illinois." Ellis answered, "You have really unfettered discretion to consider what is cause for impeachment," and, injecting a metaphor, "the line to impeach has never been drawn at criminal activity alone." For the committee's record, Fritchey reiterated again that the committee did not have to infer criminal activity (99).

Ellis continued his summarization of the criminal complaint and moved to the allegations related to the vacant US Senate seat. In a rapid, almost dizzying fashion, Ellis told of the various scenarios Blagojevich had discussed with John Harris, which included five possible candidates and what he could get in return for appointing each one. It was clear that Blagojevich was interested in money and a future position for himself. Rod Blagojevich was tired of the duties of being governor, the steady stream of negative press, and his deteriorating relationship with the legislature. And because of his extravagant lifestyle, he needed money. He stated in the conversations recorded by the FBI that his decision regarding who would fill the vacant seat was based on "our legal situation, our personal situation, my political situation." Harris responded that the legal situation was the hardest, but Blagojevich remarked that he could solve that by appointing himself to the senate seat (117).

At the end of a lengthy recitation of those sections of the complaint that dealt with Blagojevich's efforts to barter the senate seat, Lang and Fritchey again asked questions to clarify what Ellis had presented. Lang's question was of a legal nature and concerned the role of probable cause as an element in charging a defendant. He asked Ellis if the US Attorney's Office had a time limit to receive an indictment from the criminal complaint. Ellis responded that within a certain amount of time, the courts had to show probable cause to charge. "My understanding is you get probable cause from an indictment from a grand jury or through a preliminary hearing from a judge," he answered. Ellis reminded the committee that the governor had a preliminary hearing scheduled for mid-January (132). Since probable cause of criminal activity had not been formally established, the committee was hearing a recitation from a criminal complaint that would perhaps, with review, go forward to an indictment. John Fritchey added that the complaint was signed by an FBI agent, Daniel Cain, and that Cain's signature alone attested to the accuracy of the information. Agent Cain had expressed that there was probable cause to believe that the governor had committed the crimes stated in the complaint, Fritchey explained, then asked Ellis if this was correct. Ellis responded affirmatively and added that a federal magistrate judge, Michael Mason, had also signed the criminal complaint. Fritchey again emphasized that the criminal process differed from what the committee was undertaking, but that the criminal complaint attested to by the FBI and signed by a judge was reason for the committee to believe that the crimes had been committed. Ellis said that Fritchey's remarks were a "fair statement" (133).

Ellis moved on to the so-called "pay-to-play" components of the criminal complaint—the charges related to extorting money in return for official acts. In detail, he summarized three areas: attempts to extort $500,000 from highway contractors, an attempt to extort $50,000 from Children's Memorial Hospital in Chicago, and an attempt to receive $100,000 from horse-racing interests for signing a bill that the horse-racing lobby backed. Blagojevich, he charged, when contemplating spending $1.8 billion for tollway improvements, had subsequently contacted a highway contractor. The governor told the contractor he was excited about the project and then switched to discussing fund-raising. He informed the contractor that contributions had to be received prior to January 1, when the provisions of HB 824 would become law. The amount of the project was flexible, and the governor later was recorded as saying, "I could have made a larger announcement but wanted to see how they perform by the end of the year. If they don't perform, f—— 'em"

To the hearing-room audience, made up of politicians, political practitioners, and observers, the language taken from the criminal complaint used in the arrest of Blagojevich seemed incredible. The cognitive dissonance caused by the contrast between the reality of our political process and our liberal democratic values, of exchanging favors or deference for campaign support, could normally be accommodated. The political process has always been one of reciprocal arrangements. "One hand washes the other and both hands wash the face," say the old precinct workers in Chicago. Most people acknowledge that friendship and support are realities of the political process and have an existential faith that the public good is ultimately served. But extortion—the blatant demands for cash in exchange for public duties—could not be reconciled.[13] The crude, vulgar babble between the governor and his associates stunned the audience. They sat in silence.

Ellis moved on to a topic that proved to be the most resonating of the pay-to-play charges: the attempt to extort money from Children's Memorial Hospital. The legislators on the committee and everyone in the audience found the governor's statements inconceivable. Blagojevich plotted to extort money from Children's Memorial by withholding $8 million in state funds for pediatric care reimbursements unless hospital executives made a donation of $50,000. Recorded in several conversations with a person identified only as Deputy Governor A, the governor discussed how to motivate someone referred to as Hospital Executive 1 to contribute before January 1. Deputy Governor A assured Blagojevich that the funds were discretionary, and the governor responded that the money could be "pulled back" because of budget concerns. The hospital executive failed to respond to calls from Deputy Governor A, and a frustrated Blagojevich was recorded as saying, "What are we going to do with this guy?" (139).

At the end of 2008 Illinois' horse-racing industry was interested in the governor signing HB 4758. For years the subject of Illinois gaming had been hotly debated. The legislature had authorized casino gambling more than a decade before, and the horse-racing industry claimed that the expansion of gaming had caused the tracks to experience a drop in revenue. Over the years several bills had been introduced in the legislature dealing with the gaming industry, and the common question at the end of each legislative session was whether there would be a gaming bill. Every year dozens of lobbyists descended on Springfield in the last days of the legislative session, each promoting the interests of their clients. The self-interest initiatives of the various gaming interests—casinos, video gaming, and horse racing— were usually unable to reach a compromise, and the bills would fail to move. During the regular session of 2008 HB 4758 managed to survive and was considered during the veto session. A compromise was reached, and HB 4758 was passed by both chambers and sent to the governor for signature. Blagojevich saw a chance to profit before the end of the year.

In 2008 Balmoral Park, a horse-racing track located in south suburban Chicago, had hired Alonzo "Lon" Monk as a lobbyist. A former sports agent in California, Monk had been Blagojevich's law school buddy. He was a trusted confidant, and upon taking office, Blagojevich appointed Monk as chief of staff. Trading on his relationship with the governor, Monk left the Blagojevich administration and became an Illinois lobbyist. It was well known that anyone who wanted access to the governor hired Lon Monk. He soon had a long list of clients and was reportedly making more than $1 million a year after leaving state government.[14] Monk was later identified on the FBI recordings as Lobbyist 1.

Quoting from the criminal complaint, Ellis reported on conversations between the governor and Monk concerning a contribution of $100,000 from an owner of Balmoral Park. The recorded conversation made it clear that the contribution was in exchange for the governor signing the bill. It was also clear that Blagojevich was fully aware of the extortion. In one segment of the recordings, Monk urged the governor to call the racetrack owner personally, and Blagojevich suggested what he should use as his "reason" for the call (140–41).

Moving to another portion of the criminal complaint, Ellis told the committee of two individuals named in the complaint, Ali Ata and Joseph Cari. Ata had served as the executive director of the Illinois Finance Authority. Cari was a former Democratic National Committee finance chairman and a director with Health Point, a private equity firm that had received $35 million in investment contracts with the Illinois Teachers Retirement System in 2003. Both men were entangled in Operation Board Games, the federal government's ongoing investigation of the Blagojevich administration, and both pleaded guilty to federal crimes and testified against Blagojevich confidant Tony Rezko.[15] As part of his cooperation agreement, Ata pleaded guilty to making false statements to the FBI and to tax fraud. He testified that he had given a total of $50,000 to Blagojevich as payment for a position with the IFA. Cari pleaded guilty to attempted extortion of JER Partners, a real estate investment firm that was seeking investment capital from the Illinois Teachers Retirement System (151–57).[16] At the time of Blagojevich's arrest, both men were cooperating with the government.

Portions of the testimony Ata and Cari provided to the federal prosecutors were included in the criminal complaint and offered ample evidence of the involvement of Rod Blagojevich in both the selling of the IFA position and the attempted extortion of JER. Ellis recounted the numerous meetings and discussions among Blagojevich, Ata, and Rezko. He also reported Ata's testimony that he had handed money to Rezko, who later, in Ata's presence, gave the money to Rod Blagojevich. Cari testified that he had been involved with Blagojevich, Rezko, and fund-raisers Chris Kelly and Stuart Levine and had been told that he could profit from raising money for Blagojevich. He had been told, he testified, of a plan for Chris Kelly and Tony Rezko to pick consultants for the businesses that receive contracts from the state. Rezko informed Cari that he had a personal relationship with Rod Blagojevich and that the governor's chief of staff, Lon Monk, would work to ensure Rezko's choice of consultants. Business firms would be required to hire consultants picked by Rezko and Kelly, and those consultants would then funnel part of their fees to the Blagojevich campaign. Rezko also informed Cari that in exchange for raising money for Blagojevich, the administration would be financially helpful to Cari (154–57).[17]

Having reported the numerous charges of wrongdoing, Ellis was now finished with the summary of the criminal complaint. Surprisingly, given the deeds that had just been presented, the audience did not react with shock or amazement. For many in the audience, the array of charges was familiar. Because of the almost continuous media coverage since the arrest, the coverage of the recently concluded Rezko trial, and the ongoing reporting of the investigations and alleged investigations of the governor's office, the public had become well acquainted with the exploits of Blagojevich and his co-conspirators. Here it all was, neatly laid out in the criminal complaint and summarized by the house counsel.

Barbara Currie informed Edward Genson that the committee would be happy to "hear some brief remarks." Genson incredulously responded, "Brief?" and Currie replied calmly, "Please." A feeling of expectation seemed to spread through the room. How would Blagojevich's counsel respond? Ed Genson sat looking rumpled and at times befuddled, hunched over his papers, moving occasionally with lurching motions. The audience was not fooled by his deliberately expressed confusion and awkwardness; perception was an essential part of the courtroom lawyer's performance. Genson knew he was in unfamiliar territory, and he had to try to achieve as much leverage as possible despite the committee's restrictive rules.

It became immediately clear that Genson was not going to be given any courtroom leeway. The committee rules did not give the defense the opportunity to cross-examine witnesses, but the seasoned defense attorney began his remarks by questioning the validity of Ellis's use of the criminal complaint as the source of the charges presented. In hectoring tones, he began questioning Ellis. Ellis asked Genson if he was being questioned. Genson replied that he was, and Ellis objected, stating that the committee rules did not provide for the governor's representatives to cross-examine him. Currie sustained Ellis's objection and informed Genson that cross-examination was not allowed.

Appearing to reluctantly accept his limitations, Genson seemingly acquiesced to giving a brief statement but immediately referred to what he called "inaccuracies" and again presented a question to Ellis. Again Ellis appealed to Currie that he was being cross-examined. The room became tense. Genson, given the circumstances, was doing his best to challenge the basis of Ellis's statements, the criminal complaint. He postulated that probable cause had not yet been determined from the criminal complaint, pointed out there had been no indictment, and challenged John Fritchey's earlier remarks that probable cause had already been determined.

Careen Gordon, a Democratic committee member and a lawyer, jumped to the defense of Ellis. A former Grundy County prosecutor, she voiced that probable cause had been determined and had been the basis for the wiretaps. The conversation grew heated when Gordon told Genson that he should go back to practicing criminal law and Genson responded that Gordon should go back to law school. Genson contended that the content of the wiretaps should not be allowed as evidence in the hearing, because under the standards of due process, his client had not been given the opportunity to test their accuracy. He claimed that Rod Blagojevich had not heard the wiretap recordings and that he could not determine whether the statements in the criminal complaint were taken out of context. He also argued that for the committee to proceed using a summary of the wiretaps before they could be examined and rebutted by defense counsel "was unfair and illegal" (170).

Next, Genson brought up the mysterious identification of people in the wiretapped conversations, referred to as Hospital Executive 1 and Deputy Governor A, and asserted that he was not able to discover who these people were. In regard to selling the US Senate seat, he claimed that there was no proof that any illegal exchange had occurred. Jack Franks interrupted. Franks and his father, who was also an attorney, were both acquaintances of Ed Genson's, and Genson made a polite reference to their relationship. Franks told Genson that the committee's purpose was not to find guilt and that perhaps Genson's argument should wait for "a different forum" (172). Genson responded that he was requesting due process from the committee. He did not have subpoena power but argued that if he did, he would call the mysteriously identified people and question them. The use of hearsay as evidence was unfair, and it was unfair to use anonymous people, he said. To deprive Rod Blagojevich of the right to confront his accusers was also unfair. Genson attacked the accusations made by Ata and Cari and reminded the committee that Ali Ata is an admitted perjurer and that Joe Cari is an admitted extortionist. Stuart Levine, Genson told the committee, was facing life imprisonment. He was involved in bribery, tax fraud, defrauding the estate of a business associate, and using illegal narcotics. "This is the character of the statements of Mr. Levine," Genson said (179–80).

The defense counsel continued to summarize his argument against the criminal complaint. He talked about the criterion for impeachment— *cause*—and recalled Ellis speaking of "the line that had to be crossed." The line had never been drawn before, Genson said, the criterion for impeachment was nebulous, and he did not know of any record of case law that defined the standard of cause. The line for impeachment should be based on evidence and based on due process and, he added, based on confrontation.

Cause, he asserted, must mean something. Speaker Madigan had spoken about due process in his press conference on Monday—in fact, everybody was taking about due process—but due process, Genson reminded the committee, meant consideration of the evidence. To sit and listen to hearsay upon hearsay was inappropriate, he said. He went through the charges offered in the criminal complaint. None of the accusations regarding the Tribune Company had been corroborated. All that had been presented was a man who said he could do something, but there was nothing to prove that the man had talked to anyone, and Tribune Company officials were not at the hearing to confirm or deny the accusation. "Just people jabbering," Genson said (183).

With regard to Children's Memorial Hospital, there was "no evidence that anyone did anything wrong," and concerning the US Senate seat, Genson again stressed that there was no evidence that anyone had done anything wrong. The lawyer concluded by telling the committee that he could not convince them that he was right in the short period of time allotted to him and that it was incumbent that the panel members read the charges "one at a time and determine whether it's just somebody who says inappropriate things in a two-month wiretap" (184). The committee, he said, was a jury, and each member had to decide whether what he or she heard was sufficient to "kick a guy out of office" and "whether it's enough and whether it's time" (185). The standard for impeachment in Illinois had never been set. It was not a visceral standard, not intuitive, but a standard that the impeachment panel had to determine.

The reaction to Genson's remarks was difficult to measure. His remarks did not end the day's proceedings or even a portion of the proceedings. There was no pause to contemplate what had been said. The hearing continued with Currie recognizing the Republican spokesman Jim Durkin. The former Cook County prosecutor took issue with Genson's claims that the hearing did not allow due process and that the committee should not listen to hearsay. He reminded Genson that grand juries are allowed to consider hearsay and that the lawyer had been allowed "more process than anybody that's been before the grand jury representing clients" (186). Committee members were capable of "connecting the dots," and they were going to accept hearsay and make their own determination concerning the value of the documents before them (188).

Genson attempted to cast doubt on the evidence and express skepticism of the process. He did what good defense attorneys do, but the reality was that he was not in a courtroom. The committee was presented with evidence and would decide, as a grand jury, whether the governor should be tried by the senate. Rod Blagojevich did not have a supporter on the committee, and the few friends he had in the legislature had all taken political cover. The committee had been chosen by the house Democratic and Republican leadership to reach a decision to impeach. Careful consideration had been placed on geography, gender, race, and—most important—opposition to the governor.[18] Statements by the committee members to be fair and deliberate notwithstanding, the end result was predetermined. The hearing was a show, but it was not a sham. The vague language in the Illinois Constitution gave the legislature the prerogative to act as it saw fit, and the evidence supporting a resolution of impeachment was overwhelming. The house committee was holding deliberative hearings, but it was acting to begin the removal of the governor.

Administrative Charges, Part I

The third day of hearings saw a noticeably larger crowd of spectators, and there was a perceptible feeling of anticipation. Reporters congregated beneath the historic paintings that hang along the first-floor hallway of the capitol as legislators, staff, and members of the public passed through security and entered room 114. On the previous day the committee had been presented with the criminal charges leveled at the governor; now accusations of malfeasance and maladministration would be offered and representatives of the Blagojevich administration would appear. The committee needed these accusations to build its case and give credence to the cause for impeachment. The committee and David Ellis did not have time to build a case based on evidence derived from any further investigations; they had to go with already available evidence of the governor's past misdeeds.

The accusations Ellis put before the committee were well-documented incidents concerning the ongoing dispute between the Joint Committee on Administrative Rules (JCAR) and the governor's office over the expansion of the state's FamilyCare program, a botched flu vaccine purchase from a foreign manufacturer in violation of US law, and a controversy over the importation of drugs from a foreign country as part of ongoing state health insurance programs, also a violation of US law. Evidence of the flu vaccine purchase and the importation of drugs was contained in an auditor general's audit, performed in response to an investigation by the house

State Government Administration Committee and a subsequent resolution providing for an audit, introduced by committee chairman Jack Franks. A second, routine audit of the Department of Central Management Services, also performed by the Auditor General's Office, uncovered discrepancies and possible wrongdoing concerning the methods used in granting contracts and selecting vendors.

The controversy over the governor's refusal to comply with the decisions of JCAR regarding the FamilyCare expansion was the most recent and well-known incident, so it seemed wise to begin the hearings with that. It was ongoing, received extensive press coverage, and served the committee's purpose: to cast the Blagojevich administration as operating contrary to the law, violating the principle of separation of powers, and usurping legislative prerogative. Currie and Ellis initially sought to legitimize their claim of malfeasance, wrongful conduct by a public official. To add credence to the contention, the committee asked Professors Andrew Morriss and Robert Rich to appear as witnesses and to explain and justify—from a scholarly perspective—the concept of balance of power, the provisions of the Illinois Constitution, and the authority of JCAR. The committee was well aware of JCAR and its functions, and in fact, some members of the investigative committee were concurrently serving as committee members of JCAR. The professors' appearance was meant to legitimize the claim of malfeasance to the general public, to provide sanction of Illinois' system of rule review by a respected academic institution, and to show that the governor was ignoring the system by usurping a legislative prerogative and was conceivably violating the Constitution.

Andrew Morriss was the first witness. The law professor carefully explained JCAR's structure and Illinois' rule-making process and procedures. It was important, for public acceptance, that the committee establish the institutional validity of the JCAR process to uphold the charge that the governor usurped legislative prerogative. Morriss, a lawyer with a PhD in economics, met the committee's expectations. His scholarly recitation, delivered in a measured and professional manner, served to legitimize the JCAR incident as a valid inquiry by the investigative committee.

Robert Rich next gave his testimony, which focused on the particulars of the FamilyCare controversy. Rich provided facts and figures that would result from the program's expansion and also speculated about potential welfare fraud being attributed to state workers who enrolled someone for a state subsidy that exceeded the limits of the program established by the legislature. He further asked whether doctors who treated people and then billed the state could be party to welfare fraud and whether they would ever be paid. If the state refused to pay the bills, he wondered, would applicants be subject to economic hardships? And where would the state obtain the $200 million projected to be the costs of expanding FamilyCare? "In my judgment what was done here represents a real problem," Rich said, and "in my judgment these actions are irresponsible, not consistent with appropriate, constitutionally provided checks and balances" (208–9).[19] Ed Genson sat quietly but took note of Rich's remarks.

To present the functions of JCAR, again for the benefit of public observers, the committee invited Vicki Thomas, JCAR's executive director. Thomas was a career bureaucrat who had served in that capacity for seventeen years. She grew up in Olney, Illinois, and after graduating from Southern Illinois University, she followed the suggestion of a career counselor and applied for a position with the Illinois senate Democrats. She was hired and worked on the staff of the senate president, Phil Rock. When Rock retired, she became executive director of JCAR. The methods and mannerisms of Vicki Thomas exemplified the epitome of a competent and dedicated public servant. She managed JCAR in a precise and scrupulous fashion. She was an ideal witness to expound on the authority of JCAR and to provide solid, factual evidence for the committee to use in constructing impeachment charges.

Similarly to the two professors, Thomas reinforced the legitimacy of JCAR and presented an overview of the intricacies of its workings. Her testimony, advised by Democratic members of the committee, consisted of a meticulous review of JCAR's functions, including the number of rules submitted each year, the relationship to the General Assembly, and the process of filing and modifying rules—JCAR 101, as she called it (224).

She focused especially on past difficulties her agency had experienced when dealing with the Blagojevich administration. Reciting the particulars of JCAR's operations and describing specific incidents when the governor attempted to obfuscate his actions or ignore JCAR's role resulted in Thomas giving extended testimony. To some in the audience, Thomas's statements had become tedious. Currie politely asked the witness to get to the point: the emergency rule and JCAR's rejection. Lou Lang, one of Thomas's advisors, came to her defense and informed the chairman that what Thomas was relating was critical. Attempting to move things along and maintain unity, Currie instructed Thomas to "carry on." Thomas reminded the committee that she had been asked to put the FamilyCare incident into "a framework of past experience to lead into the actions of the Department of Healthcare and Family Services (HFS)." Currie encouraged her to "go right to that" (232). Thomas presented a step-by-step review of the emergency rule, JCAR's rejection of the rule, the impact to the state budget of the expanded program, and the response of HFS.

Although Thomas's testimony was lengthy and went into great detail, it met the committee's objectives. She gave the impression of a consummate bureaucrat representing a legislative agency struggling to accomplish its tasks in accordance with established legal procedures, within the context of the Constitution, and in spite of political interference from the governor. She further institutionalized the role of JCAR and demonstrated that what HFS had attempted usurped legislative prerogative, was fiscally irresponsible and unconstitutional, and demonstrated poor governance. Her presentation helped sanction the charge of malfeasance. Ellis and Lang later apologized to Thomas for the committee's confusion over the scope of her remarks.[20]

The investigation then moved on to the most publicized element of the JCAR controversy. The prosecution witnesses were plaintiffs in the Caro case, Ron Gidwitz and Greg Baise, and their attorneys, Tom Hecht and Claudette Miller, from the Chicago law firm of Ungaretti and Harris. The Caro lawsuit had been covered by the press since its filing a year before, but it had emerged as a major topic in the last few months. Originally filed by Riverside attorney Richard Caro, the lawsuit was joined by Gidwitz and Baise, who in turn retained Ungaretti and Harris. Ron Gidwitz was a well-known Chicago-area businessman who had been active in Republican politics since the 1980s and had developed a reputation for his work in civic and charitable organizations. Greg Baise was a veteran of state government and the president of the Illinois Manufacturers' Association (IMA), a leading business trade association. Both Gidwitz and Baise served as symbols of the business community and became parties to the Caro litigation as Illinois taxpayers. The involvement of Gidwitz and Baise brought financial resources and a team of lawyers to the case. The Caro lawsuit expressed the substance of the committee's argument regarding the JCAR controversy: by ignoring JCAR and expanding the FamilyCare program without legislative approval and appropriation, the governor was acting in violation of the Illinois Constitution. The Caro case had not yet been settled, and Gidwitz reviewed the details of the proceedings to date.

To emphasize the investigation's impartiality and balance the testimony presented by the University of Illinois professors, the executive director of JCAR, and the litigants in the Caro lawsuit, the committee invited representatives of HFS, the defendants in the Caro case, to give testimony. The nature of the testimony presented by the preceding witnesses had been advised by the committee. In contrast, HFS was provided short notice and received the committee's request to appear only the day before. The department seemed to be a crew adrift without a captain. After Currie requested that the department appear, little thought or direction concerning the committee's request was forthcoming from the governor's office, where things were in disarray. Ed Genson was only peripherally aware of the JCAR controversy. Who made the decision that HFS would comply with the committee's request to appear is difficult to ascertain. Barry Maram, the director of HFS, agreed to appear voluntarily. He later would not comment on the decision to attend the impeachment hearings and declined to discuss his role.[21] The committee had subpoena power and could have exercised it, but committee members felt that Maram was confident that he could deal with the committee's questions. Maram, HFS chief of staff Tamara Tanzillo Hoffman, and attorney Larry Blust were sworn in before the committee.

Maram and Hoffman were the first and only representatives of the Blagojevich administration to appear before the committee. Their appearance did not serve to support the governor's position. The committee was intent on establishing, for the record, that the governor was responsible for the decision to ignore the verdict of JCAR and proceed with the expansion of the FamilyCare program. The committee also intended to show that no funds had been appropriated by the legislature for expansion of the program, that the expansion had cost Illinois taxpayers millions of dollars, and that the governor had been fully aware of the consequences, as illustrated by his own press statements. If the committee could prove that the governor had engineered these violations, then it had proof of administrative malfeasance.

Maram began his testimony with a tedious review of the federal government's State Children's Health Insurance Program (SCHIP) and reported that actions by the Illinois legislature, Congress and President George W. Bush had reduced the program. The committee and the audience immediately sensed that Maram's initial remarks were an attempt to obfuscate the JCAR issue with a recitation of known facts. John Fritchey, a member of JCAR who was familiar with the facts, quickly interrupted and focused on the committee's interests. He asked Maram why, instead of submitting an emergency rule to restore only the people dropped from the FamilyCare program because of the federal pullout, the administration had sought to expand the program. Trying to implicate Blagojevich specifically, Fritchey wanted to know who had made the decision to expand the program.

Fritchey repeatedly asked who had made this decision, but neither Maram nor Hoffman gave a definitive answer. Fritchey was a respectful interrogator, but as the questioning continued, the witnesses seemed to become unnerved. At one point, addressing the subject of lawyer-client privilege, given as a reason for not answering Fritchey's question, Hoffman sputtered, "I'm a lawyer. I don't—I don't know the rules about privilege and what is or isn't. My parents worked most of their lives two—you know two jobs for me to have my law license, and I don't know the parameters of what the code presents" (261–62). Maram and Hoffman said they could not recall any specific directions having come from the governor or the governor's office. They recalled discussing FamilyCare but could not recall who was in the meetings or any specific conversations with individuals concerning the expansion of the program, and they continued to dodge questions and give vague answers. They told Fritchey that they would check their notes, if they had them, and get back to the committee.

The witnesses appeared evasive and at times obviously befuddled. Their refusal to answer questions played into the hands of the accusers. The audience members became fascinated, and several shook their heads in disbelief. The witnesses were representatives of the Blagojevich administration, and the spectacle before them reinforced what many had long suspected: many of the governor's administrators were not dedicated, professional public servants but devious bunglers. Ellis, as the committee counsel, could not have picked better witnesses to serve his purpose. The ineptitude displayed by the representatives of HFS bordered on buffoonery and provided an impression of the governor's administration as incompetent, evasive, and hubristic.

Mike Bost, a Republican committee member from Murphysboro, continued the line of questioning taken by Fritchey and received the same vague answers from the witnesses. After a few awkward moments, Maram asked Currie if he could continue his testimony, claiming that "other people have had the opportunity to make statements" (268). Currie said he could but cautioned him to be brief and to stay on topic. Maram's statements again began to wander off topic, relating known facts, and again Currie interrupted and reminded him that the question was the governor's authority to expand the FamilyCare program without the authorization of the legislature. He could finish his statement, Currie said, as long as he stayed on topic.

Maram continued, contending that the department's action to expand FamilyCare was taken pursuant to statutory authority and that the department had the right to set maximum income limits. The expansion, he said, was not a "huge expansion" as claimed by the plaintiffs in the Caro case and resulted in an increased enrollment of less than five thousand before the department was ordered to suspend expansion because of the ongoing Caro litigation (272). The costs of the expansion had not exceeded $6.3 million and were partly offset by premiums collected from the participants. Maram attempted to refute the Caro plaintiffs' claim that HFS lacked statutory authority to promulgate the expanded regulations and that the regulations were invalid. He argued that the courts had never contended that HFS did not have the authority to set rates based on income levels. Maram finished by reviewing statistics on previous raises of income levels and past JCAR approvals of income raises based on the impact of federal programs.

Lou Lang took up the questioning for the house majority. Lang was also a member of JCAR and was very familiar with the controversy. He wanted to establish for the record that a number of people were added to the FamilyCare program *after* JCAR prohibited the expansion and that the legislature had appropriated no funds for the expansion. Lang was a familiar voice in committee meetings and on the house floor. The tone of his questioning often bordered on sarcasm mixed with sanctimony, and he could be hectoring and at times seem irritating. His style of debating could annoy opponents, but he was skilled and his arguments were strong. Lang warned Maram that if they did not answer his questions, he would interrupt and ask the question again. He asked how many people were added to the FamilyCare program after the governor expanded it, and Hoffman responded that at one point there were five thousand and now it was about four thousand (280). Lang pounced on her answer and again asked how many people were added after JCAR prohibited the expansion of coverage. Lang wanted to establish that the department had ignored JCAR's authority and continued to enroll people in the program. He persisted, and after several back-and-forth questions and answers, the witnesses agreed to provide the committee with the true number by the end of the day.

Lang then asked Maram why the department had failed to respond to a past Freedom of Information Act (FOIA) submission by the Caro case attorneys with a similar request. Hoffman responded that the request had been denied. She said that she had seen the response letter from the department, but she could not remember what was in the letter or the reason for the denial. It was her understanding that the request had been denied "in the context of litigation," and she asked for the opportunity to consult with the attorneys involved to make sure that what she was saying was accurate (285). Lang tried to involve the governor by asking if anyone from the governor's office ever spoke to Hoffman or Maram about the FOIA requests. The witnesses responded that they had no knowledge of that but would talk to their attorneys.

Intently hunched over his notes, dressed in a white shirt and tie, with his left hand held to his forehead, Lang turned his questions to funding and asked how HFS was paying for the program expansion. Sitting erect, tense, and vigilant of his opponent's next move, Maram parried that the expansion was being funded through internal efficiency initiatives using available funds from the department's budget. Lang asked, incredulously and with a hint of sarcasm, whether the department would have a $6.3 million surplus if the program had not been expanded. Maram did not answer. Returning to the decision to go ahead with the expansion of FamilyCare, Lang asked directly if the expansion had been Maram's idea. Maram said it had not been initiated by him, but after review he was comfortable with the expansion. Lang, showing some interrogatory skill and trying once again to solicit a response that would implicate the governor, quickly asked Maram who had initiated the idea to expand the FamilyCare program. The director did not take the bait; he held firm and responded yet again that he had "no exact knowledge."

Lang continued to press the witnesses, trying to get them to admit that the governor was involved in the decision to ignore JCAR and establish that he had been aware of the financial consequences. He quoted from a November 2007 Associated Press article placing the number of caretakers and parents that would be added with the FamilyCare expansion at 147,000 and quoting the governor as saying, "I'm going to do what I think is right, and that's one of the good things about being governor . . . you can do things like this." Addressing both Maram and Hoffman, Lang asked how, in view of the extensive press coverage, it was possible that the representatives of the department could not remember anything about meetings or discussions regarding the FamilyCare expansion. Hoffman readily admitted that she had been involved in those meetings, and Lang asked who was at the meetings (293). Initially Hoffman evasively replied, "lawyers and staff," but then, bafflingly, she became specific (297). The governor had attended some meetings, she said. Pressed for the names of the people who attended the meetings, Hoffman was again evasive and said she would look for any meeting notes, and if she had them, she would forward them to the committee. Lang seized on what Hoffman had just said: that the governor was present at some meetings. He asked her if she remembered any conversations with Blagojevich concerning rule-making. Hoffman said she had told the governor that there was precedent for the emergency rule but did not talk to him about "specific rule making" (300).

Lang asked why HFS had included the expanded program in an emergency rule and then ignored JCAR's decision to reject the rule. He asked if Hoffman disagreed with Vicki Thomas's previous description of the Family-Care expansion as "cavalierly" dealing with emergency rule-making. Larry Blust, who was acting as counsel to HFS, attempted to deflect the question and interjected that it was not the function of the department to "do those kinds of things," but to the surprise of everyone, Hoffman cut him off in midsentence (302). She disagreed with Blust and said that it was the department's responsibility to determine when an emergency exists. It was odd to see the witness disagree openly with her own counsel, and the exchange reinforced the comedic appearance of Blagojevich's staff. The hearing began to take on a circus atmosphere and the audience became amused. Lang, the careful ringmaster, appeared to take no notice of the spectacle before him and continued with his questions for the record: Did Hoffman think JCAR was advisory? Had any court upheld that JCAR was advisory? When did HFS start to enroll people after the expansion was rejected? Though no definitive answers came from the witnesses, it had become clear that HFS had ignored JCAR's ruling and continued with the expanded program.

Other committee members continued with Lang's line of questioning. Republican Patti Bellock from Westmont, referring to the press conference in November 2007 that Lang had noted earlier, quoting the governor as saying JCAR does not have constitutional authority to block the expansion rule and that he was moving ahead with signing up families at a cost to the state of $43 million. Bellock's point was that the governor intentionally went ahead and dismissed JCAR's authority. Chapin Rose, a former prosecutor from the east-central Illinois town of Mahomet, was confrontational. Like Lang, he sought to establish that no court had denied the authority of JCAR and attempted to discover who had made the decision to go forward with the expansion. Maram and Hoffman again deflected his questions. Jack Franks also attempted to have the witnesses state who initiated the expansion, but to no avail.

The investigative committee sought to portray the Blagojevich administration as being fully aware of the consequences of expanding FamilyCare. It tried to identify the governor or his office as the impetus for the decision to ignore JCAR's decision, and it attempted to show that the expanded program had no funding authorization from the general assembly. The witnesses from HFS facilitated these intentions. They were unprepared to face the questions posed by the hostile committee. They had no appreciation for the committee's intent, and their evasive and bewildered manner portrayed the image the committee wished. The committee requested that the University of Illinois professors and the attorneys for the plaintiffs in the Caro case return for follow-up questions from the committee. Currie dismissed Maram and Hoffman. The committee had all it needed from them, but as it was preparing to question the previous witnesses, Sam Adam Jr., an attorney assisting Genson, asked to be recognized. He asked Maram, after Blagojevich disregarded JCAR's decision, "how many brother and sister, Illinois citizens' lives were saved as a result from that moment on? How many lives were saved because of his policy to go forward and give healthcare?" This diverged from the track of questioning by lead attorney Genson, whose questions and comments addressed points of law and established courtroom procedures. Adam's questions, posed in street vernacular, represented an abstract attempt to solicit irrelevant emotion from a specific audience and present a different characteristic to Blagojevich's defense. Genson argued points of law, while Adam was a showman. His style was confrontational, and he relied on sensationalism and intimidation (364).[22]

Lou Lang immediately objected to the question. Currie agreed and had the committee move on to follow-up questions for the University of Illinois professors. Lang and other committee members questioned Andrew Morriss and Robert Rich for the record. The questions and answers reaffirmed the authority of JCAR and the separation of power among the legislative and executive branches.

Genson attempted to challenge the qualifications of the professors who claimed that Blagojevich should be impeached for ignoring JCAR's ruling. Durkin objected and stated that Genson's questions, as prescribed in the committee rules, should be of a clarification nature only. What Genson was doing, Durkin claimed, was cross-examination. The discussion between

Genson and the committee grew heated, with members making objections to several of his questions and statements, but the lawyer endeavored to make his point: the JCAR case was not settled, the professors were merely speculating and giving their opinions, and thus there was no legal basis to justify Blagojevich being impeached. In a court of law his point would have relevance, but here it did not matter.

The investigative committee next turned to the most powerful evidence supporting the charge of maladministration: the results of the audits of the flu vaccine, the I-SaveRx program, and the activities of the Department of Central Management Services (CMS). These audits had provided indisputable evidence of mismanagement and malfeasance, gleaned meticulously by independent professionals and substantiated by hard data. Auditor General Bill Holland summarized the audit findings. Holland was well known to the committee and well respected. A former member of both the house and senate staff, he was one of them.

Holland addressed the two audits separately, beginning with the CMS audit, which focused on the administration of the efficiency initiatives program created by the legislature to seek efficient operations throughout state government. He quickly reviewed the legislative intent of the initiatives and the program's structure as defined by statute. In sonorous tones, he related what the audit had uncovered: CMS was not complying with the efficiency initiatives statute. The audit found that CMS had overbilled the state agencies, and the money was then used to pay outside vendors and consultants picked by the governor's office (418–21). As run by the Blagojevich administration, the efficiency initiatives had resulted in circumventing the legislature's appropriation process.

Holland took note of one particular company, Illinois Property Asset Management (IPAM), which received a $30 million, no-bid contract award before the company even existed. In another case, McKinsey and Company was awarded a $14.7 million contract to review the state's procurement process after McKinsey donated $52,000 to the Friends of Blagojevich, and the contract was awarded by a CMS employee who was a former employee of the company (458–59).

Jack Franks had anticipated Holland's testimony. Since the State Government Administration Committee investigation of the flu vaccine episode in 2005, and the resulting audits of CMS, the flu vaccine, and I-SaveRx in 2005 and 2006, Franks had called for further action by the legislature. Now his efforts and the findings of the audits would at last be acted upon. He was ready.

Franks interrupted Holland and began to ask questions that reinforced the findings of the audits and extended speculation of nefarious activity. Was it not true that 44 percent of contracts were not awarded to the lowest bidder? Did the company Team Services give a large contribution to Blagojevich and then receive a $5 million no-bid contract? And was it not correct that no performance guarantees were included in the IPAM contract? He asked Holland to elaborate on IPAM and if he remembered what the governor's response to the CMS audit was. Holland deferred to Franks, who answered his own question, paraphrasing the governor's statement: "this is a prize fight amongst accountants—a lot of noise but not a lot of muscle" (434). Thoroughly familiar with the audit, Franks made another supporting point: 77 percent of $708,000 of expenses examined were questionable (436).

Holland continued that in seven out of the nine contracts examined in the CMS audit, people from the governor's office had attended the selection committee meetings. Lang asked if that was unusual, and Holland answered, "Very unusual." Holland said that when the audit was performed in 2005, he had thought some of the problems were the result of "simply inexperience with the procurement process," but the events of the last nine days put what he had uncovered in 2005 in a new perspective. "In light of some of the disclosures that we see recently," he said, "maybe in retrospect this audit is a lot more valuable and a lot more relevant than what we anticipated." Lang remarked rhetorically that the committee had to face whether the actions of CMS were "simply incompetence or whether it goes beyond incompetence to some pattern of behavior that would relate to a conclusion or not as to whether the Governor was involved in an abuse of power with the distribution of contracts—the awarding of contracts at CMS" (447–50).

Indeed, the CMS audit presented tangible, indisputable evidence of misfeasance. The efficiency initiatives program was being used to create funds to award contracts to selected vendors and consultants. In light of what had been discovered, the conduct of the governor's office was cause for serious concern. The hearing-room audience listened intently as Holland related the audit findings. Many began to understand Jack Franks's passion and the investigative committee's motives.

Holland next turned to the flu vaccine and I-SaveRx audit. He briefly went through the scenario of events leading to the governor's office agreeing to purchase flu vaccines from the UK-based Ecosse Hospital Products. "The administration knew that the importation of flu vaccine was not legal," he told the committee. Although the Centers for Disease Control located sufficient flu vaccines to cover the state's priority population, the state increased the order for the number of doses to a total of 254,000. Holland pointed out that three weeks after agreeing to purchase the vaccine, the state had still not executed a contract. The governor's special advocate for prescription drugs, who negotiated the purchase, claimed that he did not know a contract was required and had been informed that the flu vaccine would be paid COD. Holland told the committee, "I know of no other product, service, or contract ever paid COD—cash on delivery—for any service in the State of Illinois—certainly not for something that was in excess of $2 million" (466–67). A contract was signed by deputy governor Louanner Peters on January 13, 2005, two days after receiving a bill from Ecosse (489). Further, the state negotiated supplying other governments with flu vaccine and increased its order with Ecosse to 773,000 doses, but no agreements with other governments ever came to fruition, so the state was left with a total liability of $8.2 million. A troubling aspect of the report, Holland related, was that high-ranking officials were aware that the vaccine would never be delivered, "even prior to being billed by the vendor and executing a contract" (468). Ecosse filed suit to recoup $2 million, and at the time of the impeachment hearings, the suit was still in litigation.

A second section of the audit concerned the I-SaveRx program, set up by the governor to provide prescriptions from pharmacies in Canada, the United Kingdom, Australia, and New Zealand. Holland testified that outreach activities for the I-SaveRx program were "primarily coordinated" by the governor's office (470). The program had not been approved—in fact, the FDA had informed the governor in writing that it violated the law. But the governor ignored the FDA's warning and expanded the program "to state employees and their dependents" (471).

Franks again asked clarifying questions. He drew the committee's attention to a visual timeline of the flu vaccine procurement and went over the events step by step. Franks asked for Holland's confirmation of doses ordered, dates, and agreement that the governor's office had signed the contract knowing the drugs would never be delivered. Holland concurred. Instead of seeking an avenue to be relieved of the contract, because it was illegal, the governor donated the $2 million worth of vaccines to the government of Pakistan, Franks claimed. Holland again agreed.

Lou Lang continued with questions for the committee record. Concerning the flu vaccine procurement, "Where was the money to come from?" Holland answered, "One of the trust funds within the Department of Public

Aid." "Assuming all of the transactions were legal," Lang asked, "would that have been appropriate?" Holland referred to a letter from Deputy Comptroller Keith Taylor to the governor's chief of staff, Lon Monk, dated January 31, 2005. The letter expressed that the comptroller's office did "not believe the Governor's office can obligate . . . another agency's appropriations to make payments for its own contract liabilities" (491–93).

Holland entertained a few random questions from the committee, but his testimony was finished and the clarifying questions exhausted. The most powerful evidence for administrative cause had been presented. David Ellis and the committee had what they wanted—tangible evidence of administrative incompetence and a pattern of suspicious behavior that more than hinted at wrongdoing.

The day was growing late, but one more set of witnesses was still to come before the committee. A growing concern throughout Blagojevich's terms in office was the disregard of requests submitted by various government watchdog groups under the Freedom of Information Act (FOIA). Several witnesses—Jay Stewart, executive director of the Better Government Association; Don Craven, appearing as a private citizen; and Paul Orfanedes, director of litigation for the conservative organization Judicial Watch—were to testify regarding the many FOIA requests, denials, and resultant ongoing litigation. But the hour was late and the committee members had expended their enthusiasm. Currie asked the witnesses to be brief. The witnesses reinforced a negative attitude toward the Blagojevich administration but provided no solid evidence. Although the FOIA denials displayed a pattern of reticent behavior, the court cases were not yet settled.

It had been an exhausting day. After a few questions from committee members, Currie announced that the committee would meet again on December 22 and cautioned members to prepare for two days of hearings. To everyone's relief, the committee adjourned.

Administrative Charges, Part II

Three days before Christmas, when the committee reconvened, the trappings of the holidays were on full display in the state capitol. The outside dome was festooned with colored lights, and a large Christmas tree adorned the center of the first floor of the rotunda. But the holiday atmosphere did not pervade the building. Inside room 114, it was business as usual. House staff was busy preparing for the meeting, doing the things that had been done hundreds of times for committee meetings. Documents were passed out and microphones checked as committee members began to drift in. It had been thirteen days since the self-assured governor was last seen shaking hands in the federal court, and despite the national media focus and widespread speculation that he would resign and reach a compromise plea with federal prosecutors, he had not. Instead, the governor had engaged in a national media campaign, attacking leaders of the house and senate and proclaiming his innocence.

Over the previous four days, through the weekend, the committee staff had worked nonstop. The cause for the impeachment resolution was beginning to take shape. The resolution would include the allegations contained in the criminal complaint, but impeachment based solely on the criminal complaint, without an indictment, no matter what degree of probable cause could be demonstrated; would be difficult. The impeachment resolution had to include incidences of misconduct or the unlawful execution of lawful acts that had occurred during the governor's administration. The previous hearing had provided what the committee needed—tangible evidence that there had been constitutional violations, the governor had usurped legislative prerogative, and he had possibly engaged in criminal activity. It was expected that the prosecution would continue to add to the growing administrative charges.

The governor's defense attorney had questioned the legality of using the federal wiretaps in the impeachment hearings, and the house counsel felt that it was important to reinforce the use of the tapes as evidence of probable cause. To justify the federal government's use of wiretaps, the committee invited retired assistant US attorney John Scully to testify. Scully was not involved with the Blagojevich case, but he was an ideal, credible witness for the prosecution. A US Naval Academy graduate, he had gone on to law school and served as a lawyer in the navy. After retiring from military service, he joined the Department of Justice. Scully was familiar with the procedures required to obtain court permission to install wiretaps, and his experience and integrity were beyond reproach.

The committee had chosen Republican Jim Durkin to be the lead interrogator to question Sully. Durkin was a seasoned trial prosecutor who was also familiar with the procedures necessary to install wiretaps.[23] His purpose was to ask questions and elicit answers that would serve to validate the necessity of, and establish a justifiable cause for, installing wiretaps. Scully's testimony would walk the committee through the process of review by the US Attorney's Office, court review, and authorization. To further legitimize Scully's testimony regarding wiretaps, Durkin started with basic questions: What were the types of intrusive devices, bugs, and wiretaps, and what did it mean to be a cooperating witness wearing a wire? Scully dutifully answered. Could he explain the process of obtaining permission to install a wiretap? Scully reviewed the steps necessary within the US Attorney's Office to prepare an affidavit and apply for court permission to install a wiretap (555–97).[24] "What you are trying to do . . . is establish probable cause, that there is evidence that various federal felonies are being committed," he said (565). Scully's testimony accomplished the committee's intent: to establish that the wiretaps had been installed only after thorough review and approval by a federal judge and that the recordings had been obtained based on probable cause.

There was little Genson could do to challenge the validity of Scully's re-marks. Instead, he attempted to use the witness to his advantage. He lauded Scully's experience and cited the many awards that Scully had received during his career with the Department of Justice. He asked Scully a series of questions concerning wiretap procedures, not to probe but to solicit affirmation and show that he and the witness were in agreement. Then Genson turned the questioning to the Blagojevich case. Scully confirmed that he had played no part in the preparation of the documents necessary to install the wiretap, had not read the application, and therefore never made a judgment as to the existence of probable cause.

Genson then asked if Scully knew whether the governor's defense coun-sel had been given the affidavits used in the Blagojevich case, eliciting an immediate objection from Jim Durkin. Durkin did not know the objective of the lawyer's question, but he was not going to provide the shrewd Genson any latitude. He objected because the question was not relevant and the witness had already stated that he had no knowledge of the Blagojevich case. Genson disagreed and continued by reading a section of a federal statute regarding the restrictions on the use of wiretaps. The lawyer was challenging the use of the wiretaps by the investigative committee and perhaps looking toward the eventual trial. He was attempting to use Scully's reputation and prestige to support his claims, but Currie and the committee stopped him. Calling his questions and statements irrelevant, and saying they exceeded the limits of clarification, Currie informed Genson that the committee would be happy to accept the statute he cited or any statistics he may wish to present to the committee, but his line of questioning was inappropriate.

The committee next swore in Matt Brown, executive director of the Procurement Policy Board (PPB) from its creation in 1998, and Ed Bedore, a member of the PPB since its founding, as witnesses for the prosecution. As members of the PPB, which has oversight over the state's procurement process, Brown and Bedore could provide intimate details about highly suspicious activities of CMS in the award of contracts and leases since Blagojevich had taken office in 2003. The audit of CMS published in 2005 provided circumstantial evidence of administrative wrongdoing, but the committee needed solid evidence. The legislature was well aware of the problems the PPB and Brown were having dealing with CMS and the Blagojevich administration. Jack Franks had been investigating the procurement deficiencies since Blagojevich had taken office and on several occasions had engaged in verbal altercations with CMS personnel and had publicly criticized the governor. Lou Lang had kept in touch with Matt Brown concerning his ongoing problems with CMS.

The committee had informed Brown and Bedore beforehand what it wanted them to discuss in their testimony. Hoping for tangible evidence, the committee had asked the witnesses to elaborate on sole source contracts where CMS or departments determined that the vendor was the only qualified supplier, cases where state leases had expired but the state continued to occupy the property (holdover leases), standards for leasing and building improvements, and the state's conducting of business with offshore companies that paid no federal or state tax. The committee was focused; the areas selected had been the subject of investigations by Jack Franks and his State Government Administration Committee and had long been sources of controversy between the governor and the legislature.

Like Bill Holland and Vicki Thomas, Brown was a consummate bureaucrat. He studiously addressed the problems that the PPB had encountered with CMS and the discrepancies in procurement procedures. His testimony was short but specific. He discussed Executive Order No. 2003-10, which consolidated all decision-making and administration for real estate under CMS. While promoted by Blagojevich as a cost-cutting move, the executive order had resulted in all decisions on contracts being under one agency, where they could easily be directed by the governor's office. The PPB had repeatedly requested operating rules to accompany the administrative change but had been ignored.

Brown also told the committee of the lack of transparency and justification of sole source procurement awards. The PPB had requested justification for "hundreds of [sole source] awards every year" (601). In many cases CMS simply canceled the awards rather than submit justification. The awarding of contracts was slipshod at best, but to many it reeked of corruption.[25] Brown told the committee what most already knew. He reviewed the number of holdover leases, noting the increase since Blagojevich took office, and described the problems for the state. He said that the PPB had requested the adoption of rule revisions that would identify which improvements for leased facilities were permanent and which were temporary. The purpose of the rules would be to prevent lessors from making permanent improvements on their properties with state money. No rules were ever adopted. The PPB suspected that the refusal to negotiate new leases and to adopt rules, along with allowing wide latitude to lessors, was a conscious effort designed to reward lessors for campaign contributions. While Brown's testimony was intriguing, raised speculation, and highlighted areas for future investigations, it provided no specific evidence of wrongdoing.

Ed Bedore was called to add detail to Brown's remarks. A former aide to Chicago mayor Richard J. Daley, grandfatherly in appearance, and with a reputation for financial acumen, he had the respect and confidence of both Republican and Democratic members of the committee. Bedore proceeded to give facts and figures and pointed out specific instances related to millions of dollars' worth of potential waste that the PPB found at CMS because of incompetent or intentional mismanagement. Referring to past *Chicago Tribune* articles that mentioned the price of influence to the Blagojevich administration, Bedore told the committee that everyone had heard about the $25,000 club, but the owner of one of the properties he cited in his testimony was a member of the $50,000 club. Emphatically, he stated that the examples he presented to the committee "have cost or would have costs to the people of the State of Illinois approximately $6 million in additional costs," and then cited Sam Adam Jr., one of the governor's attorneys, who said, "If the people of Illinois suffer, the governor will step aside." Bedore started to elaborate on Adam's remark when Genson interrupted. "This is inappropriate. This whole topic is inappropriate and this gentleman's statements are inappropriate," he said. Currie agreed that the remarks were "a bit over the top." Trying to emphasize the connection between campaign contributions and CMS procurement, Bedore concluded that the PPB review had gone back just a few years and had saved $6 million by not approving leases because "the rates were too high or the space [rented] was too much" (612–13).

The committee needed more than emotion and *Chicago Tribune* stories, however. It needed specifics, tangible evidence of quid pro quo, of pay to play. Lou Lang, a designated committee monitor, probed the witnesses. He set the tone of his questions by first explaining that he needed to review the testimony and distinguish between gross incompetence and "something else." The witnesses responded with statements that confirmed the difficulty of dealing with CMS but did not provide any hard evidence of wrongdoing. Bedore said that the PPB checked the backgrounds of those who represented the building owners and any contributions made as a matter of protocol; however, a review was not always made, and ownership and contributions were difficult to assess because of the many legal types of ownership. PPB did not retain the information on ownership and contributions. Several committee members then asked penetrating questions, and the answers continued to discredit CMS's methods and cast suspicions on the agency. But the witnesses could offer nothing concrete; in judicial parlance, there was no smoking gun.

The PPB witnesses were followed by Cindi Canary, director of the Illinois Campaign for Political Reform, a nonpartisan public interest group that primarily addresses the role of money in Illinois politics and monitors campaign contributions. Canary had monitored Blagojevich's campaign fund since 2003 and could provide information and describe questionable patterns related to the pay-to-play allegations. Canary defined "pay to play," in broad terms, as "asking for an inducement in exchange for an administrative action taken by a public official." She provided the committee with a list of individuals and corporations that had given large contributions to the Friends of Blagojevich and subsequently obtained contracts or jobs. Unlike the federal law, Illinois' law placed no restrictions on the amount of money or the transfer of money between campaign committees that could be given to officeholders or candidates. Illinois required only disclosure. She pointed out that convicted felon Chris Kelly was responsible for a $650,000 contribution to Blagojevich's early efforts to run for governor. Kelly became a key advisor to Blagojevich and was named a special agent representing the governor to the Illinois Gaming Board. At the time of the investigative hearings, Kelly was charged with tax fraud related to gambling debts. Rod Blagojevich had raised more than $58 million in the eight years since he had formed the campaign committees. The *Chicago Tribune* identified 235 checks written for exactly $25,000 and dubbed the donors the "$25,000 club." Canary said the *Tribune* had discovered that three-quarters of the checks came from people who had received something favorable from the

Blagojevich administration. An examination of the records kept by the State Board of Elections showed that 440 donations of $25,000 or more accounted for $21 million in receipts. Canary noted "a troubling, apparent correlation between donations and state actions" (664).

After Canary's testimony, Currie and Lang clarified for the record that what she had illustrated was not that the governor was a good fund-raiser, but that there appeared to be a correlation between making contributions and receiving contracts and jobs. Several members followed with random questions, but nobody commented on the amounts Canary had mentioned in her testimony. She had detailed what everyone knew: play to play was a reality in Illinois politics, but in the past six years the state had experienced pay to play on steroids. Contributions had gone from politics as a process of reciprocal exchanges to the unabashed selling of official action. Campaign contributions were necessary to run successful campaigns. Officeholders solicited campaign contributions, and those who represented interests in the public policy debate made contributions to support their friends and gain access and deference. But where was the line between mutual support and bribery? The patterns reported by the news media and now articulated by Canary left no doubt: Blagojevich's conduct had violated a basic tenet of the core American creed—equality—by granting special privilege to those who would or could pay. To the veteran politicians and political practitioners in the hearing-room audience, who had read the frequent newspaper articles and were aware of the methods of the governor's office, Canary's testimony shone a spotlight on the obscene conduct of the last six years. Now they showed little outward reaction as they sat in wordless contemplation. It was up to the silent onlookers in the hearing room to reconcile the reality of politics and the ideal of their values.

The testimonies of Brown, Bedore, and Canary publicly confirmed what many legislators had suspected for years: the Blagojevich administration had systematically engineered state government into an enterprise to benefit Rod Blagojevich and his close advisors. Everything was for sale: state contracts, appointments, jobs. The recent trial of Tony Rezko had laid bare the interworking of those close to the governor, and with the PPB witnesses' descriptions of questionable circumstances regarding state contracts, it was clear that the Blagojevich fund-raising octopus extended deep into state operations. But the day's testimonies had reported only suspicious behavior and circumstantial evidence. The examples presented by Brown and Bedore would require a prolonged investigation by branches of government outside of the legislature to uncover tangible evidence and possible charges. Cindi Canary's testimony and the recent newspaper reports revealed patterns of pay to play, but there was no hard evidence that any contract awarded or job given had been based on quid pro quo. The hearing adjourned until after Christmas.

The house staff continued working over the holiday, but the investigative committee received a welcome break. The interlude was interrupted for Jim Durkin, however. On Christmas Eve he received two frantic messages on his cell phone from a lobbyist who had arrived in Springfield with the Blagojevich administration and was close to the governor, asking Durkin to meet him in a hotel lobby in Oak Brook, a western suburb of Chicago. The former prosecutor thought the messages seemed "curious" and a bit suspicious. Durkin did not return the calls.[26]

The Defense

On Monday, December 29, two days before New Year's Eve, the committee reconvened to hear Ed Genson, the governor's defense attorney, answer the charges. The week between Christmas and New Year's is normally a time when the pace of Illinois government slows, and posts in the state capitol are manned by skeleton crews. But this was not a normal day. The entire day would be devoted to hearing and debating Genson's contradictory arguments. The governor's counsel would present the argument for the defense, and the committee would hear questions or rebuttal from its members. Genson was not allowed to cross-examine previous prosecution witnesses or call witnesses to offer testimony for the defense, nor would the prosecution call any witnesses or present further evidence. In legal circles Genson had a reputation as a persuasive defense attorney, and the anticipation in the hearing room was palpable.

During the past two weeks Ellis and his legal team had constructed a case for impeachment based on the allegations in the criminal complaint and administrative transgressions, which were substantiated by tangible evidence of malfeasance and misfeasance that had occurred during Blagojevich's terms in office. The governor should be impeached, they maintained, because he had improperly executed lawful acts, committed wrongful conduct, and failed to perform his official duties.

Genson began his remarks by renewing his request to subpoena four witnesses: Valerie Jarrett, a Chicago executive and close friend of president-elect

Obama; Rahm Emanuel, an Illinois congressman and the designated chief of staff for Obama; Illinois congressman Jesse Jackson Jr.; and Nils Larsen, an employee of the Tribune Company.[27] He told the committee, "It's our understanding that Valerie Jarrett will testify that she received no requests, nor did she request any quid-pro-quo relative to her possible appointment as senator." He said that each witness would confirm that he or she was never involved in arrangements where political or public action was dependent on financial support. It was his understanding that the US attorney was opposed to subpoenaing the witnesses, he said. He claimed that the requested witnesses would contradict what US Attorney Patrick Fitzgerald alleged in the criminal complaint and at the press conference he held immediately after the arrest. Predictably, Currie refused. She responded that the investigative committee did not want to jeopardize the US attorney's "opportunity to pursue the criminal investigation that is underway against [Genson's] client." Genson deemed the remarks by Fitzgerald inappropriate (737–38).[28]

Genson attempted to define the debate within the confines of courtroom standards. Throughout the previous two weeks of hearings the wily defense attorney referred continually to Barbara Currie as "Your Honor." There was a method to his misstatements; he was subliminally suggesting that the legislative hearing was governed by courtroom decorum. His aim was to establish a legal standard for impeachment and that the criteria required burden of proof. He told the committee that he looked to other states that, like Illinois, did not have constitutional standards, "to other law," and argued that there was a "general understanding" that the standard for impeachment was "a functional equivalent of high crimes and misdemeanors" (745). The only governor to be impeached in the last seventy-four years had been Arizona governor Evan Mecham in 1988, and he was not impeached until after he was indicted. Genson argued that impeachment must be based on egregious criminal conduct and dismissed any other cause.

Speaking from notes but mostly extemporaneously, the trial lawyer moved rapidly from one topic to another. He reminded the committee that "freedom is threatened when one branch of government is able to control or ignore the independence of another branch," and speaking of those elected to office, he noted that "the suitability of their performance is entrusted to the determination of the electorate" (752). Genson urged the committee to look to the impeachment investigation of Justice Heiple. "The best document that exists that shows what impeachment should be in the state of Illinois is the House of Representatives impeachment opinion of Justice Heiple," he claimed. The investigative committee report in the Heiple case "suggested to the whole House not to do it," and Genson recommended that the report be required reading for the entire Blagojevich investigative committee (748).

He contrasted the Heiple hearings with his present situation. Heiple was permitted counsel and informed of the allegations being investigated, but Genson received information "mostly on the day I was presented with it." Heiple's counsel was able to cross-examine witnesses and was given subpoena power. That remark caused Chairwomen Currie to interrupt, and she informed Genson that the rules of the investigative committee were identical to those followed in the Heiple hearings. Heiple's counsel also had been limited to clarification and not allowed cross-examination. Undeterred by Currie's correction, Genson continued to contrast the Heiple case with what was being allowed for Blagojevich. The Heiple hearings had begun with testimony from constitutional experts, who presented criteria for standards of impeachment and the burden of proof. The committee investigating Judge Heiple concluded that they must render their decision based on "clear and convincing evidence" (749–53).

Genson's defense focused mainly on the criminal complaint. He addressed the wiretaps that produced the criminal affidavit used in Blagojevich's arrest and spoke of the press conference Fitzgerald held afterward. His choice of words was calculated. Attempting to diminish the validity of the wiretaps, he referred to the "opinions" and "feelings" of the FBI agents listening to the taped conversations and called the reaction to Fitzgerald's press conference "cataclysmic." He conceded that the publicity generated by the press conference had to be "dealt with" but stressed that it was necessary that the committee hearings "be conducted with due process" (740–41). He bemoaned that the committee had told him there were no rules of evidence and that no objections would be allowed because the committee was not a courtroom. Genson regretted that hearsay was admissible and that the committee had allowed "uncertified transcripts, unsworn statements and even newspaper articles." No one had come before the panel "to tell us what the standards of impeachment are" or "to talk to us about the burden of proof." Before the hearings began, some committee members had made statements suggesting "they were not predisposed to rule in favor of Governor Blagojevich," he said (743).

Genson had filed a motion before the committee to preclude the introduction of the wiretaps because he had not had access to them, and in fact, the committee did not have access. The people speaking on the wiretaps were not identified, and Genson claimed that "the introduction of those snippets" of recorded conversations was not legal. The committee had sent a letter to the US attorney asking that the identities of the people speaking on the recordings be revealed, but he did not respond. Without knowing who was talking on the tapes, the allegations against the governor were based on hearsay. In emphatic tones, Genson said that he was "fighting shadows," noting, "We don't know if the quotes are accurate. We don't know if they've been cherry picked." He labeled the conversations related in the criminal complaint "just talk" and said there was no proof that anyone had been propositioned. "There is no corroboration," he appealed. The question was, "Is that clear and convincing?" (763–68).

Genson then turned to the three individuals who had made statements cited in the criminal complaint: Ali Ata, Joe Cari, and Stuart Levine. All three had pleaded guilty to federal crimes and were cooperating with the government in order to have their sentences reduced. Ata was a longtime contributor to Blagojevich campaigns, but he was also a convicted perjurer, who had lied under oath multiple times, and he was asking for probation in exchange for providing testimony against Blagojevich. Was the statement of Ali Ata, a convicted perjurer, who asked for probation in exchange for testimony against the governor, "clear and convincing?" Genson queried. Joe Cari was an admitted extortionist who also had been told that he could ask for probation if he would cooperate and make a statement regarding what the governor had said. Genson then spoke of Stuart Levine, who was going to get a sixty-month sentence for admitting he extorted money from a medical school. Levine pleaded guilty to income tax evasion, bribery, election fraud, and defrauding the state of business, and he used narcotic drugs. Commenting on remarks that Levine supposedly made to Cari and noted in the criminal complaint, Genson asked, "Is that clear and convincing?" He reminded the committee, "Those are the allegations that are set forth in this hearing that are used as a basis for impeachment" (768–71).

The defense moved to the administrative charges presented by the committee counsel. Genson stressed that though some committee members thought the charges "so serious," they were in fact noncriminal matters. He addressed the JCAR controversy by noting that nine other states had found that similar legislation was unconstitutional. The professors who testified did not have constitutional law expertise and were simply stating their opinions on how valuable JCAR was, he said. One professor thought the governor's actions were impeachable but could not say why. Another said it was for fraud but could not say what fraud it was. Referring to the Caro case, Genson said that Scott McKibbin (actually Ron Gidwitz; Genson misspoke here) and Greg Baise, parties to the litigation, "were not exactly bleeding hearts, but they were indignant that they might have to pay some more tax dollars because of this program. Indignant. Strutted in, said we should impeach, and strutted out" (772–74).

Attempting to establish legal credibility to his claim that the JCAR incident was not cause for impeachment, Genson turned the committee's attention to the two-page report submitted by Ann Lousin (misspelled as Lucine in the impeachment transcript). Genson noted that she was a professor of law at the John Marshall Law School, a research assistant at the 1970 Constitutional Convention, a staff assistant to the state house Speaker and a house parliamentarian in the 1970s, and a staff member of the house Constitutional Implementation Committee. The defense counsel declared that Lousin, the only constitutional law expert to submit comments to the committee, had said that the governor should not be impeached based on the JCAR incident.

Next, Genson characterized the decision to purchase the flu vaccine as an error in judgment and pointed out that no money had been paid. In an attempt to obfuscate the actions of the governor's staff, he said, "Nobody paid money not knowing that the drugs would not be allowed to come into the United States." Although it was bad judgment, a mistake, it certainly was not impeachable. Attempting to distance Blagojevich from the actions of his agencies and decisions by his directors, Genson noted that "nobody talks about the governor" (780–81).

Genson again asked the committee to follow the law and use the same standard for impeachment that the Heiple committee had used. He again stated that he was "fighting shadows," fighting people who had been convicted, and fighting preliminary hearings that had yet to take place. There had never been a legislator removed from office while an indictment was pending. Genson said he understood Currie's deference to the US attorney and her desire not to interfere with the investigation, but referring to Fitzgerald's disallowing of defense witnesses, he said it was not fair to write up a complaint and then refuse to talk about it. "It's just not fair," he emphasized (788–89).

The rumpled Genson shifted the papers and notes before him. Restricted by the committee rules, he had said all that he could. Now he summarized: The committee and Patrick Fitzgerald would not allow him to subpoena witnesses who could refute the criminal complaint used to arrest the governor. The wiretaps that were used to produce the affidavit were illegal—neither he nor the committee could examine them, and the people speaking on the recordings had not been identified. The committee should be conducted with due process, under established rules of evidence, and require a burden of proof that established clear and convincing evidence. It should follow the standards and procedures set in the Heiple hearings and apply the same to Rod Blagojevich. All the people mentioned in the criminal complaint lacked credibility, as they were convicted felons who were attempting to have their sentences reduced by cooperating with the federal government. JCAR was before the courts, and a recognized legal scholar had reported that the committee should not act before the courts decided the case. The JCAR controversy was not an impeachable offense, the flu vaccine incident was just an error in judgment, and there was no proof of the allegations of procurement or campaign finance wrongdoing.

The sagacious defense attorney paused and searched for more to say. The interruption caused many in the audience to turn their attention toward Genson, and the room became quiet. Sitting in his motorized chair, surrounded by notes and stacks of paper, Genson knew the outcome. He knew that no matter what he said, the committee was going to send an impeachment resolution to the full house.[29] He concluded, simply, with one final plea: "I'd ask all of you not to impeach in this case" (790).

Currie thanked Genson and said she wished to make "just a couple of points." Her statement portended the committee's response. They would challenge the defense's contentions. In regard to Genson's reference to shadows, Currie said that the governor had been invited to appear before the committee and could have identified who was speaking on the recordings. Concerning JCAR, the governor could have gone to court if he thought it "invades the integrity and the prerogative of the chief executive" (790–91). However, the governor had signed legislation increasing JCAR's authority in relation to his own, and Currie reiterated that JCAR was constitutional unless the courts ruled otherwise (790–92).

After a brief exchange with Genson about these points, Currie recognized Jim Durkin, the Republican spokesman on the investigative committee, who offered some remarks in rebuttal. Durkin was influenced by his time in the narcotics trial unit, when, as a young attorney, he honed the instincts of a trial lawyer. "I was a young and inexperienced lawyer and up against the best defense attorneys in Chicago—you learn," he recalled. Now, once again, he was facing the best. [30] Durkin wanted to clarify that whatever the committee decided, it would not remove the governor from office. The committee was similar to a grand jury, and should it decide to recommend impeachment, an impeachment resolution would be decided by the full house. He also wanted to make it clear that what Genson had experienced before the committee was "more than due process." The committee had allowed the defense attorney to participate in the committee process and had allowed him to call witnesses. He stressed to Genson that he could have called his client, the governor, as well (797). He reiterated, "We've extended an invitation to your client to come before this committee," and since it was "not a criminal proceeding," the committee had the "right to draw a negative inference from his not . . . participating." Addressing the wiretaps used in the affidavit, Durkin said, the US Attorney's Office was acting within its proper authority to obtain the information. The use of wiretaps was within the legal boundaries established by the US Supreme Court. He stated emphatically that the committee was not "bound by anything that was done in Heiple." He repeated that the committee was like a grand jury and could use hearsay. If the committee and the full house decided that impeachment was warranted, then the senate would hold a trial (800–803).

Genson, not surprisingly, disagreed. The committee was not a grand jury, and its procedure should be guided by the Heiple proceedings and require clear and convincing evidence. And he added that it was his hope that the committee would consider the governor's constitutional right not to testify.

Currie next acknowledged Lou Lang. Like Durkin, Lang expressed that he wished to comment on Genson's remarks rather than ask questions. Lang knew what had to be accomplished. His remarks were for the record, as well as for public consumption, and were a direct rebuttal of the statements offered by the defense. He needed to challenge and disparage Genson's remarks, point by point, and legitimize the committee's case for impeachment. Lang noted that Genson's defense primarily addressed the charges contained in the criminal complaint. "He's a criminal attorney," Lang later explained.[31] But Lang wanted to focus on the administrative indiscretions presented to the committee in the prior two weeks. They were supported by clear evidence, and in Lang's view, they constituted violations of the constitution.

Genson had spoken of the importance of the separation of powers, and Lang found that "a curious argument." He asked, "Isn't that what this hearing is all about?" He reminded Genson that Blagojevich's attempt to expand the FamilyCare program without legislative authorization was a violation of the constitution.[32] The governor's disregard of the auditor general, the handling of the FOIA requests, and the flu vaccine and the controversies associated with the Procurement Policy Board all indicated, Lang posited, that he did not respect the independence of other branches of government and the law. In an attempt to establish that the administrative incidences constituted impeachable offenses, Lang attacked Genson's argument that the allegations needed to rise to the level of a criminal allegation. "A non-criminal violation of the Constitution is still a violation of the Governor's constitutional oath," he declared. "And therefore," he said, justifying the apparent consensus of the committee, "if this committee finds that the Governor has violated his constitutional oath for whatever reason, that would be cause or grounds for possible impeachment" (810–12).

He also disagreed with Genson's contention that the governor had been denied due process and wished that the governor would come in and testify. He defended the use of the wiretaps, stating that they provided evidence "as to the state of mind of the Governor" (807). Lang admonished Genson and claimed he had insulted the committee members by speaking publicly of their "railroading" the governor and characterizing the process as "a witch hunt." The Heiple investigation had no bearing and did not set any precedent for the investigative committee. Clear and convincing evidence was not a standard the committee was bound by. Regarding Genson's claim that "we need to have probable cause, no, that's not the standard," he said. The Illinois Constitution contains "a simple word, cause. Not probable cause, not clear and convincing evidence, cause" (808–9).

In vociferous tones, interspersing criminal charges, constitutional violations, and administrative discretions, Lang went through the allegations that had been presented to the committee in the preceding two weeks. Genson had called the discussions on the government recordings "merely talk," but Lang challenged the defense attorney to deny that it was the governor speaking and reminded him that it was a crime to perform a public act for personal gain. The committee was deciding not on the incompetence of the governor but on violations of the constitution and possible wrongful acts. "But this committee is honor-bound and duty-bound and constitutionally bound to put politics aside, to put our petty grievances with the Governor aside, to put our concern about whether he's a competent manager of state government aside, and just deal with the issues that are before this committee," he declared (813–16).

The governor's defense asked to respond. With some annoyance, Currie instructed Genson not to repeat his previous remarks. He answered that his comments would be "brand new" and quipped that "Mr. Lang is very inventive." He maintained that his statements calling the investigative hearings a "circus" were directed at the newspaper coverage and editorials and that the term "witch hunt" was "apropos." Genson referred to Lang's interpretation of what cause was and was not and his statements that the Heiple investigation had no bearing on the Blagojevich investigation "Lang's rules of order." Genson would not put his client before the committee until he understood what the charges were. He again mentioned that the courts had not ruled that the governor did anything inappropriate in his dealings with JCAR. Concerning the taped conversations, he asserted that the governor "has made no offer to anyone according to that tape." Regarding the auditor general's audits and the PPB, Genson pointed out that no one had ever spoken directly to the governor (817–19).

Genson's remarks were brief. They were followed by statements and questions from the committee that ranged across the charges and defense arguments. The committee's questions were relentless. Genson attempted to parry the onslaught: the tapes were illegal, misconduct must rise to the level of criminal conduct, JCAR was still before the courts, the tapes relate just jabber, the governor had not offered anything to anybody, and the committee should look to the Heiple case for guidance. His arguments were in vain. It was clear: Rod Blagojevich had no supporters on the committee.

Lang again asked to be recognized. During the committee's questioning the legal staff had time to discuss and respond to Genson's retort to Lang's rebuttal. Interjecting some comic relief in what had been a serious day, Genson quipped; "Didn't you have your turn already?" Lang smiled and rejoined sarcastically, "Sorry, Mr. Genson." Again the attorneys sparred. Lang wanted to state again—for the record—that the Illinois Constitution "refers to cause and only cause. It doesn't say clear and convincing, it doesn't say probable cause, it just says cause." Further, speaking of the precedent of the Heiple case, there was no prohibition against a legislature changing its mind. Concerning Genson's claim that the tapes were illegal and should not be considered by the committee, and the defense attorney's claim that "nothing wrong" was discussed on the tapes, Lang asked, "If the tapes display that your client has done nothing wrong, what's the big deal, sir?" Genson responded forcefully, "The big deal is that there are laws and the laws have to be followed." It was "incumbent upon" him, he stated, to remind the committee that it was "considering tapes illegally" (860–61).

Lang then asked that a series of newspaper articles criticizing the governor's actions in the JCAR incident be entered into the committee record, and Genson quickly responded that the committee should not make a decision regarding impeachment based on polls or editorials and questioned the impartiality of the committee. Verbally battered and frustrated, Genson asked rhetorically; "Is anyone here going to stick up for the Governor . . . ? I mean this is the impartial panel that we all swore to . . . ," his voice trailing off. Currie quickly responded that the committee would be happy for the governor to come before them and "stand up for himself" (865). The day for the defense was over.

The Final Proceedings

Over the New Year's holiday the Speaker and his staff had to make some decisions. Since the first conversation between Ellis and Madigan on the day of the governor's arrest, both men were conscious of the political ramifications of what was taking place. The impeachment resolution had to justify cause, not only for the house to concur but also to satisfy enough members of the senate to convict the governor and remove him from office. Looming above legislative tactics was the perception of the public and the media. The decisions weighed heavily. Never before had the Illinois legislature removed a state officeholder, and the world was watching. The reason to remove had to be convincing. The house investigative committee had considered tangible evidence of maladministration; both the auditor general's audits and the JCAR controversy provided solid criteria. Contracts and procurement involved tantalizing circumstances but would require further investigation to develop concrete evidence. Negotiations with the senate had started concerning the senate's trial rules. Removal of Rod Blagojevich had shifted into high gear. It was time to end the investigation, pass the impeachment resolution, and start the senate trial.

The governor's defense counsel chose not to attend the January 7 hearing. Genson had put on his defense; there was nothing more he could do. Without opposing counsel, the investigation committee met to consider one more investigative report that could provide damaging evidence of Blagojevich's misdeeds. In 2006 Ray Long, a reporter for the *Chicago Tribune*, disclosed a 2004 report by the governor's inspector general, Zaldwaynaka "Z" Scott, which found that Blagojevich's office circumvented hiring laws.

The report found that the governor's office had falsified hiring records, ignored veterans preference requirements, hired unqualified employees, and falsified some employees' experience and qualifications.[33] Z Scott's report was from Blagojevich's first term, but the confidential report had not become known to legislators until it was leaked to the press in 2006. Blagojevich was running for reelection when the irregularities were reported in the *Tribune*, and Illinois attorney general Lisa Madigan confirmed that a federal probe of "endemic hiring fraud" was under way.[34]

That fall the Blagojevich administration began to come apart. Confidants Chris Kelly, Tony Rezko, and Stuart Levine were subjects of the federal investigation called Operation Board Games, and all had been named in federal indictments. All three would later be convicted. Even Blagojevich's wife, Patti, was the subject of an investigation concerning commissions paid to her real estate company by individuals who received state contracts. A most troubling issue was a $1,500 check given to Blagojevich, ostensibly as a birthday present for his seven-year-old daughter, by a job seeker. Nevertheless, Blagojevich won reelection and began his second term.

Barbara Currie explained that the report, under state statutes, was confidential. The investigative committee had subpoenaed the full Z Scott report from the Executive Ethics Commission, which then consulted the attorney general for direction on whether to comply with the committee's subpoena. The attorney general found that the information in the report was necessary for the committee's work, which took precedence over confidentiality.[35] The dependable Lou Lang summarized the findings for the committee. The report focused on complaints occurring in the Department of Employment Security. The report concluded that the governor's Office of Intergovernmental Affairs had directed the department to bypass state protocol.[36] Lang read off a litany of irregularities, including the firing of a human relations director for hiring a qualified employee rather than following the direction of the Office of Intergovernmental Affairs to hire the person it had chosen. Lang was precise, reading off page and paragraph numbers from Z Scott's report. His presentation was damning and showed hard evidence of wrongdoing as standard procedure in the governor's department. The committee had another arrow in its quiver.

During the New Year's break, Ed Genson had engaged in back-channel discussions with members of the legislature concerning an arrangement whereby Blagojevich would temporarily step down from his post, as provided in the Illinois Constitution.[37] He would still be paid and retain his bodyguards. Lieutenant Governor Pat Quinn would assume the duties of governor, the impeachment would be suspended, state government would go on, and Blagojevich could concentrate on the criminal indictment that was sure to follow. Genson also advised his client not to make an appointment to fill the vacant US Senate seat created by Barack Obama's election. He did not want his client to take what could be interpreted as a presumptuous and hostile action, given the governor's circumstances.[38] But Genson's entreaties to Blagojevich were ignored. It was becoming clear to Genson that the governor preferred the more aggressive approach and flamboyant style of the Adam father-and-son legal team. The client was disregarding his seasoned defense attorney's advice more and more, and the relationship between Genson and the Adam team was becoming strained. In fact, Blagojevich had not been returning Genson's phone calls.[39]

In consultation with Sam Adam Jr., Blagojevich decided to appoint Roland Burris to succeed Barack Obama in the US Senate. Burris's name was well known in Illinois politics. He had held the offices of Illinois comptroller and attorney general and had run against Blagojevich during the 2002 primary election for governor. He was African American, a necessity seen by some for Barack Obama's successor, and he was not one of the individuals identified in the taped conversations. But as Durkin put it, Roland Burris was not "pure as the driven snow" as many claimed.[40] The 2002 primary had been a three-way race among Blagojevich, Burris, and a former Democratic senate staffer and former Chicago school superintendent, Paul Vallas. Vallas had been running well, and it was rumored that Burris was thinking of withdrawing from the race. But then Burris mysteriously received a loan for $1.2 million from a Mr. Stroud, a name not well known in political circles, and he stayed in the race and ostensibly took votes away from Vallas. The loan was never repaid.[41]

Over the New Year's break Blagojevich announced the appointment of Burris to Obama's seat, and it started a national media frenzy. Burris traveled to Washington to meet with Democratic leaders in the senate. They were not pleased. Burris, surrounded by reporters, photographers, and his attorney, held an impromptu press conference after meeting with Illinois senator Richard Durbin and US senate leader Harry Reid. He expressed astonishment that anyone would challenge his integrity. "You know me, I'm Roland," he said. Republican Jim Durkin immediately sent a letter to David Ellis requesting that Burris appear before the committee. Durkin recalled that the initial reaction by the Democrats was dispassionate. Lang told Durkin that Burris had nothing to do with the charges being explored by the committee and that he would not receive any new information.[42]

Durkin was adamant. The Democrats had controlled the entire investigative hearing. Republicans had not been consulted concerning witnesses, played a minor part in forming the committee agenda, and had little input in the final committee report. It was business as usual for the Republicans. The Democrats had controlled the Illinois house for decades, except for a short two-year period when the Republicans gained the majority and Lee Daniels, the Republican leader from Elmhurst, was elected Speaker. Michael Madigan had been Speaker since 1983 except for those two years. Democratic control had become institutionalized and became the legislative temperament, and it could be sharp elbowed. Blagojevich's appointment of Burris was an embarrassment to the Democrats; legislative leaders had discussed the political fallout of a Burris appointment since November. Durkin seized the opportunity to exploit the situation and have a Republican moment in the sun. The Democrats had little choice but to accede to Durkin's demands. Thus on January 8, the last day the investigative committee met, Burris was called as a witness.

The Burris appointment had become an extension of the Blagojevich circus and soon became a national media event. For Republicans, it was a chance at last to score political points. For the Democrats, the Burris appearance was something to be endured. They opted for a "rope-a-dope" defense. Burris's appearance satisfied Durkin's insistence, and Democrats attempted to simply intercept any political fallout. The only enthusiastic inquisitors were Republicans. Prior to the meeting the Democratic staff had already distributed the final committee report. The committee had what it needed; the investigation was over.

Durkin began the questioning by exchanging pleasantries with Burris and then asked him what his thoughts were on hearing of the governor's arrest. The question was immediately challenged by John Fritchey, and the room became tense. It rapidly became clear that the Democrats intended to protect the witness. Interrupted by challenges from Fritchey, Lang, and Burris's attorney, Timothy Wright III, Durkin attempted to establish Burris's business connections and background, including the state lobbying he had performed during the Blagojevich administration and contributions he had made to the governor's campaign. Burris said that he had no conversations with the governor after his arrest until he was offered the senate seat. He testified that he had received a call from Sam Adam Jr. in the late afternoon on December 26; Adam had something important to discuss and later that evening stopped by Burris's home. Burris claimed that Sam Adam Jr. was like a son to him and he had known him for years. Later that evening Adam asked if he would accept the appointment to fill Barack Obama's senate seat. Burris said he talked it over with several friends, and two days later he confirmed with Adam that he would accept the senate seat. The governor called a short while later and offered the seat.[43]

Durkin turned to the controversial loan of $1.2 million from a Mr. Stroud under the name of the company Telephone USA Investments. The loan to the Burris campaign was suspicious; it was the largest exchange of money to a campaign committee in Illinois history, and the only other campaign contribution from Telephone USA Investments was one for $100,000 to Blagojevich in 2006. Burris responded that the $1.2 million was a loan and it was never paid back because the campaign committee was dissolved. The loan was still outstanding. Lang, the committee monitor, immediately objected to the relevance of Durkin's questioning. Durkin kept probing, and Currie suggested that Durkin end this line of questioning quickly.[44] Burris was unswerving; he had not had conversations with Stroud about repaying the loan, and his campaign committee was dissolved. Durkin continued to verbally spar with the Blagojevich appointee, asking hypothetical questions and soliciting opinions as he tried to establish a past connection with Blagojevich, but he had scored all the political points he could. Burris was not offering anything that Durkin did not know, and the Democrats wanted the exercise to end.

Attempting to discredit the Burris appointment, the Republican members continued to ask follow-up questions. But the exercise seemed procedural. The history and possible mischievous deeds of Burris and the governor would remain a mystery. They would not be discovered through questioning from the Republican committee members. An exchange between Republican representative Roger Eddy of Hutsonville and Ed Genson drew little audience attention but portended future events. There was major tension between the defense counsels. Addressing Burris, Eddy said he thought it curious that the governor's defense attorney, Sam Adam Jr., would play any role in the appointment of Barack Obama's successor. Genson and Adam were both in attendance for Burris's appearance. Somewhat irritated, Genson interrupted and emphatically stated that Sam Adam Jr. was not a defense attorney. "Mr. Adams [sic], Jr., does not, has not, and will not represent Governor Blagojevich in the criminal case," he said.[45]

Later events would prove Genson's statement to have been a sad misconception. Genson had misjudged his client and fellow attorneys. He had brought Adam and later his father into the case, and their subsequent conduct prompted him to leave the case.[46] The Adamses' approach to the defense differed dramatically from Genson's, and Blagojevich made his choice. He ignored Genson's advice not to appoint Barack Obama's senate successor, taking the advice of Adam and appointing Burris. Genson counseled restraint and dignity. Instead, Blagojevich hired a public relations firm and made appearances on *Late Night with David Letterman*, *The View*, and *Larry King Live*, taking his appeal to a national audience.[47] There he attacked Patrick Fitzgerald, Michael Madigan, John Cullerton, and the Illinois legislature. The Burris appointment was a sign of what was to come: Adam and his father would represent the governor in his criminal proceedings, and Genson would leave the case.

Prior to his appearance, Burris had filed a sworn affidavit with the committee. After the committee hearing, he filed another affidavit to supersede the original one. Madigan ask the Sangamon County state's attorney to investigate, but an investigation did not follow. After some complimentary statements by Democratic members, meant to show partisan support, Burris was excused. The committee went into recess.

When the committee reconvened after the recess, it met for the last time. One item was still outstanding. The house Democratic leadership was conscious of Blagojevich's popularity in the African American community and worried about black house members balking at a vote to impeach. They were especially concerned about black members in the senate. Monique Davis had served in the house since 1987, represented a district on Chicago's far South Side, and had been appointed by the Speaker to the investigation committee. She introduced a written statement from Brenda Gold, who had been terminated from the Illinois Department of Transportation for allegedly investigating hiring practices that discriminated against African Americans. "There are a lot of African American people who feel that this Governor has been extremely good and kind to them," she said, "but when they look at these kind of practices, and this is just one example, they will know that this Governor carried his vendetta against people for no reason to a large extent, which was very harmful to the state."[48] Gold's statement became the committee's Exhibit 70 and provided justification—cover—for wavering members.

Currie briefly summarized the committee report. The sixty-one-page *Final Report of the Special Investigative Committee* was carefully constructed to build a case for impeachment based on multiple incidents of possible criminal conduct, taken from the criminal complaint, and of maladministration uncovered by investigations and audits. The totality of evidence provided cause. The litany of charges began with the most resonating ones: that the governor had attempted to trade the appointment to the US Senate for personal gain, had conspired to grant financial assistance from the Illinois Finance Authority to the Tribune Company in return for firing members of the *Tribune* editorial board, and had attempted to exchange the signing of a bill favorable to the horse-racing industry for a campaign contribution. Additionally, the governor had announced a $1.8 billion tollway project and then pressed someone identified as Highway Contractor 1 for a $500,000 contribution. He had made a commitment of $8 million in pediatric care reimbursement and demanded in return a $50,000 contribution from an executive with Children's Memorial Hospital in Chicago. Ali Ata had given campaign contributions for an appointment to the Illinois Finance Authority. Using Joe Cari's testimony from the Rezko trial, the report detailed how Tony Rezko, Chris Kelly, and Stuart Levine plotted to pick contractors and then solicit for campaign contributions. Turning to administrative cause, incompetency, and maladministration, Currie noted that the report also contained the ongoing JCAR incident, flu vaccine procurement, the I-SaveRx program, the so-called efficiency initiatives, and the inspector general's report finding that the governor had violated state and federal laws regarding hiring and firing of state employees.

There was no discussion. Everyone knew what was in the report and everyone supported it. Durkin remarked that the investigation had been fair and that the governor had been allowed due process. Genson and Adam had left the hearing room; they knew there was no point in being present. Durkin, speaking for the minority Republicans, moved that the committee adopt the report. The partisan sparring that had taken place moments before was replaced by a unified determination to remove Blagojevich. Led by Barbara Currie, each member of the committee gave a short explanation and voted aye. All twenty-one members voted aye to adopt the committee report. The house investigation, the first step of removing Blagojevich from office, was over. It was time to present the resolution to impeach the governor to the full house.

Chapter 4

The Impeachment Resolution

On January 9, as house members began to take their seats and prepared to consider House Resolution 1671—the resolution to impeach Governor Rod Blagojevich—the gallery was crowded but strangely quiet. The elderly men who served as part-time gallery attendants seemed unsettled. Democratic chief of staff Tim Mapes had instructed them to keep order and restrain any outbursts from the galleries, but there was little reason to worry; the audience was not of a boisterous bent. In fact, spectators were greeted by an unfamiliar silence as they looked to find an open seat. Those in the house gallery that afternoon were not the familiar faces of regular visitors, the Springfield lobbyists who often watched the floor action from discreet vantage points or sat on the sofas and chairs along the sides of the house chambers waiting for a particular bill, bargaining with legislators and other lobbyists or just killing time. The large chandeliers that have graced the house chamber since the late nineteenth century seemed slightly dimmed, adding a somber vagueness to the scene below. Noticeably absent were the normally ubiquitous house staff and pages whose activity ordinarily caused constant distraction up and down the chamber's aisles. A few members talked on their cell phones, and some spoke to each other in hushed tones, but most did not speak at all. Those in attendance, the curious and interested, were ordinary folks, the general public—the people.

The house was meeting not to debate the impeachment resolution but to present it, hear restrained comments, and pass it. The Republican and Democratic caucuses had discussed the resolution and the conduct and decorum expected from the members; everyone knew what was about to take place. The resolution had been filed with the house clerk the day before, the same day the *Final Report of the Special Investigative Committee* was released. Speaker Michael Madigan, Chairwoman Barbara Currie, minority leader Tom Cross, and Jim Durkin, the Republican spokesman on the Special Investigative Committee, were the resolution's chief sponsors. Impeachment had received overwhelming support in the house. When the resolution was filed with the clerk, 107 members immediately requested to be added as co-sponsors. In the words of a senior Democratic staff member, "It was a done deal."

The five-page resolution synthesized the sixty-one-page report and justified the findings of the investigative committee that Rod Blagojevich should be impeached. The resolution reiterated the purpose of the Special Investigative Committee: to investigate alleged evidence of "misfeasance, malfeasance, and nonfeasance and other misconduct of Governor Rod Blagojevich." It spelled out the findings detailed in the committee's report and presented thirteen reasons—cause—for impeachment. The first eight findings covered the criminal acts discussed in conversations recorded by the FBI in the months leading up to the arrest. The other five findings dealt with incidences of mismanagement and the abuse of power, maladministration, and violations of federal and state law and Illinois' Constitution. The resolution stated that the governor had displayed an "utter disregard of the doctrine of separation of powers" and refused to recognize the authority of the Joint Committee on Administrative Rules (JCAR). The committee found that the governor had exceeded his constitutional authority, violated the law, and obstructed legislative oversight by bypassing the ruling of JCAR and implementing a program that expanded health care benefits without legislative authority or funding appropriation. The resolution expressed a pattern of criminal allegations, violations of state and federal law, and willful mismanagement.[1]

When the session was called to order, the Reverend Milton Bost, pastor of the Chatham Baptist Church and the brother of Republican state representative Mike Bost, set the tone for the day. His invocation called on "Almighty and sovereign God" to "grant Speaker Madigan and each Member of this House a mindset and a resolve to initiate correction and healing within the government of our state" (1).[2] Speaker Madigan chaired the proceedings and recognized Barbara Currie to present HR 1671.

With a calm and measured voice, Currie justified and summarized the actions of the Special Investigative Committee. Her selection of words revealed her emotions. It was the "perfidy of one man, Rod Blagojevich," that brought the house to this day. After his arrest the house had given the governor a week to "do the right thing," to resign. Instead, the governor had chosen to "fight, fight, fight." Currie cautioned that what the house was doing was the beginning step in overturning an election and was "not something that should be undertaken lightly." She noted the vagueness of the Illinois Constitution and insisted that the committee had taken action because of "allegations of serious infractions, serious betrayals." Currie offered evidence of maladministration within the Blagojevich administration and blamed the governor for disregarding the prerogatives of the legislature, and she briefly reviewed the offenses (3–4).

But the mainspring for the impeachment resolution was not maladministration; it was the criminal allegations. In the minds of many citizens, expanding health care was a good thing and could be defended no matter what administrative avenue was taken to achieve it. The flu vaccine fiasco could have been excused as a mistake, a lack of oversight, or just politics as usual. The trigger for impeachment was the arrest of the governor and the evidence of taped conversations between Blagojevich and his cohorts, planning various schemes to enrich themselves and the governor. After years of confrontation with Blagojevich, at last the legislature had justification to remove him. Referring to portions of the taped conversations contained in the criminal complaint, she gave an account of the alleged criminal offenses and pronounced, "They show a public servant who has chosen not to serve the public but only his own interests. . . . They show a public servant . . . who is prepared to turn public service into an avenue for private benefit" (5).

Currie's presentation was short, to the point, and presented with certitude. Her remarks were carefully designed to establish the seriousness of Blagojevich's misconduct and the criteria needed to follow the Constitution's requirements to show and justify cause for impeachment. Intently, Currie concluded that the governor had chosen not to answer the allegations against him. "His silence in this grave matter is deafening," she said (5).

Following protocol, Tom Cross was recognized next. The remarks from the Republican minority leader were obligatory. He thanked everyone—committee chair Currie, Republican spokesman Jim Durkin, staff, and Republican counsel Tom Durkin, Jim Durkin's brother—for working together. Cross said that the emotion he felt was anger; the governor had violated the trust invested in him when he took the oath of office. He urged all members to read the committee's report and said, "Unfortunately or fortunately, however you want to look at it, we have no choice today but to vote yes on this Resolution" (12). The remarks served to diminish any doubts that the resolution would pass with unanimous Republican support.

The house leaders and the lawyers who had provided counsel, conducted the investigative committee proceedings, and written the committee's report were well aware of the potential for future court challenges from the governor, and they presented and managed the proceedings with careful attention. They wanted to explicitly express, for the legislative record, that the reasons and methods used to bring about the impeachment action complied with the terms set forth in the Constitution.

Republican Jim Durkin followed Cross, and like Currie, he reinforced the legitimacy of the resolution and the methods of the investigative committee. As the minority spokesman on the investigative committee and an assistant minority leader, he expressed the unity of the house. The committee had performed its duty "in a truly bipartisan manner," he said. Durkin focused on the committee's methods and stated that its purpose had been to determine "whether there is an existence of cause to impeach the governor." Addressing criticism from the governor's attorney that Blagojevich had not been afforded due process, he argued that the Constitution did not state that the governor's attorney for was permitted "to participate in the hearings," "to question witnesses, "to rebut or mitigate the evidence" presented by the committee, or "to call witnesses," but that the committee had afforded those privileges in its quest to ensure "that we were going to be fair." Like Currie, Durkin remarked that "the Governor failed to participate in those proceedings; we invited him." He also pointed out that "the Governor's attorney failed to rebut any of the evidence which was presented before this committee." The former Cook County prosecutor told the house that "the evidence was overwhelming." Durkin recounted the allegations in the resolution and concluded that the action of the house would ensure "that a system of checks and balances works and is also the best form of government" (13–14).

Deputy Majority Leader Lou Lang now took the floor in the role of prosecutor, speaking as a well-informed lawyer and continuing to establish the legislative record. He reminded the house that the Illinois Constitution requires that the governor be responsible for the "faithful execution of the laws" and that the governor had violated his constitutional oath. Reiterating Durkin's remarks, he reported that during committee hearings, the governor's attorney had argued that the governor was being denied the right of due process. Lang again emphasized that although the Illinois Constitution does not specify any provisions for due process in the impeachment process, the governor was given an "extraordinary, unprecedented level of due process." The committee, he said, allowed the governor to have lawyers attend and participate in the committee hearings, and he contrasted their level of participation with the procedures followed in the Clinton impeachment trial. "We afforded them the opportunity to ask questions and afforded the opportunity to challenge exhibits, to challenge witnesses," he noted (17–18).

Lang cautioned that the investigative committee was not a "criminal tribunal" but that the governor's failure to refute the allegations could "be used against him" in the impeachment proceedings. The governor's attorney had tried to impose the standards of proof for criminal proceedings, "beyond a reasonable doubt, clear and convincing evidence, even a preponderance of the evidence, but," he pointed out, "the fact is that the Constitution of the State of Illinois says none of those things." He reminded the house that the Constitution states "one word as a standard" for impeachment, and "that word is cause." And "cause means whatever the 118 members of the house individually think it might be." Emphasizing the administrative indictments of the resolution, Lang cautioned that the governor's administrative conduct was just as important as any criminal allegations. The governor had violated his "gubernatorial oath," and he emphasized, "a violation of the Constitution is the same level whether it was an abuse of power because he committed a crime or an abuse of power because he violated the separation of powers or an abuse of power because he fraudulently . . . purchased flu vaccine for the State of Illinois knowing he would never take possession of it" (18–19).

The governor was charged by the federal government with allegations concerning criminal activity, but Lang wanted to establish that the charges of maladministration determined by the investigative committee were as important to the impeachment process as were the pending federal allegations. "The criminal is more emotional, the criminal is sexier, the criminal is something people want to talk about, but as it relates to this chamber and this Governor and this decision we must make, the fact is that what he has done within government separate and apart from any crimes is just as important as the criminal allegations," he concluded (20).

Next to speak was Susana Mendoza, a five-term state representative from Chicago's Near Northwest Side and a designated alternate member of the investigative committee. She had attended every committee meeting, sitting in the area designated for legislators, intently focused on the proceedings. At times Mendoza sat with the committee and asked questions of the witnesses. She took a particular interest in the proceedings. When Blagojevich took office, the bright, young, and idealistic Mendoza had been an enthusiastic supporter of the Democratic governor. She supported his legislative initiatives and attended press conferences with him. Over the years, as she came to learn of his misdeeds and manipulations, her support turned to disappointment and then to anger. When the investigative committee was formed, she went to the Speaker and asked that he appoint her as a member.[3]

Her remarks on the house floor seemed to synthesize the feelings of the entire house, reflecting a sense of sadness, anger, and shame. "Today we're one day closer to healing the gaping wound inflicted upon the State of Illinois by Governor Rod Blagojevich," she said. Her poignant delivery riveted the attention of the house chamber. Her choice of words also expressed her emotions: "Our state's reputation has been sullied and, worse yet, people in our state have been seriously hurt by the unmeasured rapaciousness of this Governor." She expressed outrage at Blagojevich's "greed and arrogance" and his "brazenness and recklessness," and she declared that it was "amazingly fitting" that Blagojevich should be impeached on the birthday of his "self-admitted hero Richard Nixon" (21–22).

Mendoza said that as an alternate committee member, she had listened to all the testimony and studied all the evidence with care and consideration, and she concluded that the only course was immediate impeachment to end the "continuing threat to the health of our state." She was particularly incensed by the governor's alleged extortion of Children's Memorial Hospital and called the deed "repugnant." Mendoza had sponsored HB 5331, the bill that provided the grant to the hospital. "Governor Blagojevich promised those physicians that money so that they could care for our sickest children," she said. "Those sick children, Governor, they're still waiting." With measured anger, she amended her earlier statement: "Repugnant is too kind a word to describe [the governor's] action." She then spoke directly to the governor: "Rod Blagojevich, you should be ashamed of yourself, but I won't pretend to think that you feel any [shame]. You've already shown us that you have none." With that, Mendoza asked the house to "all vote" for the resolution and impeachment of the governor (22–24).

David Miller, a veteran legislator whose district included several southern suburbs of Chicago, was then recognized and began to ask Currie and Durkin some clarifying questions. Miller was respected by members of both parties, and many assumed that he also was simply trying to support the resolution. But his questions seemed dissonant and disjointed; he was hesitant and unsure. The night before, Miller had been a guest on WVON radio, a popular station among Chicago's black community. The program featured a call-in format, and several of the callers expressed anger and skepticism about the upcoming impeachment. Miller took note. His district was predominantly minority populated, Miller himself was African American, and he was aware of the importance of the occasion. "The whole country was watching," he later confided.[4]

Blagojevich was popular in the black community. He attended black church services, appeared at black-sponsored events, and appointed African Americans to positions in government. The black community was important to his electoral success. The governor's personal narrative was that he had come from immigrant parents who worked in the steel mills with no advantage in life and had worked his way up, always struggling, fighting the odds, perpetually the outsider. He insisted that he was the crusader of good and truth, fighting for the people. Now he was again being opposed by the established powers, an evil cabal of greedy politicians. Blagojevich's narrative resonated within the black community, and many could identify with what he was saying. Many black people felt that Blagojevich was being railroaded by the established powers. Miller's radio appearance the night before provided him with an instant poll of black feelings. The reaction of listeners prompted some trepidation, and he felt he had "to get these things out." He had whispered to Currie, "I'm going to ask you some questions."[5]

He posed two questions to Currie and Durkin. The first question, "Why now?," was straightforward. The second question seemed imprecise, somewhat curious. Speaking of the abuse of power that Lang had discussed, Miller asked, "How does that reflect in the criminal issues that Mr. Blagojevich is facing now? Does that have a bearing on this?" Currie explained that the criminal complaint "sparked the flame that led to the creation of the committee" but cited that other administrative actions such as that related to the flu vaccines along with the disregard for legislative authority, taken together with the criminal allegations, constituted justification for impeachment. Miller responded by stating that the governor had not been granted the right of due process under the US Constitution. "Haven't we circumvented it?" he asked. Currie reiterated what she had expressed many times in the impeachment hearings, that the investigative committee was not a criminal jury and that "nothing in our Constitution nor any State or Federal Constitution suggests that our standards should be a criminal one." Currie argued that the governor "spent a lot of time figuring out how to sell state actions and state money for his political and personal benefit" and that the testimony before the committee was "not refuted." Taken as a whole, Currie said, Blagojevich was not "fit to govern and he should be removed from office." Miller agreed and said that the points made by the investigative committee, taken by themselves, did not constitute grounds for impeachment, but taken as a whole, "collectively," they represented "a slow train wreck moving that has all sort of accumulated to our actions that will be today." Currie agreed that Miller's analogy was "exactly the way to think about it" (27–29).[6]

Wishing to conclude his questions, Miller began to make a statement on the "matter at hand today," but Durkin sought recognition. The former Cook County prosecutor was aware of the importance of the moment. He knew that everything he said and everything the house did would be analyzed and dissected, and he knew the world press was watching. He wanted to expand on Currie's remarks. Miller had asked "a few questions," he said, and he wanted to add clarification. Addressing the "why now" question, he explained that the governor's criminal allegations might take two to three years to be settled in federal court. In the meantime, the governor could still make appointments and sign laws and would have all the rights and authority he had under the statutes and the Constitution. Durkin stated that the impeachment process was "strictly a legislative process." He also reiterated that although the state Constitution does not provide for due process in the impeachment process, the investigative committee had afforded the governor "due process plus." Durkin said that a federal agent had signed and sworn an affidavit attesting to the accuracy of the recordings of the governor, and a federal judge had authorized the wiretaps contained in the criminal complaint. The committee had weighed the evidence carefully and paid particular attention to the affidavit concerning the wiretaps, he said, because the governor's attorney Edward Genson "went to great length . . . to challenge the integrity of that document." Due process was afforded, Durkin said, but the governor and his attorney did not avail themselves of it. "That's their decision," he said. Durkin then answered Miller's first question by saying, "Because I think we have to right now" (29–30). Durkin's comments provided the rationale—the political cover—many needed to vote for impeachment.

Miller said that he agreed with the committee's report and that as a member of JCAR, he had voted to reject the governor's health expansion program "time and time again." "The end doesn't justify the means," he said, and it was his responsibility as an elected official to work with others to "lobby Members on both sides of the aisles, in both chambers to hopefully agree upon things that I feel that is [of] value to my community and the State of Illinois." Miller then called for support of the impeachment (31).

Discussion of most important issues brought up before the Illinois General Assembly is generally accompanied by a degree of political posturing, with for-the-record speeches that establish positions for constituent consumption or are intended for use in future press releases, but on the occasion of this momentous resolution, the political rhetoric and bombast were limited. Tom Cross and Jim Durkin were the only Republicans to speak, and the other random speakers on this issue limited themselves to a few brief remarks.

Barbara Currie delivered brief closing remarks. She declared, "This Governor has violated his oath of office. This Governor has breached the public trust. This Governor must be impeached." The house did not need to hear anything further. Most were deeply saddened by what was about to take place. Speaker Madigan then posed the question: "Shall the House adopt House Resolution 1671?" (44). The tally was 114 voting yes, 1 voting no. Before the vote, Madigan had asked Ellis how he should announce the results. Ellis told him to simply say that the governor was impeached.[7] Now the Speaker announced the vote: "The House does adopt House Resolution 1671 and Governor Blagojevich is hereby impeached" (44).

The results did not immediately register with all observers, perhaps because the house announces thousands of vote results in the course of a session in the same staccato cadence with which the results of HR 1671 were officially announced. But in a few moments the magnitude of what had just happened became clear, and the legislators slowly left the house floor. It was the first time in the state's history that the house had voted to impeach a governor. There were no cheers among the members or in the galleries. Those present did not feel joy, just relief, sadness, and regret.[8]

Chief Justice Thomas Fitzgerald being escorted into the senate chamber. Senate sergeant at arms "Joe" Dominguez is to the chief justice's immediate right. *Photo by Jay Barnard. Courtesy of the Illinois Senate Republican Caucus*

Senator Frank Watson. *Photo by Jay Barnard. Courtesy of the Illinois Senate Republican Caucus*

House prosecutor David Ellis. *Photo by Jay Barnard. Courtesy of the Illinois Senate Republican Caucus*

House assistant prosecutor Michael Kasper. *Photo by Jay Barnard. Courtesy of the Illinois Senate Republican Caucus*

Senate minority leader Christine Radogno. *Photo by Jay Barnard. Courtesy of the Illinois Senate Republican Caucus*

Governor Rod Blagojevich. *Photo by Jay Barnard. Courtesy of the Illinois Senate Republican Caucus*

View of the Illinois senate floor during the trial. *Photo by Jay Barnard.*
Courtesy of the Illinois Senate Republican Caucus

Senator Dale Righter. *Photo by Jay Barnard. Courtesy of the Illinois Senate Republican Caucus*

Senator Matt Murphy. *Photo by Jay Barnard. Courtesy of the Illinois Senate Republican Caucus*

Senator David Luechtefeld. *Photo by Jay Barnard. Courtesy of the Illinois Senate Republican Caucus*

Speaker Michael Madigan (*center*). To the Speaker's right is state representative Constance "Connie" Howard, and to his left is state representative Frank Mautino. *Photo by Russ Nagel. Courtesy of the Illinois House of Representatives Democratic caucus*

Defense attorney Edward Genson, before the house Special Investigative Committee. *Photo by Russ Nagel. Courtesy of the Illinois House of Representatives Democratic caucus*

Speaker Michael Madigan (*center*), with Constance Howard to his right and state representative Lou Lang to his left. *Photo by Russ Nagel. Courtesy of the Illinois House of Representatives Democratic caucus*

Department of Healthcare and Family Services (HFS) chief of staff Tamara Tanzillo Hoffman (*left*) and director Barry Maram (*right*), being sworn in before the house investigative committee. Hoffman and Maram were the only members of the governor's administration to appear before the committee. *Photo by Russ Nagel. Courtesy of the Illinois House of Representatives Democratic caucus*

Representative Susana Mendoza. *Photo by Russ Nagel. Courtesy of the Illinois House of Representatives Democratic caucus*

(*left to right*) Cullerton's chief of staff, Andy Manar; senate president John Cullerton; senate secretary Deb Shipley; and senate counsel Eric Madiar. *Photo by Brandy Renfro. Courtesy of the Office of the President of the Illinois State Senate*

Chapter 5

Senate Preparations

I n early December 2008 the newly elected Democratic senate president John Cullerton had a great deal on his mind: numerous meetings and decisions to select a staff and organize the senate. His initial task was to plan the swearing-in ceremonies. "I had to worry about everything, even ordering flowers," he recalled. He was also attempting to focus on the immediate legislative issues that faced Illinois, mainly a capital bill to fund the state's crumbling infrastructure. He had reached out to the new Republican senate minority leader, Christine Radogno, and the two agreed that they could start with a "clean slate" and not continue the hostile relationship that had existed between Emil Jones and outgoing Republican leader Frank Watson. They felt that they could do better than their recent predecessors.[1] Animosity between Jones and Watson was well known, and in the past year tension between the party leaders had gone from bad to worse. When Watson became ill and Radogno called Jones to go over the day's legislative agenda, she recalled, Jones would not speak to her.[2] Party politics in Illinois had developed a rough edge, and the earlier give and take, compromise, and camaraderie between Democrats and Republicans, when they would negotiate and come up with a compromise over coffee, a drink, or dinner, seemed lost memories of a bygone era.

Deep animosity also existed between Rod Blagojevich and Michael Madigan, often resulting in vituperative rhetoric and open hostility. Blago-jevich used every opportunity to embarrass the Speaker. He openly mocked the Speaker in front of other legislators and staff, and on Democrat Day at the Illinois State Fair he bused in demonstrators to heckle Madigan. Cul-lerton felt that he could help "bridge the gap." He and Blagojevich spoke infrequently, and in fact, the new senate president recalled only two conver-sations of substance during the governor's six-year term in office. Cullerton represented the governor's home district, he was from the neighborhood, and he had been supported by the governor's now-estranged father-in-law, Chicago alderman Dick Mell, but his political relationship with Blagojevich was strained. Cullerton, however, was optimistic that he could provide some common ground between the governor and the Speaker.[3]

John Cullerton's election as senate president deviated from the usual pattern of someone moving into the leadership position. He was not the leader of a minority party that had gained the majority. He did not hold a position on the leadership team of outgoing senate president Emil Jones. He did not have a new leadership team in place, and by early December he had not made two important appointments, his chief of staff and his chief legal counsel. In late November he focused on two individuals, Andy Manar, the current senate Democratic budget director, and Eric Madiar, an attorney in private practice in Springfield. Madiar had legislative experience with house Democrats and with a state agency. The arrest of Rod Blagojevich and the prospects of a senate trial presented an added challenge to Cullerton's already full agenda.

In the days after the governor's arrest Cullerton and Democratic senator Don Harmon, from Oak Park, had urged Emil Jones to form a committee to begin developing rules for conducting a senate trial. Jones would be senate president until January 14, 2009. An ally of the governor, Jones was hesitant. John Cullerton was in an awkward position; if Jones refused to form a committee, Cullerton would have to do it alone, with no official staff and no official sanction by the senate. Rules for a senate trial needed to be in place quickly. The house was moving to impeach. After some discussion, Jones relented. Senate Resolution 966 created a committee to develop trial rules in the event that the governor was impeached. The resolution was passed by the senate the same day that the house held its first investigative hearing.[4] The committee consisted of five Democrats and four Republicans, and Cullerton was named committee chairman.

Cullerton felt that when the house impeached the governor, it was important to hold a trial quickly. The thought of Blagojevich being impeached by the house and continuing to hold the position of governor while legislation was debated and passed was unacceptable. An array of negative scenarios could be contemplated. The trial had to be held immediately, as soon as the Ninety-Sixth General Assembly was sworn into office.[5]

Eric Madiar, a Springfield lawyer with the Chicago firm of Freeborn and Peters, had worked for the Illinois house Speaker from 2000 to 2003. He then worked as an attorney for the Illinois Commerce Commission before entering private practice. Madiar was a meticulous, detailed attorney, familiar with administrative law but also politically astute. He had watched the leadership change in the Illinois senate and felt that it was a good time to return to government. A few days before Blagojevich's arrest, he began to talk with Cullerton about the position of chief legal counsel. He presented the incoming senate president with research concerning the potential appointment of Roland Burris to fill the vacant US Senate seat of president-elect Barack Obama. Blagojevich's appointment of Burris had been rumored ever since Obama's election, and many Illinois Democrats felt that the appointment "would be a blemish" on the party and the state.[6]

Madiar and Cullerton met again a few days after the governor's arrest to discuss how the senate would conduct an impeachment trial. Impeachment of the governor was by this time imminent. The structure of Illinois' government and its Constitution had changed since the 1833 impeachment trial of Supreme Court justice Theophilus Smith. A format and procedures for a trial were undefined. A careful lawyer, Madiar was conscious of the vagueness of the Illinois Constitution concerning impeachment, but he was also conscious of the law and potential political fallout. Impeachment is a rarity in the United States, and the procedures for state impeachment vary based on the requirements of individual state constitutions. Illinois' Constitution treats impeachment as a political action, but the subsequent senate trial, Madiar believed, had to be conducted in a judicial fashion. Madiar looked to the US Senate trial of President Clinton and the 1988 Arizona senate trial of Governor Evan Mecham as examples. He even reviewed the procedure and rules used during the 1833 trial of Judge Smith.

He reasoned that even though the Smith trial had taken place long ago, the case might provide some precedent. Madiar worked on the trial rules but had not yet been appointed to the senate staff. While in Chicago over the Christmas break, as he was buying a gift for his son, he received a call officially informing him that he would be hired as chief legal counsel. He immediately began working with the special committee.

The full rules committee met a few times over the Christmas holidays in Chicago. The committee gained some direction from the Mecham example and even the much outdated Smith proceedings, both cases that involved criminal charges. But mainly the committee relied on the procedures of the Clinton trial, modified and shaped by its own deliberations. The rules governing the senate trial were the senate's prerogative, with no constitutional provision establishing what the rules should include. The house staff and counsel provided input and negotiated some of the rules. The house leadership was adamant that the formal rules of evidence, used in Illinois and federal courts, would not be used in the trial before the senate, which was not a court of law. Conversely, the senate committee insisted that no member of the house serve as house prosecutor. A house member had served as house prosecutor during the Smith trial, but Cullerton wanted to maintain the senate's independence from the house. By the senate trial rules, the counsel to the house investigative committee would be named house prosecutor. By early January, after many drafts, the final version was complete.

On January 14 the Ninety-Fifth General Assembly adjourned and the Ninety-Sixth was sworn in. The swearing in of a new legislature is ordinarily a festive time in Illinois' capital city. Legislators' desks are piled high with flowers, friends watch from the galleries, and families accompany members to the chamber floor, where they take the oath of office. Hotel rooms are at a premium, restaurants are booked, and parties and receptions are held to celebrate the election winners and the beginning of a new term. Party politics are put aside, animosities are tempered, and governance, for just this one day, is in abeyance.

But celebration was not on the minds of the house and senate leaders. The first day of the Ninety-Sixth General Assembly was different. The governor's arrest, the national media attention of the preceding five weeks, the investigative hearings, the pending senate trial, and the imminent removal of the governor collectively served as the proverbial elephant in the room. Merriment was tempered; house and senate leaders had much on their minds. Madigan and his legal staff discussed the validity of the senate of the

Ninety-Sixth General Assembly acting on the resolution impeaching Blagojevich, which had been passed in the previous general assembly. They decided
to pass another impeachment resolution as soon as the Ninety-Sixth General
Assembly was sworn in and send the resolution immediately to the senate.

The momentous day created logistics considerations. Because of the
crowds, the ceremony of swearing in the house had been moved several
years before from the house chamber to the nearby auditorium of the University of Illinois' Springfield campus. The house prosecutor would have
to travel from the university campus to the capitol to exhibit the article
of impeachment. In the senate contingency planning was taken to an ex-
treme level. Blagojevich's circumstances and personality led senate leaders
to contemplate bizarre potential scenarios and try to "outthink crazy."
They had to be ready for anything. The governor, by the Constitution, was
responsible for presiding over the swearing in the new senate. What if he
refused? Madiar asked. What if Blagojevich just announced that a quorum
was not present and gaveled the senate to a close? What if he simply did not
show up? There would be no senate to hold a trial.[7] Four Illinois Supreme
Court justices would be there, however, and Madiar argued that *Robert's
Rules of Order* seemed to sanction one of the justices presenting the oath.

The house decided to reconstitute the special investigative committee
in case further committee action was required. HR 4, which reauthorized
the investigative committee, passed unanimously as soon as the house was
sworn in and organized. The impeachment resolution became HR 5, an
exact copy of the previously passed HR 1671.[8] With the Speaker presiding,
the festivities of inauguration day were suspended, and Barbara Currie
introduced and explained the resolution to the new house. Jim Durkin
spoke for the Republicans and addressed the process of the investigation.
He emphasized the fairness of the committee rules and the seriousness of
the charges. Only Currie, for the Democrats, and Durkin, for the Republicans, spoke. HR 5 was passed with 117 voting yes and 1 voting no. Deborah
Mell, the daughter of Alderman Dick Mell and the sister of Patti Blagojevich, had been elected to the Illinois house in November. It was the first
time she had been present for the vote on impeachment, and she voted no.
Afterward, to protect her from the swarm of media, she was escorted out
of the auditorium. The senate was informed that the resolution had passed
and that the house prosecutor was on his way to the capitol.

Meanwhile, Blagojevich did attend the senate inauguration. It was
awkward for the governor, the senators, and everyone else in attendance.

Few were smiling. The governor attempted some levity. Blagojevich and some staff were waiting in the anteroom behind the senate dais for the swearing-in ceremony to begin. Madiar recalled Blagojevich quipping to his staff, "When they came to arrest me, I should have jumped out of the window and ran to Cullerton's house. Then they would have had to arrest me at Cullerton's house." The staff laughed. Madiar did not think it was funny.[9] The governor walked to the senate podium and presided as appellate court judge Mary Jane Theis administered the oath of office to the senators, and then presided over the vote that elected Cullerton president of the senate. He then invited Cullerton to come to the podium to take charge of the senate. There was a pause and another awkward moment. Blagojevich, the consummate politician, had to speak. But his remarks were political bunkum, empty words to fill an empty moment: "We live in challenging times," he said, hoping "we can find our way, as we deal with other issues, to find the truth and sort things out, to put the business of the people first." He followed the veiled plea with two safe topics that were not in the least controversial and would gain approval, reminding everyone that they would soon celebrate the bicentennial of Abraham Lincoln's birth and mentioning the upcoming presidential inauguration of Illinois' Barack Obama.[10] Cullerton then made his way to the rostrum. After a quiet exchange of pleasantries, the governor left the senate.

Cullerton made a few obligatory remarks, recognizing dignitaries in the audience, then focused on the economic challenges that Illinois faced. Perhaps in a veiled reference to the pending removal of the governor, he said, "Things today are not going well," and "Times are not so good."[11] In deference to the governor, he consciously made no direct reference to the imminent senate trial. After the Republicans elected Christine Radogno as minority leader, and the leadership teams of both parties were announced, the senate finished its organizational business. The senate stood at ease while the guests left the senate floor. After a short period the senate began the serious work of conducting a senate trial. The senators moved to adopt the trial rules developed by the special committee in the form of a senate resolution that was sponsored by Cullerton. To present the resolution, Cullerton resumed his seat in the senate, and Senator James DeLeo, a veteran legislator from Chicago's Northwest Side who was appointed to Cullerton's leadership team, assumed the chair. Cullerton presented the trial rules as Senate Resolution (SR) 6. After a short explanation and no debate, SR 6 was approved by a unanimous vote of 58 to 0.[12]

The senate then took up SR 7, the schedule for the impeachment trial, and again adopted the resolution with no debate and by a unanimous vote. The senate was united and prepared to proceed.

Meanwhile, the house was meeting across town, at the University of Illinois, and coordination was problematic. Andy Manar and Eric Madiar were in touch with Ellis and members of the Democratic staff to keep Cullerton informed. The senate paused, waiting for word from the house that the impeachment resolution had passed and that Ellis was on his way to exhibit the resolution to the senate. DeLeo returned to his seat and Cullerton assumed the chair. After an awkward several minutes, a commotion was heard at the rear of the senate, and Cullerton called the senate to order. People ended their muffled conversations, and the senate chamber went silent. Cullerton appointed six senators, three Democrats and three Republicans, to accompany the house prosecutor into the senate chamber. The large mahogany senate doors opened, and the house prosecutor, David Ellis, and his senate escort walked in a solemn procession down the red carpet of the chamber's center aisle, hesitant, eyes downward, shuffling silently, like dour monks escorting the bishop to an excommunication. They were followed by an entourage of attendants pushing carts heavy with boxes of evidence. Several senators stood and looked at the scene in silent fascination. The audience appreciated the grave reality of the situation. Just moments earlier they had witnessed the inauguration of a new senate, and with the new organization came a new beginning. But the celebratory mood had abruptly transformed into the somber ritual of removing a sitting governor from office.

Like many others, Pamela Althoff, the Republican senator from McHenry, described the scene as surreal and said her feelings were mixed. She shared the excitement, the adrenaline rush, of being part of history being made but also the terribly low feeling of sadness that Illinois had come to this point. She told of another feeling that was difficult to describe: having "no emotion," almost as if she were "an observer in a different dimension."[13]

As the muffled scene played out, Ellis informed the senate that the Speaker had directed the house prosecutor "to exhibit the Article of Impeachment which had been preferred by the House of Representatives against Rod R. Blagojevich."[14] Ellis's utterances were strange words never heard before in the Illinois senate. This was not the familiar syntax of political debate, but an odd terminology that contributed to the dreamlike nature of the moment. Ellis read the impeachment article, requested that the senate "take over for a trial," and asked to withdraw. The entire episode took less than five minutes. Then Ellis was escorted out, and Cullerton appointed a new committee to escort Illinois Supreme Court chief justice Thomas Fitzgerald into the senate chamber. Cullerton administered the oath to preside over the senate trial to Fitzgerald, who in turn instructed the senate secretary, Deb Shipley, to read the oath necessary for the senate to serve as an impeachment tribunal. Afterward, each senator's name was called and each responded in the affirmative. Procedurally, the senate had "resolved" itself into an impeachment tribunal and adopted the trial rules and schedule. After some minor procedures, the senate quickly arose from sitting as an impeachment tribunal and adjourned.

Chapter 6

The Trial

The First Day

Hours before the trial began, lead prosecutor David Ellis and the prosecuting team received some reassuring news. The house assistant prosecutor, Michael Kasper, called Ellis from Chicago and said, "You won't believe what I'm holding."[1] The prosecution had been asking for access to the FBI recordings since the investigative committee was formed, but the US attorney, Patrick Fitzgerald, was reluctant. He did not want to divulge any information that would jeopardize the federal government's upcoming criminal case. Just before the trial, Fitzgerald compromised and agreed to release four limited segments of the tapes. Ellis was elated. The small segments gave him what he needed—the governor's actual voice, incriminating himself.

In addition, Daniel Cain, the FBI special agent who had signed the affidavit attesting to the accuracy of the recordings, was given permission to provide restricted testimony. With Special Agent Cain, Ellis had a real person before the senate who could address the criminal affidavit. He would not need the testimony from the house members he had earlier identified as potential witnesses. His trial strategy now was established: he would develop cause by presenting the criminal arguments contained in the affidavit used to arrest the governor, aided by the governor's own words and with Cain's testimony to validate the recordings; introducing the sworn testimonies of the convicted Blagojevich fund-raisers Ali Ata and Joe Cari to establish the governor's involvement in pay-to-play activity; and establishing maladministration and malfeasance using the ongoing JCAR case and the audits concerning the flu vaccines and I-SaveRx program.

At exactly 12:01 P.M. on January 26, 2009, the senate was called to order. On normal session days, senators slowly amble into the chamber, and after the customary prayer and Pledge of Allegiance, those present press their desk buttons to record their attendance and press the buttons of their colleagues who have not yet arrived on the senate floor. As the schedule for the day's business is decided, one can hear muffled floor discussions and people talking on phones, while staffers move up and down the aisles. This day was different. Every senator was at his or her desk, and a limited staff was instructed to remain at the rear of the chamber. The room was silent, and the face of each senator illustrated the solemnity of the task at hand. For only the second time since statehood, the Illinois senate was about to convene a trial to remove a state officer. The silent audience members in the galleries were merely spectators watching the drama playing out before them, but they were fully engaged and aware of the momentousness of the occasion. Before them Illinois history was being created, not with loud alarms, trumpets blaring, and passionate speeches, but with the solemn dignity, formality, and precision of a courtroom.

Access to the senate galleries was restricted, partly because of the many house members and state officers who wished to witness the historic event, partly because of public demand, and partly for security reasons. Attendance at the trial was subject to approval by the senate president's office. Andy Manar, chief of staff for the senate Democrats, arranged to have letters of admittance and plastic gallery passes prepared.[2] Gallery passes were strictly controlled. Senate staff members set up tables outside the entrance to the president's gallery, on the fourth floor behind the senate rostrum, and the gallery at the rear of the senate to distribute credentials. Guests turned in their credentials to staff posted outside the galleries when they left and retrieved them when they returned.

In what would be the procedure for the next four days, the Illinois senate was convened as a regular session, the chief justice was escorted into the senate chamber, and the senate then resolved itself into an impeachment tribunal. The first business on the first day was to administer the oath necessary to serve on the tribunal to Senator Frank Watson, who had been absent from the January 14 inauguration, when the other fifty-eight senators took the oath.

John Cullerton and Eric Madiar understood the importance of following senate protocol and adhering to the trial rules. They were aware that the governor might challenge the trial proceedings and were careful to offer the governor the opportunity to participate. Following the precise script prepared by Madiar, the senate tribunal established that on January 14, in conjunction with the trial rules, Blagojevich had been served with a summons, through his deputy general counsel, instructing the governor to file an appearance and answer the charges contained in the article of impeachment. The trial schedule required that the governor reply by January 17; failure to reply would constitute a plea of not guilty. Blagojevich did not reply. Also, for the record, it was noted that neither the governor nor his counsel filed any motions to dismiss or challenge the article of impeachment.

The secretary of the senate, Deb Shipley, read into the record that the house prosecutor had requested that four individuals who had appeared before the house investigative committee be called as trial witnesses: University of Illinois professor Andrew Morriss, Auditor General Bill Holland, JCAR director Vicki Thomas, and John Scully, who had provided testimony on wiretapping during the house impeachment investigation. In addition, Ellis had requested that eight house members be called as witnesses, chosen carefully to show wide geographic and ethnic inclusion in the removal effort. From the Republican investigative committee, he chose Chapin Rose, from downstate Mahomet; and Jim Durkin, the party's spokesman on the committee. From the Democratic investigative committee, he chose Representative Constance "Connie" Howard, an African American from Chicago; David Miller, from suburban Cook County; Jack Franks, from upstate Marengo; Lou Lang, from suburban Skokie; and alternate committee member Susana Mendoza, from Chicago. Ellis also requested that Representative Gary Hannig, a Democrat from downstate Litchfield, be called as a witness. Ellis was unsure what role these witnesses would play, but it seemed necessary to have the charges that had been developed by the investigative committee expressed by "real people," rather than present only an abstract concept of the committee's findings.[3]

The Trial

After establishing the pretrial activity in the trial record, Chief Justice Thomas Fitzgerald instructed a group of senators to escort the house prosecutor and the governor into the senate chamber. The governor was not present, and Fitzgerald noted for the record that "the Governor has chosen not to appear either in person or by Counsel" (15).[4] The governor's strategy was becoming clear. Genson had left the case, and Blagojevich had decided to plead his case not before the Illinois senate, but to the American public. Blagojevich ignored the senate's activities, perhaps anticipating the outcome. Instead, in a series of public appearances and statements, he attempted to develop the persona of a national celebrity in the style of Robert Blake and O. J. Simpson, both of whom were acquitted in murder trials.[5] As late as Saturday, two days before the trial began, he appeared on *The Don Wade and Roma Show* on Chicago radio station WLS. Possibly anticipating his upcoming criminal trial, he focused on how unfair it was to remove him, saying that if he were given the chance to bring in witnesses, they would show that he was innocent. He admitted that it was his voice on the FBI tapes and apologized for the use of profanity, but he stayed on message, ignoring the criminal aspects of the recordings. He employed the same political rhetoric that had served him for the past six years, portraying himself as fighting for the people, trying to do good things, and being the victim of evil elements in state government, led by Michael Madigan and John Cullerton.

Now, Ellis was recognized to explain the prosecution's motions for changes in the original witnesses identified and evidence submitted. With newly acquired access to segments of the FBI audio recording evidence, along with permission from the US attorney to call Special Agent Cain as a witness, Ellis had his "real person" and informed the senate that house witnesses Durkin, Mendoza, Hannig, Miller, and Franks would not be called. He was still planning to call Chapin Rose, a former county prosecutor, to review the testimony of Ali Ata and Joe Cari related to their pay-to-play and extortion pleas; Lou Lang, a member of the JCAR committee, to testify to the governor's "refusal to provide any information related to the FamilyCare program"; and Connie Howard, to speak about the adverse effects on the state as a result of the governor's previous actions and arrest (28).

Ellis explained that on January 22 Patrick Fitzgerald, the US attorney, had indicated that he would allow Cain to provide testimony before the senate, but it would be restricted. Cain would only swear that what was contained in the affidavit was true and accurate, and he could answer general questions about his role as an FBI agent, but he could not divulge any other information. Ellis told the senate that the governor would be indicted in April and that the federal investigation was still ongoing.

The prosecutor methodically outlined the case that he would present to the senate. In addition to testimonies from Lang, Rose, and Howard, Scully would testify about the process of securing a court-authorized wiretap, Holland about the audits related to the flu vaccine procurement and the I-SaveRx program, Thomas about the governor's "defiance" of the Administrative Procedure Act (27), and Morriss about the illegality of the governor's conduct. Ellis would play four intercepted phone conversations that would provide evidence of specific acts of pay-to-play activity. To address the issue of probable cause for the wiretap authorization, Ellis would introduce an excerpt from a transcript where US district court Judge Holderman made clear that the US government followed procedures and the law. To highlight sections of the criminal complaint, the prosecution would use visual transcripts of pertinent quotes from the wiretap.

Ellis would introduce all supporting documents related to the CMS audits and asked to be allowed to introduce as evidence an amendment filed in Congress by Illinois congressmen Mark Kirk, a Republican, and William Foster, a Democrat, which called for restrictions on federal stimulus funds coming to Illinois as long as Rod Blagojevich was governor. He also asked that the January 24 recording of the radio program where the governor admitted he was speaking on the tapes be admitted as evidence. To show a motive for the governor's desire that members of the *Chicago Tribune* editorial board be fired, the prosecutor introduced several *Tribune* editorials and stories critical of Blagojevich. Concerning the governor's attempt to obtain personal gain from an appointment to Barack Obama's vacated senate seat, Ellis introduced a description of the little-known organization Change to Win, with which Blagojevich had allegedly sought a position in exchange for appointing Obama's choice.

When Ellis finished his opening remarks, the senate chamber was silent. The range and complexity of the prosecutor's evidence was difficult for many senators to grasp. The charges involved both criminal allegations, including selling positions in government and extortion, and administrative acts such as misappropriation of funds, violating state law, and constitutional violations. Cullerton and Christine Radogno asked the chief justice for a party caucus, to discuss what the house prosecutor had presented and to formulate questions. The senate recessed for one hour.

The Trial

As established by the senate trial rules, the questions were written and submitted to Chief Justice Thomas Fitzgerald, who then read each question to a witness or attorney, alternating between parties. These questions were the first expression from the Illinois senate, and they were mixed. Illinois is a racially and culturally diverse state, and its senate reflects that diversity. Each senator viewed the trial and events from his or her own perspective. Some questions initially revealed support for the governor. Senator Rickey Hendon, an African American from a district on the Near West Side of Chicago who was a former alderman and a Blagojevich ally, asked, "Isn't the Kirk-Foster amendment a political amendment that further prejudices the case against the governor?" Ellis countered that although it was a political amendment, it was relevant because it was "probative" and illustrated that the governor's actions were injuring the state (40). Hendon remained skeptical. He stated that Ellis had introduced new evidence and asked if Ellis was under any obligation to present evidence that would exonerate the governor. Ellis said he would. Hendon asked if "giving health care to children is an impeachable offense." Ellis responded that the senate would decide what an impeachable offense was (54). Hendon also questioned why all the charges were "lumped together in one article of impeachment." He said his research could not find other impeachment cases where all the charges were contained in one article and asked why the house had "decided to go against precedent." Ellis countered that there was precedent for charges based on a pattern of abuse of authority and said that the house had decided to present the article of impeachment based on a pattern of abuse. He recalled the impeachment of Supreme Court justice Samuel Chase (57–58).[6]

Hendon, who was known for his flamboyant style of imagery and rhetoric, would not relent. He cited the impeachments of Andrew Johnson, Richard Nixon, and Bill Clinton and said all were examples of charges being divided among separate articles. Why had the house constructed one article of impeachment? Wasn't the house restricting the senate's right to judge the charges separately? He asked why Ellis was opposed to separating the charges. Hendon was not known for in-depth historical research, and his questions led to speculation that he had been supplied with them. Ellis replied that he did not believe that presenting the charges as one article restricted the senators. He maintained that the house had prepared the article and that he could not change a decision by the house (59–61).

Some Republican questions were veiled attempts at partisanship. But the partisanship should not be dismissed as mere tribal gamesmanship. The

Republican senators had chafed under the yoke of Emil Jones for six years. They had long complained and debated the state's fiscal policies and the way the state was being managed, but Jones only dismissed and resented them. The partisanship snipes were the outpourings of pent-up frustrations and genuine anger. The Republicans were saying to the Democratic senators, this was your party's governor, and your leadership allowed this to happen.[7]

Senator Kirk Dillard, a Republican from DuPage County, asked why Democratic US Senate leader Harry Reid was not subpoenaed. Reid had spoken to Blagojevich and discussed the senate vacancy, and Dillard queried, "Wouldn't the Democrat leader in the US Senate be in a premier position to know the behind-the-scenes of who would join his caucus?" Ellis responded that he had no knowledge of the content of the tapes that were not released and that the house prosecutor could not subpoena the tapes (41–42).

Republican senator Chris Lauzen, from Aurora, brought up the Z Scott report, paragraph 13 in the house impeachment article. The report addressed hiring and firing practices, but no witness was slated to address the report. Lauzen asked why. Ellis responded that the report had been a collaborative effort and the prosecution did not have a witness that had personal knowledge of the report. The house investigative committee had attempted unsuccessfully to have Z Scott testify, but Ellis felt that the report spoke for itself (46–47).

Senator William Haine, a Democrat and the former state's attorney from Alton, asked Ellis if Cain would testify as to whether exculpatory statements had been made by the governor or anyone acting for him on the tapes *not* heard by the senate. A seasoned prosecutor, Haine was concerned that the case developed before the senate remain fair and impartial. Ellis responded that he would highlight such statements and that when examining Cain, he would "make it a point of drawing those out of him." He assured Haine, "You have my commitment to that" (50).

When the questions from the senate were finished, Cullerton asked that the senate grant leave for all the motions requested by the house prosecutor to be voted on with one roll call. Rickey Hendon objected to Cullerton's request. He was opposed to the Kirk-Foster amendment, restricting federal funds coming to Illinois, being accepted as evidence. The amendment had not passed, and Hendon felt that the amendment would be injurious to the state. With Hendon's objection, leave was not granted. The senate voted separately on the motion to submit the Kirk-Foster amendment as evidence, and it was accepted with 48 voting yes and 11 no. Through separate votes, the senate approved all the remaining motions presented by the house prosecutor. With all pretrial motions complete, the senate took a short recess and prepared for the trial.

Since the governor's arrest, the days and nights seemed to run together for David Ellis. A few days before the trial, he left his Springfield home and moved into the downtown Hilton Hotel, because his wife had developed a severe cold and feared he would be infected. Ellis could not afford to be compromised; he was working nonstop, first with the impeachment investigation in the house and now as the house prosecutor in the senate. The trial was the most important professional event the young lawyer had ever undertaken. Fortunately, he could turn to others on the prosecuting team: attorneys Heather Wier Vaught, Cindy Grant, and Michael Kasper. Vaught and Grant were members of the house Democratic staff, and Kasper was an experienced trial lawyer who was no stranger to Springfield. He was a former chief counsel to the Speaker, and most of all, he had Madigan's confidence.

When the senate was called back to order, Chief Justice Fitzgerald, without fanfare, simply recognized Ellis for an opening statement. It took a moment for the room to adjust; the trial had begun. After the obligatory statements of gratitude for letting him appear before the senate, Ellis thanked the senators for undertaking the "awesome task" of an impeachment trial. He knew, he said, that the senators did not take the duty of holding a trial lightly and recalled "the look on all the faces" surrounding him and "the utter silence in the Chamber" as he entered the senate on January 14 to exhibit the article of impeachment. The assiduous house prosecutor had crafted his opening remarks to establish a feeling of unanimity between the house and senate. The house and senate were acting together; they had the same purpose. He established unity between the legislative chambers by drawing a parallel between the serious attitude displayed by the senate and the way the house deliberated over the impeachment resolution. The house had "accumulated a great volume of evidence, heard a great deal of testimony and deliberated on it." The result, he told the senators, was a house vote of 117 yes and 1 no, for "a single Article of Impeachment alleging a pattern of abuse of power" (68). Ellis spoke in a manner that conveyed professionalism and detachment, showing little emotion to detract from what he was saying. His tone was devoid of theatrics, his pitch was steady, and he did not stress words.

The nebulous, problematic word *cause* in the Constitution, and the varied understandings and interpretations that the word can generate, prompted Ellis to initially provide a definition of impeachment that would justify the actions taken by the house. He cautioned the senate that impeachment and removal were not criminal proceedings. "We are not here to punish Governor Blagojevich." Rather, "the purpose of impeachment is [to] remediate . . . to protect the citizens of this state from the abuses of an elected officer." The prosecutor announced that he would not attempt to prove that the governor had committed any particular state or federal crime. The criminal proceedings were months, perhaps years, away. Proving the criminal case would be the responsibility of the US attorney. Ellis said that the prosecution would show that "the Governor repeatedly and utterly abused the powers and privileges of his office," a justifiable cause for removal. He would illustrate a pattern of abuse by using both things that "came to light from the ongoing federal investigation" that prompted the governor's arrest and evidence that was "entirely unrelated to that investigation" (69–70).

December 9, the day of the governor's arrest, had become an indelible event etched in the memory of every senator. The astute house prosecutor took his audience back to the moment of the arrest. Everyone in the senate chamber, listening intently, recalled vividly the shock and shame of that morning and the disgraceful scene of Illinois' governor being led away by FBI agents in handcuffs. Ellis explained why the arrest happened: the FBI had been secretly recording conversations, and those recordings, he assured the senators, will be "front and center in our case." The recordings would contain the governor's own words and show the governor directing people. The legitimacy of the actions by the law enforcement agencies remained unquestionable, and Ellis used this sentiment to emphasize the upcoming testimony of Special Agent Daniel Cain. He told the senate that Cain would declare that everything contained in the affidavit was "true and accurate." He would play segments of the tape recordings so that the senators could hear the governor attempting to exchange the signing of legislation for political contributions. The governor's words, he said, "may shock you. At times, they will probably disgust you" (70–71).

The prosecutor then brought up what many felt was the most egregious charge against the governor: the selling of Barack Obama's senate seat. The senate would be presented with evidence that Blagojevich plotted to obtain something of value, "like a sports agent shopping a star athlete to the highest bidder." Ellis discussed the governor's options at length. At first Blagojevich had high hopes, perhaps a cabinet-level position or an ambassadorship. He did not meet with success, and as his hopes were dashed, he began to explore a position with Change to Win, a union interest organization. When that option dissolved, he became frustrated and tried to obtain paid appointments on corporate boards for his wife. Finally, he was reduced to scheming for "good old-fashioned political contributions." Ellis used a refrain that by now each senator was quite familiar with. It was the governor's creed for political operations, his words to his advisors that were heard on the FBI recordings, the standards and criteria used to benefit Blagojevich: everything had to be "legal, personal, [and] political" (72–75).

Ellis told the senate that he would demonstrate how Blagojevich abused the power of his office by attempting to trade official acts for personal or political gain. He told of the governor's attempts to coerce the Tribune Company to fire members of the editorial board, to extract more contributions from road contractors by promising larger allocations for tollway improvements, to prompt horse-racing track officials to make contributions in exchange for his signing legislation that would benefit the tracks, and perhaps most repugnant, to withhold an allocation for pediatric care from Children's Memorial Hospital unless hospital officials made a political contribution. All the charges that Ellis spoke of had been recorded and discovered during the ongoing federal investigation. "The stuff we've talked about so far, these are the issues that were caught on tape" (75–77).

The house prosecutor then seamlessly turned to the impeachment charges that were unrelated to the ongoing criminal investigation. The senators would hear of Ali Ata's sworn testimony that he had received his position as executive director of the Illinois Finance Authority in exchange for a campaign contribution. The convicted Joe Cari would "testify that the Governor flat out told him" he could obtain political contributions from those who received state contracts. Ellis told the senate that the governor not only appointed people to the Health Facilities Planning Board but also "controlled how they voted." At the recent trial of Tony Rezko, "it was corroborated by a number of people" that Blagojevich "switched the vote of his block from no to yes on a permit application by a hospital after that hospital agreed to give the Governor a campaign contribution" (78–79). The house prosecutor's charges, with one corrupt incident after another delivered in rapid succession, had a noticeable impact on the senate. The senators sat transfixed.

But Ellis had more. He transitioned to the incidents that had received the most attention of the house investigative committee: the flu vaccine and I-SaveRx audits and JCAR. The audits would "show that the Governor liked splashy ideas, big ideas, headlines," Ellis said, "but when it came to implementing his policies, he consistently violated state law and federal law, often jeopardizing the safety of our citizens" (80).

Finally, the house prosecutor addressed the rules governing the senate proceedings. The rules were modeled after the Clinton impeachment trial, he said, and, emphasizing the fairness of the rules, the presidential trial had resulted in an acquittal. Once again, employing the prestige of the law enforcement agencies involved in the governor's arrest, he stressed that the governor's own words would be verified by Special Agent Cain. Ellis closed by noting that there was one person who could "refute any charges that he was capable of refuting," who had "absolute personal knowledge of all of the information contained in this complaint." That was the governor, and the rules permitted him "to testify in his own defense." The governor had "betrayed the public trust" and "violated his constitutional oath," and thus "he should be removed from office" (81–82).

Immediately after Ellis's opening remarks, Chief Justice Thomas Fitzgerald spoke. Again, for the record, the chief justice intoned, "Is the Governor present? Is counsel present on behalf of the Governor?" His questions were met by silence. Fitzgerald then asked that the record reflect that the governor had "chosen not to make an opening statement" (82).

The first witness for the house prosecutors was John Scully. Scully's task was to verify the legitimacy of the wiretap, which was the foundation on which the impeachment was based. The house prosecutors made sure Scully's background in the military and with law enforcement agencies was not lost on the senators; they passed out a copy of his "curriculum vitae" (86). Michael Kasper questioned Scully about his experience, the types of recordings, and the procedures necessary to obtain court permission. Then for the record, Fitzgerald asked if the governor or his counsel wished to cross-examine the witness. Again his inquiry was met with silence. After a short recess to formulate questions, only the Republicans chose to ask anything of Scully, with a few general questions concerning the particulars of wiretaps and the procedure necessary to obtain permission. The day was over. The purpose of Scully's appearance had been to substantiate the legitimacy of the wiretap evidence, and there was no dispute from the senators.

The Second Day

Throughout the house investigative hearings, Ellis had relied on the criminal affidavit as the source of the major charges for impeachment and removal, referring to it when he opened the house hearings and as he gave his opening arguments before the senate. He had stressed the importance of the testimony of Special Agent Daniel Cain, someone who was a participant in the ongoing criminal investigation and who could attest that the contents of the affidavit were accurate. Although highly restricted by the US attorney, it would provide Ellis the opportunity to use the actual language of the affidavit, giving him the ability to paint graphic scenes that the senators could easily envision.

Ellis, the ever-meticulous attorney, was ready. The night before and early that morning he had met with the other prosecuting attorneys to go over the affidavit, and they decided which remarks, corroborated by Cain, would confirm the prosecution's claims. Before beginning the interrogation of his witness, Ellis introduced the senate to Assistant US Attorney Tom Walsh, who would sit next to Cain during his testimony. If the questions from Ellis or the senators were deemed beyond the scope of verifying the accuracy of what the affidavit contained, Walsh would instruct him not to answer.

After the obligatory background questions to establish the credibility of the witness, Ellis read a paragraph from the affidavit that informed the senate of Cain's knowledge of the criminal investigation. The investigation involved many government agencies, and Cain had worked with agents from those agencies. He had interviewed witnesses and analyzed reports, and he had been involved with the investigation for an extended period of time, long before the governor's alleged wrongdoings were discovered by wiretapping.[8] The paragraph also established that there had been ongoing investigations concerning Blagojevich and his confederates for several years.

Ellis constructed his interrogation for the maximum effect on the senate. He moved through the affidavit by subject rather than chronologically. Lawyerly instincts indicated that the first subject discussed set the tenor for the entire presentation. The first topic needed to not only prove culpability but also ignite a sense of outrage over the governor's actions. He began with Blagojevich's attempt to obtain personal benefits from the appointment of a successor to the vacant US senate seat of president-elect Obama.

For the record, but mainly for impact, Ellis emphasized the title of paragraph 86 of the affidavit: "Evidence Concerning Efforts to Obtain

Personal Benefits for Rod Blagojevich in Return for His Appointment of a United States Senator." He then summarized the paragraph, which said that through intercepted calls, evidence was obtained proving that Blagojevich had conspired with his chief of staff John Harris and others to attempt to receive some benefit for his wife and himself in exchange for Obama's vacant senate seat. In particular, revealed through the weeks of wiretaps, Blagojevich considered a range of options. He started high, contemplating a cabinet position or an ambassadorship, but as time went by, he became frustrated and his proposals became driven by monetary concerns. The governor "focused on an effort to obtain campaign contributions, up front, in consideration of an appointment" (159; para. 86).[9] Blagojevich also considered using the president's assistance to create positions within the private sector or to help place his wife on paid corporate boards. Finally, he kept open the option of filling the vacant senate seat himself. Through a series of convoluted schemes and options, with several possible choices identified in the affidavit as Senate Candidates 1 through 5, he continued to discuss the possibilities of personal monetary gain with his advisors. At the end of this and every other section Ellis read from the quoted affidavit, he asked Cain to validate the truth of his statements. Cain answered in the affirmative each time.

Many of the schemes recorded by the wiretaps seemed farcical. Initially, the governor proposed trading the appointment of a candidate—identified in the affidavit as Senate Candidate 1, believed to be Valerie Jarrett, the candidate supported by Barack Obama—for Blagojevich's appointment as secretary of health and human services. He also considered being appointed as an ambassador, but he quickly realized that the negative publicity surrounding the recent convictions of several key advisors, his nonattendance to governance, and his relationship with the legislature prohibited Obama from ever considering a direct appointment. Blagojevich then considered asking President-elect Obama to arrange for a position with a union organization called Change to Win or to persuade his wealthy supporters—including Warren Buffett—to donate millions of dollars to a start-up political action and lobbying organization. Blagojevich thought he could head the new organization and also remain politically active. On several occasions he discussed experiencing financial stress and stated that he needed to make money, even suggesting the amounts necessary. Placing his wife in paid positions on corporate boards was another possibility that he raised. Blagojevich also considered appointing himself to the senate seat (143–94; paras. 86–116).

125

Ellis continued to summarize and quote from the intercepted conversations revealed in the affidavit. From the day of Obama's election to the day he was arrested, Blagojevich and his advisors plotted to receive something of personal value for appointing the US senator. The summaries and the quotes from the affidavit clearly revealed a governor weighing various possibilities to barter the senate seat. The governor repeatedly stated that he would not give up the senate seat and receive nothing in return. To reinforce and highlight the governor's words, Ellis exhibited them on large display cards before the senate. As he moved through the paragraphs of the affidavit, staff attorney Cindy Grant changed the cards.

The prosecutor referred to a conversation that took place on November 3, 2008, between the governor and a person identified in the affidavit as Advisor A. Blagojevich stated that he wanted something in return for the senate appointment: "Unless I get something real good for Senate Candidate 1, [expletive deleted in the transcript], I'll just send myself. You know what I'm saying?" Later the governor remarked that the senate seat "is a F-ing valuable thing. You don't just give it away for nothing" (161; para. 90).

Throughout early November 2008, in a series of phone calls and conversations, the governor continued to explore various options to gain something of value. The excerpts extracted from the supporting affidavit starkly revealed the governor's motivation. On November 3 Blagojevich spoke to his deputy governor, identified as Deputy Governor A, regarding Obama's assumed choice for the vacant senate seat: "If they're not going to offer anything of any value, then I just might take it" (160; para. 89). Two days later Blagojevich was recorded speaking to Doug Scofield, identified in the recorded conversations as Advisor A.[10] The governor pronounced what became the signature statement of the impeachment: "I've got this thing, and it's F-ing golden, and uh, uh, I'm just not giving it up for F-ing nothing. I'm not going to do it. And—and I can always use it. I can parachute me there" (166–67; para. 96).

On November 7 the governor and John Harris discussed the option of having Obama intervene with the Service Employees International Union and the union-affiliated organization Change to Win as compensation for getting his choice for the senate. Harris insisted that a three-way deal would give Obama a "buffer so there is no obvious quid pro quo" and cautioned him to be careful and not make it look like "some sort of selfish grab." Blagojevich said that he was "financially hurting," and Harris responded that the governor's staff was considering what would help the governor's "financial security." The governor responded, "I want to make money" (168–70; para. 99).

Ellis summarized a conference call placed on November 10, which lasted almost two hours, involving the governor; his wife, Patti; chief of staff John Harris; the governor's general counsel; and several Washington, DC, based advisors. The participants came on and off the call, and they again discussed the many options open to the governor. The governor talked about the possibilities of making money and potentially "participating in the political arena again." He kept returning to the possibility of his wife being placed on corporate boards, and once again Blagojevich expressed how he was "struggling financially—struggling." Patti Blagojevich claimed that she was qualified to serve on corporate boards because she had a background in real estate and appraisals. Blagojevich's consultants told him to "suck it up for two years and do nothing and give this [expletive deleted], referring to the President-Elect, his senator." The governor responded, "F him. For nothing? F him." Blagojevich went on to state that he would appoint Senate Candidate 4, believed to be a deputy governor of the state of Illinois, before he appointed Senate Candidate 1 to the "F-ing Senate seat and I don't get anything." And once again the call participants discussed the possibilities of going to Change to Win and making a three-way deal (173–76).

Finally, Ellis read paragraph 116 of the affidavit, summarizing Blagojevich's motives and the viability of appointing himself to the senate seat. He was frustrated with being "stuck" as governor, and appointing himself to the US Senate was a viable option. He was aware of the possibility of indictment and impeachment, and if this occurred, Blagojevich supposed he could "obtain greater resources" to defend himself as a sitting senator than as a governor. The senate also would allow him to remake his personal image, with an eye toward running for president in 2016. If he decided to leave public office, he mused, the corporate contacts he could make as a senator would prove valuable to securing future positions and would assist in generating speaking fees. And being a member of the US Senate would also facilitate his wife's employment as a lobbyist. Cognizant of his present relationship with the Illinois legislature, he thought that by taking the senate seat, he could avoid impeachment.

The senate audience sat stunned as they listened to these words from the recorded conversations. The audacity and hubris expressed by the governor seemed incredible. The governor's schemes bordered on absurdity, but the conversations laid bare the dealings and priorities of Rod Blagojevich. The discourse went beyond politics. Everyone knew that the US Senate appointment would be made with political considerations. No one expected the governor to appoint someone who would not be advantageous to him, but the scheming and devious scenarios discussed among the governor and his aides and advisors shocked and embarrassed the audience of seasoned politicians. Few in the senate galleries had read the criminal complaint or the attached affidavit. Most of the senators had been aware of the charges but not the dialogue or language in the conversations recorded by the FBI wiretaps. Politics can be harsh, niceties are sometimes abandoned, and the words used by the participants are often direct, but the governor's base and vulgar language was inappropriate and made the listeners feel uncomfortable and awkward. His foul language notwithstanding, the governor's motives were clear. The prosecutor had scored with his first charge.

Ellis moved to another subject: the governor's attempt to coerce the Tribune Company into firing members of the editorial board of the *Chicago Tribune* in exchange for financial assistance from the Illinois Finance Authority (IFA). Funds from the IFA, Blagojevich was informed, could be distributed at the governor's discretion without intervention from the legislature. The criminal complaint alleged that the governor and John Harris attempted to "corruptly use the power and influence of the Office of the Governor to cause the firing of the *Chicago Tribune* editorial board members as a condition of State of Illinois financial assistance" (198–200; para. 71).

The wiretaps revealed that the governor instructed John Harris to inform the Tribune owner, through an individual identified in the affidavit as the Tribune Financial Advisor, that assistance from the IFA would not be forthcoming unless members of the *Tribune*'s editorial board were fired. Blagojevich believed that the *Tribune* was "driving" the notion of impeachment (201; para. 72). The newspaper had been critical of Blagojevich for bypassing the legislature to achieve what he wanted, and the governor mentioned the irony of bypassing the legislature to grant IFA funds to help the Tribune Company.

Reading from the affidavit, Ellis painted a graphic image of the developing plot. On November 3 the governor was recorded speaking at length to an individual, identified as Deputy Governor A, about the *Chicago Tribune*'s endorsement of Speaker Michael Madigan and an editorial calling for an impeachment investigation. The governor's wife, Patti, could be heard in the background, shouting to Blagojevich to tell the deputy governor to "hold up that F-ing Cubs, blank. Blank them." Later in the conversation the governor's wife spoke directly to Deputy Governor A and explained that the Tribune owner could "just fire the writers because [the] Tribune Owner owns the Tribune" (202–3; para. 73). As the discussion progressed, the governor told Deputy Governor A to put together the articles that called for removing Blagojevich and John Harris would approach the Tribune Company. "We've got some decisions to make now." Musing, he followed with "Someone should say, Get rid of those people." Blagojevich was becoming frustrated, his thoughts running together. "Someone's got to go to [the] Tribune Owner. We want to see them. It's a political F-ing operation in there" (203–4; para. 74). Recordings from later that evening had Blagojevich speaking to Lon Monk about his scheme to pressure the Tribune owner to fire members of the newspaper's editorial board.

The next day Blagojevich told John Harris to explain to the Tribune financial advisor, its owner, and the Cubs chairman that the *Tribune* was writing editorials criticizing the governor for taking actions like those the owner wanted to take concerning the Cubs and the IFA. Because of the past impeachment investigation editorials, he said, "We don't know if we can take a chance and do this IFA deal now. I don't want to give them grounds to impeach me." Slipping back into his usual vulgar vernacular, Blagojevich told Harris that the recommendation was to "fire all those F-ing people, get them the 'F' out of there and get us some editorial support" (208; para. 76). On November 5 Blagojevich conducted a conference call with Harris, Scofield, and an individual identified in the affidavit as a press spokesman. He instructed Harris to call someone at the Tribune Company and "lay a foundation with them." Harris said he would call the financial advisor. Blagojevich told Harris to say that "this is a serious thing now . . . and that the only way around it is around the legislature and that the *Tribune* is trumping up impeachment discussions because I do this stuff to get things done." He directed Harris to tell the financial advisor, "Everything is lined up, but before we go to the next level, we need to have a discussion about what you guys are going to do about that newspaper" (209–10; para. 77).

The following day Harris confirmed to the governor that he had talked with the financial advisor about the problem of going forward with the Cubs IFA assistance with the current *Tribune* editorial board in place. The financial advisor was aware of the delicacy of the issue and would discuss it with the Tribune owner, Harris reported. Blagojevich was concerned about whether the financial advisor had gotten the message that editorial board members had to be fired. Harris responded, "Oh, yeah, he got it loud and clear" (212; para. 78). However, the Tribune Company failed to act on Blagojevich's recommendations. Blagojevich and Harris continued discussions about the company throughout November, and the governor repeatedly restated his desire to remove members of the editorial board in exchange for assistance from the IFA, but nothing changed at the *Chicago Tribune*.

The prosecutor had organized and presented his accusations for maximum effect. The first two charges, the trading of Obama's senate seat and attempted interference with the *Tribune's* editorial board, dealt with information that had been gleaned from the wiretaps in November and December. Using evidence that had been gathered through years of FBI investigations and surveillance, Ellis next turned to alleged criminal activity. The prosecutor started with a topic that continues to generate disagreement: the propriety and influence of campaign contributions. Again, for impact, Ellis read to the senate the title of a section contained in the affidavit: "Evidence Concerning the Solicitation and Receipt of Campaign Contributions in Return for Official Acts by Rod Blagojevich prior to October 2008." Ellis began by relating the statements of Ali Ata. Ata was a Jordanian immigrant who came to the United States to study engineering. After graduation he held various jobs in the private sector before becoming involved in politics after meeting Alderman Dick Mell in the 1970s. He subsequently met Rod Blagojevich and had contributed to his campaign during his run for congress. Ata's foray into Illinois politics also introduced him to Tony Rezko. The two became friends and seemed to have much in common. Both were emigrants from the Middle East; Rezko was a Syrian. Ata had agreed to raise funds for Blagojevich during his race for governor, and he and Rezko had discussed a position within state government after the election. He also became acquainted with Chris Kelly and Lon Monk. Ata was duly rewarded for his fund-raising efforts and named president of the newly founded Illinois Finance Authority.[11] There is an old refrain in Springfield: Be careful when you are swimming with sharks. Ata had jumped into the pool.

In connection with the ongoing Operation Board Games, the federal investigation of corruption in the Blagojevich administration, the government charged Ata with tax fraud on $1.2 million he had received from Rezko and for lying to FBI agents. Ata reached an agreement with the government, pleaded guilty, testified as a witness for the prosecution during Rezko's trial, and agreed to cooperate with the federal government in exchange for a lesser sentence (218). Rezko was charged with and convicted of two separate fraud schemes. He was convicted of shaking down millions of dollars from firms doing business before Illinois regulatory boards and of defrauding General Electric Capital Corporation and investors in a pizza restaurant business owned by Rezko.[12] Rezko was sentenced to ten and a half years in prison.

Portions of Ata's testimony during the Rezko trial were introduced as evidence in the criminal complaint against Blagojevich and were contained in the supporting affidavit. Attempting to link Blagojevich with the newly convicted Tony Rezko, Ellis read a portion of Ata's testimony. Ata claimed that as early as 2001 he was becoming aware of the close relationship between Rezko and Blagojevich, and he related a series of incidents when Rezko had asked Ata to raise money for Blagojevich. Ata always complied.

During the Rezko trial, Ata testified that he had discussed a high-level position within the Blagojevich administration "while a $25,000 donation check to Friends of Blagojevich from Ata was sitting on a table in front of Blagojevich." Ata also testified that after another substantial contribution, Blagojevich told Ata that he was aware of the contributions, that Ata was a good supporter, and that he understood Ata would be joining the administration. He added that "it had better be a job where Ata could make some money" (221–22, 227–28; para. 16). Ata was apparently surprised at Blagojevich's response and told Rezko about it. Rezko said he was "not surprised and had heard Rod Blagojevich say things like that before" (228). Ata was eventually appointed director of the Illinois Finance Authority.

The Ata testimony linked Blagojevich with Rezko and served implicitly to revive the question of whether the governor was involved with Rezko's nefarious deeds. But the account of Ata giving contributions in return for a position also was problematic. The governor had expressed that Ata was a good supporter and that he was aware that Ata would be joining the administration. Ata supported Rod Blagojevich, and Blagojevich did what every successful politician does—he rewarded his supporter by bringing him into the administration. Politics is a process of reciprocal arrangements. Patronage, tempered by the evolving demands of government, has been and always will be a component of our particular form of democracy.[13] The only direct link of a quid pro quo was the check for $25,000 that was supposedly on the table in front of Blagojevich, and as verification that the event took place, the senators had only Ata's word. But the senate was not a court of law, and to remove Blagojevich, the senators did not have to find the defendant guilty of unlawful actions beyond a reasonable doubt. The prosecution instead sought to establish a pattern of abusive actions that made the governor unfit to hold public office. All the charges were presented to the senate in one impeachment article. The senate would decide on the totality of the article, and the Ata testimony served the purpose of linking Blagojevich and Rezko.

Ellis moved next to the Rezko trial testimony of Joseph Cari, portions of which were also included in the affidavit supporting the criminal complaint. Cari, an experienced fund-raiser on the national level, had served as the national finance chairman for Al Gore's 2000 presidential campaign. Cari had been cooperating with federal authorities since being confronted with the charge of extortion in early 2005. Initially, Cari lied to the federal agents about his relationship with Stuart Levine, but when pressed, he finally agreed to cooperate. He was the first person to provide any real evidence that Blagojevich and those around him were going above and beyond what was allowable in the fund-raising arena.[14]

Cari testified that on October 29, 2003, he flew to New York along with Blagojevich, Rezko, Chris Kelly, and Levine to attend a fund-raiser that he was hosting on behalf of Rod Blagojevich. The airplane was arranged and paid for by Levine, a member of the board of the Illinois Teachers Retirement System. The governor expressed that he was thinking of running for president of the United States and was interested in Cari's fund-raising experience on the national level. According to Cari, Blagojevich had remarked that it was easier for governors to solicit campaign contributions because they could "award contracts" to campaign contributors. He also informed Cari that Rezko and Kelly were his point people in raising money. Additionally, Blagojevich said that contracts and other Illinois work could be given to contributors who "helped Rod Blagojevich, Rezko and Kelly," and that "Rezko and Kelly would follow up with Cari." On the plane ride, Levine informed Cari that a plan was in place where Rezko and Kelly would choose what consultants would do business with state boards, and afterward the consultants would be solicited for campaign contributions. At a subsequent meeting among Rezko, Levine, and Cari, Rezko told Cari that Lon Monk, then the governor's chief of staff, "would help implement" Rezko's choices of consultants, and that "in exchange for" Cari's help in fund-raising, the Blagojevich administration would be "financially helpful to Cari's business interests" (231–33).

In March 2004 Kelly met with Cari and stated that he was following up on the conversation between the governor and Cari during the plane ride to New York. Cari testified that he initially informed Kelly that he was "not inclined" to help Blagojevich on the national level. Kelly responded "that helping Rod Blagojevich would be good for Cari's business interests and that Cari . . . could have whatever Cari wanted" (233–34). The opportunity was too great for Cari to pass up, and he became involved in an attempt to extort $750,000 from JER Partners, a Virginia-based private equity firm seeking an $80 million investment from the Teachers Retirement System.

In connection with another attempted shakedown scheme, the federal authorities were also secretly recording conversations on the phone of Stuart Levine. In early 2004 Levine and a contractor named Jacob Kiferbaum attempted to extort the chief executive officer of Edward Hospital in Naperville, Illinois. The hospital was attempting to build a facility in nearby Plainfield. Instead of cooperating with the scheme, however, the Edward executive went to the FBI, and Levine's phone was subsequently tapped.[15] Levine, one of the most disreputable characters associated with Blagojevich and Rezko, was a board member of both the Teachers Retirement System and the Health Facilities Planning Board. His criminal activities included abuse of power on both boards.[16] Levine had served in board positions in preceding Republican administrations, but upon Blagojevich's election, he quickly associated himself with Rezko and Blagojevich. Unrelated to the Edward attempt, Cari had been recorded discussing JER with Levine. The Virginia firm was balking at paying a $750,000 kickback to an associate of Tony Rezko's as a "finder's fee." Levine was upset that the firm was hesitating. Cari, who had connections with JER, intervened and urged the firm to cooperate. He sent several messages to JER "that they needed to hire a consultant and that in Illinois, the Governor and the people around the Governor pick the consultants to be used on particular deals." If JER did not hire the consultant, Cari said, then it would not receive the money from the Teachers Retirement System (235; para. 30). JER dallied; no one at the firm had ever heard of the supposed consultant, Emerald Star International, and JER became suspicious when it discovered that the consultant's fax machine was located in the Turks and Caicos Islands.[17]

Ellis now moved on to an allegation contained in the affidavit concerning the Health Facilities Planning Board. Levine and fellow Health Facilities Planning Board members Imad Almanaseer, a Park Ridge pathologist, and Thomas Beck, a former Cook County comptroller, had testified at Rezko's trial for the prosecution. All the men had been placed on the board by Tony Rezko. It was the function of the Health Facilities Planning Board to approve permits for the construction of hospitals, medical office build-ings, or other medical facilities. Entities seeking to construct facilities were required to receive a certificate of need (CON) from the planning board prior to construction. The prosecutor described how Almanaseer and Beck would receive instructions on how to vote from Rezko. Beck had testified that at times he would provide note cards to Almanaseer conveying Rezko's instructions on how to vote (232; para. 35–37).

Mercy Hospital Systems, in Chicago, wished to build an expansion and was seeking a CON from the planning board. Initially, Rezko said that Mercy would not receive a CON, arguing that it had submitted a poor application. But Levine had planned well. He had persuaded Mercy to hire Steve Loren, an outside attorney for the Teachers Retirement System and a conspirator with Levine, as well as the contractor on the project, the same one who was involved in the Edward Hospital deal, Jacob Kiferbaum.[18] Both Loren and Kiferbaum would advise Mercy to make a contribution. Levine asked Rezko if a contribution would make a difference, and Rezko responded that it might. Rezko gave the go-ahead and Mercy received a CON. Rezko later admitted that he manipulated the vote based on Mercy's agreement to contribute (238–40; para. 38n10. According to Almanaseer, Rezko stated that the governor wanted it to pass (244; para. 41).

Ellis had been before the senate for more than two hours, but his au-dience, the members of the senate and those observing from the galler-ies, remained keenly attentive. One by one the criminal allegations were paraded before the senate. Reports of Blagojevich's confederates and the federal investigation had been in the news for years. All were aware of the investigations, the parties involved, and the Rezko trial. Now the events of the past years were being synthesized before them, and the enormity of the ongoing saga challenged their moral sensibilities. Ellis's performance was arduous; the audience was exhausted. The room of seasoned politi-cians silently looked on, stunned by what they were hearing. Moral outrage permeated the staid senate chamber. Justice Fitzgerald suggested that the senate break for lunch. As the galleries emptied, each audience member seemed to be contemplating what he or she had just witnessed. Few looked at each other, few spoke.

When the trial reconvened, Ellis reminded the senate that the day before, Senators Rickey Hendon and William Haine had asked if any evidence fa-vorable to the governor would be presented. Hendon wanted to defend the governor. Haine, a former county prosecutor, knew the trial would be the subject of future analysis and scrutiny; he wanted the trial to be conducted in a fair manner. Ellis, referring to the affidavit, responded that "there are a few places in here that I think one could argue there is information favorable to the Governor" (246). In fact, there was little. The prosecutor noted only that in Rezko's discussions with the federal authorities, his recollection had differed from what Ali Ata had said about the quid pro quo for his job at the IFA. Rezko could only remember asking for one check, for $25,000 (247). The prosecutor also offered the obvious: Rod Blagojevich had denied involvement in illegal activities (250).

Ellis then returned to the FBI recordings that were submitted in the supplementing affidavit. Referring to the section of the affidavit titled "Evidence Concerning Efforts to Obtain Campaign Contributions in Exchange for Official Acts," Ellis reminded the senate that the about-to-be-revealed accusations were incidents that took place after October 2008 and had been captured on the recordings. Someone identified in the affidavit only as Individual A had informed the FBI that the governor was seeking $2.5 million in campaign contributions before the new campaign contribution restrictions became law at the end of the year. Individual A also told of a list of contributors kept by the Friends of Blagojevich and how the governor had conspired to raise the $2.5 million from those on the list. The FBI had obtained the list, and Ellis pointed out that "numerous of the individuals and entities on that list have state contracts or have received public benefits conferred by Rod Blagojevich"—adding, to remind the senate of what everyone already knew—"such as appointments to positions in state government" (254).

According to the informant, on October 6 Rod Blagojevich had told Individual A that he was going to make an announcement of a $1.8 billion allocation for tollway improvements and that he was going to have Lobbyist 1 contact an individual identified in the affidavit as Highway Contractor 1 to ask for $500,000 in contributions. The use of code names to identify individuals in the affidavit was a legal necessity but also added intrigue to the senate presentation. Blagojevich was blunt and straightforward, noting, "I could have made a larger announcement but wanted to see how they performed by the end of the year. If they don't perform, blank them" (254–55). On October 15, 2008, Blagojevich announced a plan to have new express lanes built on the Illinois Tollway for a cost of $1.8 billion (256).

Ellis told of an intercepted meeting held at the offices of Friends of Blagojevich, where Rod Blagojevich met with an individual identified in the affidavit as Fundraiser A. Later, in the governor's subsequent criminal trial, Fundraiser A was identified as the governor's brother, Robert. Also attending the meeting were two lobbyists actively involved in fund-raising, whom Ellis did not identify. Injecting a bit of theater, Ellis told the senate, "The voices on the recording are very low and at times are difficult to hear" (257). He specifically spoke of a call made by the governor to an individual identified in the affidavit as Highway Contractor 1. The contractor, later identified during the criminal trial as Gerald Krozel, was an officer in a company that supplied large amounts of concrete to the state of Illinois and was active in the American Concrete Paving Association.[19] During the call, Blagojevich told Krozel he was excited about the "tollway" and then asked the contractor to become involved in fund-raising. He went on to explain that the rules of fund-raising would change with the start of the New Year and, attempting to keep Krozel engaged, ended the conversation by saying, "Call me if you need anything" (258).[20]

Ellis had begun the litany of charges with the selling of Barack Obama's senate seat. Now, coming to the end of the criminal allegations, he presented another emotionally charged accusation: that the governor had threatened to withhold $8 million from Children's Memorial Hospital unless he received a $50,000 contribution. This had incensed the members of the house investigative committee. Ellis reiterated what he had told the house committee, but for the senate he embellished the story. The governor had first approached Children's Memorial through his brother, Robert. But things did not go well. The hospital's chief executive officer, Robert told the governor, was balking and supposedly not returning calls. "I've left three messages there so I'm going to quit calling. I feel stupid now," Robert told the governor. Blagojevich asked his brother when he had last spoken with the hospital executive, and Robert replied that it had been "two days ago." The governor responded, "If they don't get back to you, then, then last resort is I'll call" (260–61). Through the taped conversations, it was clear that Blagojevich was contemplating withholding the allocated $8 million unless he received $50,000.

In a later phone conversation, the governor asked Deputy Governor Robert Greenlee, identified in the affidavit as Deputy Governor A, "The pediatric doctors, the reimbursement, has that gone out yet, or is that still on hold?" Greenlee replied, "The rate increase?" and added, "It's January 1." "And we have total discretion over it?" Blagojevich asked. Greenlee confirmed that the governor had complete discretion. Blagojevich posed a hypothetical question: "We could pull it back if we need to, budgetary concerns, right?" Greenlee replied, "We sure could, yeah," to which the governor responded, "Okay. That's good to know" (261–62).

By mid-November, as the January deadline to raise unlimited campaign funds loomed on the horizon, the Blagojevich fund-raising team shifted into high gear. Robert Blagojevich was instructed to contact Lon Monk, the governor's former chief of staff and now a well-connected lobbyist, to discuss what they could do about the hospital executive who was not returning phone calls. A frustrated Blagojevich asked, "What do we do with this guy?" (262–63).

Blagojevich was aware that trouble was stirring. In a conversation related to the highway contractor from whom they were attempting to get $500,000, Blagojevich told Robert, who was going to talk to an individual identified as Lobbyist 2, about the contractor's reluctance to raise the money. "Now, be real careful there," the governor said. "I mean, the FBI went to see Lobbyist 2. You understand?" (263). The FBI investigations prompted some caution, but they seemed not to faze Rod Blagojevich or alter his efforts to raise money. In 2006 he had been questioned by the FBI in connection with Operation Board Games. The federal authorities asked to meet with him again in late October 2008, but his lawyer, Sheldon Sorosky, informed the FBI that the governor would invoke his Fifth Amendment rights.[21] Blagojevich knew that the government was circling and carrying on an active investigation, but it seemed to embolden him, and he took the investigations as a personal challenge. In 2006, just before his election, with Rezko indicted and Stuart Levine pleading guilty, he thought he was above it all. He appeared at a Thirty-Sixth Ward rally in Chicago and "howled, they got nothing, nothing."[22]

The prosecutor again asked Special Agent Cain if everything just stated from the criminal complaint was true and accurate to the best of his knowledge. He answered yes. Ellis then asked if the governor's voice had been identified, using the identification procedures outlined in previous questioning. Again Cain answered yes. The prosecutor was attempting to establish certainty, to leave no doubt that the governor had said the things just related. But these questions to Cain were merely procedural. For the sitting senators, there was no doubt that the governor had said those things.

Quoting from the affidavit accompanying the criminal complaint, Ellis displayed a train of criminal allegations that stretched back to Rod Blagojevich's first year in office and continued until his arrest. The governor had turned the state government over to criminal advisors, and from the affidavit, the prosecutor recounted incident after incident of extortion, including the emotionally charged efforts to barter the senate seat and withhold allocated funds from Children's Memorial Hospital.

The prosecution announced that one more topic would be addressed: the horse-racing bill. Ellis set the stage, telling the senate what they were about to hear, using a tape of the governor discussing his plot to extort money from an executive at Balmoral Park, a horse-racing track in south suburban Chicago. On November 13, 2008, when the first conversation was intercepted, HB 4758, the bill that would direct a percentage of casino revenue to the horse-racing industry, was still being debated and still being advocated by its supporters in Springfield. The governor wanted the horse-racing industry to make a contribution if the bill passed and he signed it before the end of the year. Ellis summarized a series of phone conversations between the governor, his brother, and Lon Monk regarding the squeeze play with John Johnston, an executive at Balmoral Park identified in the affidavit as Contributor 1 (266).

Ellis now informed Chief Justice Fitzgerald that it was his intent to play the tape recordings, and Fitzgerald told him to proceed as he wished. The first recording was a phone conversation between parties whom Ellis identified as the governor and his brother, Robert, obtained by using a wiretap on the governor's home phone. The senate chamber was silent, mesmerized by hearing portions of the evidence spoken by actual voices for the first time. Everyone seemed to assume the temporary persona of an eavesdropper, listening to a private conversation between the governor and his brother. The fascination with the circumstance seemed to overcome any moral reluctance.

The conversation opened with the two brothers exchanging the greeting "Hey." Then the governor got right to the point and asked, "How we doing?" Robert said they were good and that Lon had talked to John Johnston and that Johnston was "good for it." But then he added a caveat. The contribution was forthcoming but, "ya know, he didn't get it. But he said, ya know, I'm good for it." Robert explained that Johnston had told Lon Monk he just had to decide what accounts to use. "Lon's going to talk to you about some sensitivities legislatively tonight when he sees you," he told the governor, "with regard to the timing of all this." The governor was concerned: "Right—before the end of the year though, right?" Robert reassured the governor and told him that Lon Monk would give him the details that evening, "when he sees you." The governor asked if Monk would meet him that night, and Robert informed the governor that Monk would join him at a basketball game at the United Center. Attempting to rationalize the delay in receiving the contribution, the governor mentioned that Monk and Johnston were in Springfield, "pushing the bill." The governor stated, "Yeah, they're pushing a bill. So that's probably what he wants to wait on" (270–71). The exchange made clear that the governor was obsessed with getting the contribution before the end of the year, before the campaign restrictions became law.

Ellis moved on to the second tape, a conversation between Lon Monk and John Johnston recorded from Monk's cell phone. Monk called Johnston, and after the two exchanged greetings, Johnston informed Monk that he had previously called and was just "checking in." Monk asked Johnston, "Where are you right now?" Johnston said he was at the track, and Monk asked if he could come and see him. Johnston said yes, and Monk told Johnston that he would be there in about forty-five minutes. Attempting to describe evolving events, the prosecutor told the senate that the call took place at 2:21 P.M. on December 3, 2008 (271–72).

He then went on to the third tape recording, a call from Monk's cell phone to Rod Blagojevich at his campaign office, recorded at 4:11 P.M. the same day. Monk told the governor that he had asked Johnston, "What about your commitment?" Johnston answered that he would be leaving town in two weeks and would be gone for two weeks. "I know that I have to have this in your hand by the end of those two weeks," Johnston told him. Monk, expressing some concern about Johnston's delay, told the governor that he said to Johnston, "Look, there's [concern] that there's gonna be some skittishness if your bill gets signed because of the timeliness of the commitment." Johnston responded, "Absolutely not," and then hedging a bit, asked, "Do you want me to put some into the next quarter?" Monk reported to the governor that he told Johnston, "This has all gotta be in now." Paraphrasing Johnston, Monk told the governor that he said, "I hope I'm gonna have it next week, but you have my commitment. I've always been there. I'm gonna be there. I've gotta have it in the next two weeks cause I'm going out of town." At the end of the recorded conversation, the governor said to Monk, "Good job" (272–74).

The senate audience remained fiercely attentive. They were familiar with the governor and with his voice. The impact of hearing the governor seemingly totally obsessed with contributions, scheming to obtain money before the end of the year, resounded and challenged the moral sensibilities of even the most jaded among them. The tape recordings accomplished what Ellis had hoped: they provided evidence that went beyond an abstract allegation to the actual enactment of wrongdoing.

The final intercepted conversation to which Ellis had been given access was another conversation between Monk and Blagojevich recorded from Monk's cell phone. The next day, December 4, they spoke again of obtaining a contribution from John Johnston. Monk, the lobbyist for Balmoral Park, thought a call from the governor might serve to motivate Johnston to make the contribution. Blagojevich opened the dialogue with his familiar, "Hey, Lon." Monk hesitated but finally got to the point: "So one thing I was thinking about last night is that, um, you ought to give, not today, but maybe tomorrow, just give John Johnston a call and say, you know, calling just to say hello, um, you know, I'm working on the timing of this thing, but it's gonna get done." Blagojevich responded, "Okay," then asked, "Call him tomorrow?" Monk replied, "It's a two-minute conversation." Blagojevich said, "Yeah, happy to do it. Call him tomorrow, right?" The governor then questioned the strategy; "Okay. Call Johnny Johnston, or should I call—have Harris call him?" Monk hesitated and Blagojevich continued, "I mean, you want me to call him directly, I will, whatever's the best thing. I'm just a little bit—." Monk quickly said, "I think it's better if you do it. . . . It's better if you do it just from a pressure point of view." Blagojevich relented and told Monk he would call and use as a ruse that he wanted to do a bill signing downstate and they could get together and start picking some dates. Monk asked the governor what the chances were of signing the bill the next week, and Blagojevich responded, "You know, they're good." Monk reinforced that the contribution was coming: "He's—I'm telling you he's gonna be good for it. I got in his face." Balmoral Park was Monk's client, but his allegiance was to Blagojevich (274–76).[23]

At the completion of the taped call, Ellis passed out transcripts of all four calls. The prosecutor and Chief Justice Fitzgerald discussed whether the tapes should be played again with e ach member of the senate having a transcript. Ellis initially said he would like to play the tapes again but then decided not to. Fitzgerald announced, in conjunction with Senate Resolution 7, that the governor or his counsel had the right to cross-examine the witness. But neither the governor nor anyone representing him was present, and the chief justice excused Cain. John Cullerton and Christine Radogno then asked that the parties be allowed to caucus to formulate questions to ask Cain. The senate recessed and each party met in caucus.

When the senate returned, Fitzgerald announced that "the body," meaning the senate, had requested that the tapes be played again. Ellis was ready and went right to the tapes, again introducing each phone conversation. Hearing the tapes played the first time had left the senators overwhelmed; as the tapes played a second time, with the senators following the printed transcripts, the gravity of what they were hearing became even clearer.

The trial had reached the point where senate members could ask questions of the witness, and Daniel Cain resumed his place at the witness stand. According to the senate trial rules, the senators were prohibited from discussing the trial before and during the proceedings. The questioning of Cain was the first indication of each senator's individual disposition, and many seemed anxious to publicly display their inclinations. Each member of the senate who wished to ask a question was required to submit it in writing to the chief justice, who would then read the question to the witness. Cain was again accompanied to the witness stand by Assistant US Attorney Thomas Walsh. Fitzgerald explained that legal restrictions prevented the disclosure of information collected in the course of a federal crime. Cain was authorized to testify only whether the affidavit that he executed was accurate to the best of his knowledge. He was not permitted to provide additional details or any other conversations, speculate, or give his opinion. The senators had many questions, but with the restrictions in place, Cain was not able to answer the majority of them.

Nevertheless, the senators presented questions knowing that they would not receive an answer from Cain, and what they asked served to divulge their attitudes. The questions were wide-ranging but fell into four basic categories: some solicited more information than was contained in the affidavit, some addressed the procedures used to obtain the recordings, others were made as statements to disparage Rod Blagojevich, and still others seemed motivated by partisanship.

Senator Larry Bomke, a Republican from Springfield, read a section of the affidavit to reiterate a charge and asked Cain if it was correct. Cain answered that Bomke's statement was correct (304–5). Senator Michael Bond, a Democrat from Grayslake, asked if it was "fair to say" that Blagojevich did not wish to be governor (292). Senator Frank Watson, a Republican from Greenville, asked Cain if he was aware that the governor and his attorneys were given an unredacted version of the conversations referred to in the affidavit, and that neither the governor nor his attorneys would come before the senate to refute or explain the conversations. Cain would not answer or comment on either question (301–2). A moment of comic relief broke through the intense atmosphere after Senator Gary Dahl, a Republican from Granville, asked if any members of the senate tribunal were on the wiretaps. Walsh said that was a question that could not be answered, and an unidentified voice was heard muttering, "Thank God" (292–93). The remark elicited smiles and muffled laughter.

Not all senate members, however, were keen on removing the governor. Showing a reluctance to take the consequential step of removal, Senator Mike Jacobs, a Democrat from East Moline, asked Cain, "Is the Governor's ability to appoint someone to the U.S. Senate seat a thing of value sufficient to support a criminal conspiracy?" (315). Cain would not address the question. The last two questions were from John Millner, a Republican from Carol Stream, and Heather Steans, a Democrat from Chicago. Millner brought a sense of authority with his presence. He was a former police chief of Elmhurst and was genuinely liked and respected by those on both sides of the aisle. He asked a four-part question dealing with the accuracy of the governor's statements and the oath Cain took when he signed the affidavit. He suggested that Cain took his oath "very seriously" and would not have allowed statements into the affidavit that were not true. The witness seemed ready for the question and responded affirmatively. Justice Fitzgerald, surprisingly, assisted Cain's answer and asked him to read paragraph 117, the conclusion of his affidavit. Cain read the damning conclusion (324–27).[24] The final question, from Steans, was whether the affidavit "accurately reflected what was heard on the various wiretaps and microphones." Cain answered yes (327–28). With that, the senate's questions were concluded, and Fitzgerald excused Cain.

Of the sixty-three questions asked by the senators, most had not been answered by Cain, but there was a sense in the senate chamber that the verdict was already in. Outside of Jacobs's question, which seemed motivated more by reluctance to remove the governor than a desire to defend him, none of the senators had offered support for Blagojevich or questioned the accuracy of the criminal complaint.

The trial was progressing as a dynamic event with the calling of the next witness. Ellis had carefully chosen this witness, having rethought his strategy after he was given access to a portion of the tapes. The governor's decision not to participate had made the use of house members as witnesses problematic. Still, to address the pay-to-play impeachment charges that resulted from the testimonies by Ata and Cari at the Rezko trial, Ellis felt that he needed a real person before the senate to make the testimony come alive. He needed someone to ensure that the written statements of Ata and Cari had maximum effect on the senate. To address the testimony as a witness for the prosecution, it was best to have an attorney, someone who could not only address the testimony as it was presented during the trial but also interpret the events that had led up to the cooperation of Ata and Cari and explain the consequential factors that ensured the accuracy of their remarks. Chapin Rose, a member of the house investigative committee, a former assistant state's attorney from Champaign County, and most important, a Republican, seemed the logical choice. It was important that the senate trial be conducted in a nonpartisan manner, but controlling individual members was always on the minds of party leaders Cullerton and Radogno. Some of the house members introduced by Ellis the day before could have prompted some Republicans to drift into partisan posturing. The Republican Rose negated that scenario.

Rose was questioned by Michael Kasper, a former counsel to the Speaker. Competent and trusted by the Speaker, Kasper had been asked to assist in the trial on a pro bono basis.[25] Copies of Ata's and Cari's Rezko trial testimony were passed out. Before beginning to ask specific questions about the testimony, Kasper wanted to establish that the two men, both of whom had admitted to committing crimes, had been telling the truth when they testified in the Rezko trial. He asked Rose a series of questions regarding the incentives of both men to be truthful. Rose explained that the two had not been sentenced but agreed to cooperate with the federal authorities. Presumably, in exchange for their truthful testimony, they would receive reduced sentences.

Kasper took Rose through the testimony in some detail. He began with Ata's and recalled, once again, Ata's encounters with Rezko and Rezko's requests for contributions. Ata had testified that the governor, speaking of a future position for Ata, had said, "He hoped that whatever the position might be, it was one that he could make some money at." Kasper asked Rose what had taken place after the governor's remarks, and Rose said that Rezko had informed Ata that he would be offered a position with the newly created Illinois Finance Authority and that someone from the administration would contact him. Ata was contacted and met with the governor's chief budget director. After the meeting, he accepted the IFA position. Ata testified that Tony Rezko later informed him that he should report to Rezko, and Ata agreed to have regular meetings with Rezko (341–43).

The senate had heard the tale before, and it remained the weakest of all the charges. Rewarding loyal supporters was an intricate part of American politics and has been widely practiced since the country's founding. There was no evidence of a direct quid pro quo. The governor never said, "You are getting this job because of the money you donated," and Rezko never said, "If you donate the amount I have requested, you will get a job." The governor's comment about Ata making money could have been in reference to Ata's financial well-being. The exchange with the governor and the discussions with Rezko certainly cast suspicions concerning the methods of governance within the Blagojevich administration, but it would be difficult to prove that a crime was committed.

Kasper moved on to Cari's testimony, which was much more clear-cut than Ata's, with its nebulous statements. Cari's acts had involved intimidation, extortion, and a clear pattern of pay to play. Most of all, his testimony included remarks, allegedly made by the governor, about schemes to exchange contracts for contributions. Cari's trial testimony was reviewed in greater detail than it had previously been during the house investigative committee hearings, with more of it being made public. Kasper asked how Joseph Cari first became involved with the governor's "political committee." Rose answered that Cari testified that he was asked by David Wilhelm, a former head of the national Democratic Party, to meet "some of the key players around Governor Blagojevich," mainly Chris Kelly and Tony Rezko. Blagojevich was considering running for president, and Cari, who had been a former Democratic National Committee finance chairman, would be a good person with whom to discuss "what it takes to run a national campaign." Cari subsequently met with Kelly and then Stuart Levine. Later, Wilhelm called Cari and asked him to arrange a fund-raiser in New York, and Cari, whose "law firm did a lot of business with the State of Illinois," agreed. Kasper asked Rose about the plane Levine had procured to fly the governor and a small entourage to New York. Cari said he was asked to join the group on the plane. During the flight, the governor told Cari that it was better to run for president as governor than as a sitting US senator because governors "could award contracts to people who helped to raise funds." Kasper seized on the contract awards—this was definitely pay to play. With a quickened voice, he asked Rose a series of questions intended to provide the senate with a clear understanding of the type of contracts: "State contracts for legal work?" "And advisory work?" "And consulting work?" And finally, "And investment banking work?" Rose answered yes to each (344–52).

Kasper then asked Rose to read from the Rezko trial transcript. Rose read a question posed by an assistant US attorney, referring to the governor: "And what, if anything, did he say in relation to how they might help his friends?" He then read Cari's answer: "That there were contracts, that there was legal work, that there was investment banking work, consulting work to give to people who helped them." Kasper asked if Cari had explained "who he was referring to when he said 'them,'" and Rose answered, "Principally Mr. Rezko and Mr. Kelly." Rose related that in a later conversation, Stuart Levine told Cari "that there was a plan in place . . . in terms of fundraising," and the people around the governor would pick the consultants, lawyers, and investment bankers, and "those people then would be in return solicited for political contributions." Kasper asked if Cari ever said who picked the lawyers, bankers, and contractors, and Rose replied that Cari had indicated that Kelly and Rezko did. When asked if Cari's testimony addressed statements by the governor about Kelly and Rezko, Rose answered yes, the governor had told Cari "that they were trusted advisors" and "that he expected them to be with him throughout his public service career." After a short exchange designed to reinforce Cari's guilt and the involvement of Stuart Levine in the extortion of JER, Kasper had no further questions (353–58). The senate again took a short recess to formulate questions.

The appearance and testimony of Rose, a Republican house member, did not sit well with the Democratic members of the senate. The senate and the house are considered by their members as autonomous chambers, and the independence of each is a guarded principle. The senate Democrats opposed a member of the house serving as the prosecutor, and now many felt that the appearance of house members as witnesses was inappropriate. During the dialogue between Kasper and Rose, Eric Madiar informed Ellis that Rose's appearance "was not going well" and was not welcomed by the Democratic members. He suggested that the record of the house investigation spoke for itself and that the remaining house witnesses, Lou Lang and Connie Howard, not be called.[26] The official reason for the prosecutor not to call more house witnesses could be that they would simply rehash what was in the trial transcripts, and the senate members could read the transcripts. The witnesses were unnecessary.

An element of political tension was also at play. The Democratic members did not want to extrapolate on the testimony regarding Ata and Cari. Blagojevich was the sitting Democratic governor, though few felt any party or ideological kinship to his style of governance. The majority of senate

Democrats agreed that they had to act decisively, that the governor had to be removed quickly, but the whole affair proved an embarrassment. They did not wish to extend the process or draw unnecessary attention to the misdeeds of a member of the Democratic Party. Removal was obvious. They wanted to do it quickly. They wanted it to be over.

When the senate returned from the party caucuses, Christine Radogno asked Fitzgerald if they could continue the questioning of Rose the next day. The Republicans wanted time to study the transcripts of the Rezko trial, which had been handed out at the beginning of Rose's testimony. It had been a long, arduous day. The evidence put forth in the criminal affidavit and the testimony of Ata and Cari was overwhelming. The senate members were spent. Fitzgerald granted the request, and the tribunal adjourned for the day.

The Third Day

When the senate returned the next day, the Democrats announced, not surprisingly, that they had no questions for Representative Rose. The house prosecutor had agreed with Madiar's suggestion and moved to minimize the process. One by one Ellis excused the remaining house members. The latest to be excused was Representative Constance Howard, a Democrat from Chicago's South Side. A member of the house investigative committee, Howard was slated to testify concerning the committee's perception of the "injury" to the state of Illinois as a result of the governor's actions. The prosecution suggested, taking Madiar's advice, that the investigative committee's record spoke for itself and there was no reason to have additional house members testify. Ellis, the meticulous, orderly attorney, had planned the prosecution, but judicial processes are human processes and ultimately fluid events. The prosecutors had been unsure whether the governor would participate in the trial when they initially planned their strategy. Without counterarguments from a defense, their presentation of the evidence would be the only criteria that the senators would use to make their judgment. The prosecution had presented adequate evidence—in fact, overwhelming evidence—to convict. Ellis and the prosecution team had discussed the situation. With no counterarguments, and the risk that house members could prompt unintentional counterarguments or bring further embarrassment to the Democrats, the prosecution changed its strategy and decided that after Chapin Rose, no other house members were needed.

There was a sense of resentment among the Republican members of the senate, who were not happy with Ellis's decision to move quickly through the process. They wanted to dwell on the evidence as much as possible. The Democrats had been in control for the past six years, and now the Democrats were in control of the trial proceedings. All the animosities and negative experiences of dealing with Blagojevich and Jones still haunted the Republicans. Under Emil Jones the majority Democrats had enabled the errant administrative schemes of Blagojevich many times. Jones was gone and Cullerton was now the senate president, but the Republicans felt that once again they were being dismissed and denied participation. The trial offered little opportunity to express their political frustrations and to articulate that they had warned of the impending crisis several times. The questioning of witnesses constituted the only opportunity the Republicans had to make veiled partisan barbs, and they wanted to take advantage of it. The Republicans' quest for justice was focused not on particular individuals sitting on the opposite side of the chamber, but on their own past circumstances.[27]

Christine Radogno, speaking for the Republicans, stated that it was important for people to see that the proceedings were not rushed and for every member of the senate to have the opportunity to have his or her questions answered. Michael Kasper responded to the Republican leader that the prosecution was "sensitive to letting the evidence speak for itself"; they were eliminating witnesses who would merely summarize the evidence and wished to question only people with firsthand knowledge of the facts. Howard, he said, was to give only her characterization and opinions of the evidence. Cullerton, attempting to finesse an answer to Radogno's question, referred to the senate trial rules and reminded the senators that they were acting as both judge and jury and that it was the house prosecutor's obligation to present the case. Radogno was not satisfied and requested a forty-five-minute caucus to "reformulate" their questions. Cullerton did not want to allow the Republicans time to strategize and reminded the justice that they had met that morning for the purpose of asking Chapin Rose questions. Fitzgerald extended the courtesy of compromise and asked Radogno if she would accept a thirty-minute caucus. She agreed and the senate stood in recess (365–76).[28]

During the caucus, the Republicans did not so much reformulate their questions as reinforce their objective. They discussed what they would ask and at times designated people to ask specific types of questions.[29] The question period was the only chance in the trial that the Republicans would have to comment on the last six years, and they wanted to take full advantage. When the senate reconvened, exhibiting an effort to compromise and perhaps defuse the political tension, David Ellis offered that any questions from the senators pertaining to the hearing records or the affidavit that could not be answered by a live witness could be submitted in writing to the prosecutors, who would do their best to direct the senators to the relevant passages in the record or answer the questions themselves. Radogno expressed appreciation for his offer but said the Republicans wanted to ask questions of live witnesses.

As expected, the Republicans released a torrent of disparaging inquiries directed at fellow Republican, Chapin Rose. Frank Watson started by reiterating the details of Ata's meeting with the governor's chief budget director and then Rezko later telling Ata that he would report to Rezko. Watson wanted to emphasize the names of people and asked Rose whether Ata ever mentioned the names of the special advisors to the governor. Rose could remember "Mr. Kelly and Mr. Rezko" and "they may have mentioned Mr. Jay Hoffman," a Democratic state representative from Belleville (378). Most of the questions went beyond the Ata and Cari testimony and were asked only to emphasize the governor's misdeeds. The Republican senators posed questions concerning bond ratings and the state's financial condition under the Blagojevich administration. The financial questions were followed by inquiries into Blagojevich's security clearance, which had been revoked by the federal government, and the condition of the state if a disaster occurred. The Republicans then asked questions concerning the governor signing legislation and contracts with the state. Rose dutifully answered that the questions were beyond his scope of testimony, but on occasion he offered personal remarks. The senate Republicans asked Rose more than sixty questions, some with multiple parts. The questions, answered or not, included many veiled innuendos and overt accusations, and they were put in the record. The interrogators thus accomplished their goals (379–451). The short exchange concerning the reduction of house witnesses and the questioning of Chapin Rose were the only times during the trial that overt partisan differences surfaced.

The prosecution now moved to the charges concerning violations of the constitution and malfeasance—wrongful conduct by a public official. The administrative charges were important to the prosecution's case. The prior presentations had dealt with allegations of criminal activity, but they were merely allegations; the governor had not yet been tried in a court of law or found guilty of any crime. Impeaching the governor for conduct that constituted malfeasance had become a viable option, however.

Three more witnesses would be called: JCAR director Vicki Thomas, University of Illinois professor Andrew Morriss, and Auditor General Bill Holland. They would testify on specific administrative and constitutional subjects and not the intimate dealings of Blagojevich or his administration. These witnesses would not offer the Republicans the opportunity to ask ranging questions.

The prosecution's first witness to address the maladministration charges was Vicki Thomas, the executive director of the Joint Committee on Administrative Rules (JCAR). Michael Kasper resumed the role of prosecutor. As rehearsed, Kasper took Thomas through an explanation of JCAR's role in the Illinois administrative system. The questions and answers did not inform the senators; they were well aware of the functions of JCAR and the controversy that had erupted over the FamilyCare expansion. Her testimony was intended to establish the legitimacy of JCAR and to show that the governor had ignored the legislature's role and authority. When testifying before the house committee, Thomas had at times moved off subject, the result of miscommunication and conflicting advice from the committee and staff. This time the witness was focused. Kasper's questions and Thomas's answers were crisp and to the point. Thomas had provided the house investigative committee with details concerning the Department of Healthcare and Family Services (HFS) attempt to change the FamilyCare program without legislative sanction or appropriation and the resulting Caro lawsuit. Her appearance before the senate was abbreviated because the controversy over HFS's actions and the resulting Caro lawsuit had been extensively covered by the Illinois press. The senate did not need an elaborate explanation; what the governor had done had been made clear. What the prosecutors needed to do was to present the topic clearly for the trial record and for public consumption.

Attempting to establish an abusive pattern of rulemaking under Blagojevich, Kasper asked, "How often does JCAR suspend or prohibit a rule?" Thomas told the senate that from its inception in 1977, after the review of more than twenty thousand rules, JCAR had suspended or prohibited rules sixty-nine times, and thirty-three of the sixty-nine cases had occurred under the Blagojevich administration. Kasper and Thomas went through the emergency rules procedures, when an emergency rule is appropriate, and the subsequent review by JCAR. They clearly established that in the case of FamilyCare, JCAR had followed proper procedure. They established that the governor or his office instructed HFS to disregard the authority of JCAR and continued to enroll people in the FamilyCare program. Kasper asked Thomas if she believed that "by not abiding by JCAR's decision," HFS had "violated state law," and she answered yes (417–22). The senate recessed to allow members to develop questions for the witness.

The senate's ensuing questions were both procedural and historical. Republicans asked most of the questions, but this time Democrats also asked questions. Senator Rickey Hendon was the only dissenter to the prosecution's claims. Trying to drive a wedge between the house and the senate, a favorite past tactic of Blagojevich and Jones, and perhaps because he did not understand the functions of JCAR, Hendon asked Thomas if she was aware that in the past the house had "placed rule-making language on the vast majority of bills sent to the Senate, including senators' bills combatting autism, mortgage foreclosure and job losses? Is it the intention of JCAR to use rule-making language to handcuff legislation in the Senate?" The subject matter emphasized by Hendon echoed the familiar demagogic refrain of Blagojevich: helping the disadvantaged, the poor, the sick, and the disabled. Thomas did not take the bait. She did not address the question. Hendon's questions became bizarre: "Is it the intent of the Illinois Constitution for JCAR to be the chief executive of the State of Illinois?" And finally, "Does JCAR serve both the House and the Senate? Are you aware that several of the Governor's healthcare initiatives were passed and supported in the Senate? Is the House superior to the Senate in JCAR's mind?" It was clear that no one was supplying these questions to Hendon; he was acting on his own. Thomas answered no to the first question and reminded Senator Hendon that a bill becomes a law only after it passes both the house and senate and is signed by the governor. JCAR looked at what had been enacted and placed in the Illinois statutes (426–28). Responding to Hendon's questions, several in the senate galleries shook their heads, rolled their eyes, and smiled sardonically.

The remaining questions from the senators attempted to emphasize the rocky history of JCAR's dealing with the Blagojevich administration or sought to establish that JCAR had acted properly. There was no discussion of the pending Caro case or its unconstitutionality claim. Kasper had gotten what he wanted, a clear, factual account of what had occurred. Since there was no counter to his claim that HFS had broken the law, the witness was excused.

The chief justice immediately instructed the prosecutor to call his next witness, but David Ellis had a few procedural remarks before the trial continued. Lou Lang was the last scheduled house witness, and Ellis explained that because Thomas had covered all the testimony that the prosecution would have elicited from Lang, he would not be called. Fitzgerald told Ellis, "You may try your case as you wish" (439). Christine Radogno was recognized and, of course, objected. Once again she stated that the Republican caucus was concerned over the shortening of the witness list, emphasizing that the charges were serious and they wished to ensure that the governor received a fair trial. Radogno did not belabor her objections; she had said the same before, but she made her points for the record. Fitzgerald was correct: the prosecutor could proceed with his case as he wished.

Andrew Morriss, the University of Illinois administrative law professor, took the witness stand next, and another member of the prosecution team, Heather Wier Vaught, assumed the role of questioner. After establishing Morriss's qualifications and experience, Vaught quickly moved to the substance of his testimony. He had testified before the house investigative committee and was familiar with JCAR operations and the rule review systems in other states. He had been selected by the prosecution to validate the JCAR system of rule review and to comment on the legitimacy and necessity of checks and balances between the legislative and executive branches. Morriss called the separation of powers "the bedrock of the American system of government" and noted that "Article II, Section 1 of the Illinois Constitution provides that no branch of government may exercise the powers that belong to another branch." Answering Vaught's questions, Morriss testified that the legislature, consisting of the "elected representatives of the people," was responsible for policy, and policy was implemented through state agencies and departments. It was JCAR's function to ensure that policy implementation matched the intent and will of the legislature. Morriss testified that he believed that agencies and departments that ignored the decisions of JCAR were violating the law, and he knew of no past cases where the existence of JCAR was found to be unconstitutional (444–47).

Following Morriss's brief testimony, Radogno asked again for a caucus. Cullerton objected. He wanted to move the trial along and felt that senate members could ask questions without strategizing. He asked the house prosecutor to confirm that they would conclude the presentation of witnesses that day to provide the senate a time frame. Ellis confirmed that after Professor Morriss, he would call one more witness, Auditor General Bill

Holland, whose testimony would take about an hour. Fitzgerald allowed the Republicans to caucus and asked Cullerton if the Democrats just wanted to stand at ease. The senate president requested a caucus (449–51).

After the recess, the majority of questions posed to Morriss by both Democrats and Republicans served merely to confirm or clarify his testimony. The only dissenting question came, again, from Rickey Hendon. He asked Morriss if there were "any other professionals who may disagree with your opinion." Morriss's answer diminished the question: "Well, I'm certain there are a lot of professors who disagree with virtually all. There are a lot of professors. I'm not aware of any that disagree with this particular opinion, but we could probably find one," he said (456). Morriss quickly finished answering general questions from the senators, and Fitzgerald told the house prosecutor to call his next witness.

Before Holland arrived at the witness stand, John Cullerton abruptly asked for recognition. The day before, Cullerton had spoken to the press and publicly challenged Blagojevich to appear before the senate. He was angry that the governor was appearing on national television accusing the legislature of being unfair and trying to railroad him out of office. Now the senate president delivered startling news: the governor had asked to appear before the senate and give a closing statement. Clayton Harris, the governor's acting chief of staff, had called Cullerton and conveyed the governor's request to appear.[30] During the impeachment investigative hearings, Harris did not have any contact with house members or staff, but some senators, who knew him, found him approachable. Harris was a link to the governor, and there was a back-channel effort to prompt Blagojevich to resign or step aside. Resignation or stepping aside would end the senate trial, as the senate would not have to remove the governor from office. Blagojevich would have none of it, however, and Harris later said the governor "seemed oblivious to what was going on."[31]

Blagojevich had chosen to ignore the trial and did not file an appearance by the date set forth in the senate resolution. He had offered no defense, explanation, or counterarguments, but now he requested to make a statement. Cullerton wanted to make the conditions of the governor's request clear to the senate: Blagojevich requested that he not be under oath and that he not be subject to cross-examination by the prosecutor or questions from the senate. The senate chamber stirred. In the galleries, people turned and looked at each other with wonderment. The press was shocked and speculation was rampant. What would he say? Would he be contrite or aggressive? Would he challenge individual senators? Would he resign?[32]

Cullerton, Andy Manar, and Eric Madiar hurriedly discussed what procedures and documents were necessary to grant the governor his request. Above all, they wanted to ensure that the senate remained in control of the process. Since he had ignored the provisions of the trial rules, they thought it best that the senate formally grant leave, giving its permission for the governor to appear. Cullerton informed the senate that he would ask leave of the body. Cognizant of the partisan tension that had emerged over the reduction of witnesses, Cullerton had called Radogno before making the announcement. She arose after the announcement and urged everyone to grant the governor leave to appear, should he appear. Many were not convinced that the governor would come. Some senators had been informed of the governor's request before Cullerton's announcement. Earlier, Senator Dale Righter, from downstate Mattoon, was handed a note from a staff member. He looked up and asked if the staffer was kidding.[33]

Finally, Auditor General Bill Holland took the witness stand. After being sworn in and invited to take his seat, he declined and requested to stand, an unusual request for most, but not for the self-assured, no-nonsense veteran bureaucrat. He had served as chief of staff for former senate president Phil Rock and was at home in the senate chamber. Holland approached his testimony before the senate with assurance and aggression. He was a witness for the prosecution and had six years' experience dealing with the Blagojevich administration. Kasper again assumed the role of prosecuting attorney. The testimony covered the three audits that had been presented to the house investigative committee, concerning the flu vaccine effort, the I-SaveRx program, and the Department of Central Management Services (CMS), the last of which had uncovered evidence of maladministration and possibly corruption related to the governor's efficiency initiatives.

It had been more than a month since the auditor general had testified before the house, and both Holland and the prosecution team had time to refine and rehearse the presentation. They were ready. They provided the senators with summaries of the audits, packets with charts and timelines, and documents that they referred to throughout the testimony. There could be little question regarding what had occurred. The senators knew the story. They were well aware of the flu vaccine fiasco, the mismanagement and incompetence of the governor's staff, and the $2.6 million that the state might have to pay for the undelivered flu vaccines. Concerning the

I-SaveRx program, the senate had watched as the governor ignored the rulings of the federal government, violated the law, and went ahead and instituted the program. In regard to the CMS audit, senators were also well aware of the shell game that had been made of the statute that authorized the efficiency initiatives. This was the third day of the trial and Holland was the last witness. The days had been long and intense, but the senators' faces seemed to show a relaxed sense of resolve. The situation no longer seemed surreal.

Kasper began with the flu vaccine incident. He took Holland through the history of the failed initiative. The prosecutor's questions were constructed to clearly establish the facts contained in the audit and provide a clear narrative. Through his questioning, Kasper attempted to reinforce that the governor was well aware that the importation of drugs was a violation of the law. A number of the governor's top aides had been involved, and Holland named names and implied that the governor had been aware of the program by emphasizing that the aides reported directly to the governor.

Holland made it a point to stress that the Illinois Procurement Code prohibited the comptroller from processing payments without a contract on file, and Kasper highlighted the special advocate's unfamiliarity with purchasing procedures by asking Holland about correspondence that Scott McKibbin, the state of Illinois' special advocate for prescription drugs, sent to the purchasing officer at the Department of Public Aid. In the correspondence, McKibbin admitted that he was unaware that a contract was necessary and further divulged that he had been told several times by the budget office and the deputy governor that the payment would be COD. Holland commented that he had never heard of anything being paid COD by the state.

An especially damning document was an e-mail the audit uncovered in which the special advocate acknowledged that the vaccines would never be delivered and suggested that they find a way to pay Ecosse for the *service* it performed. Holland said it was clear that the special advocate's suggestion to make the payment for services rather than tangible goods obfuscated what the state would be purchasing. Holland noted a December 21 e-mail back to McKibbin from the governor's attorney Mike Lurie, who stated that changing the wording to *services* "should make our lives in dealing with the Comptroller a heck of a lot easier in terms of getting these guys paid promptly in the absence of FDA approval." Kasper noted that in the correspondence, the word *services* was in quotation marks (482–83). Kasper asked Holland whether, at the time the e-mail was sent, Illinois officials knew that enough vaccines to meet the state's needs during the flu season had been found. Holland explained that in early December, the Centers for Disease Control indicated that it had found enough vaccines to service Illinois' priority population. Regardless, knowing the vaccines were not needed and would never be delivered, the state officials still entered into a contract with the UK-based company Ecosse on January 13. Ecosse was not paid, the company sued the state, and at the time of the impeachment trial the case was still pending before the Illinois Court of Claims.

Kasper next turned his attention to the audit of the I-SaveRx program. The audit revealed that the governor had clearly violated federal and state law by authorizing the importation of prescription drugs intended to be used by state employees and state retirees. Again, Kasper and Holland went through the results of the audit. Kasper asked Holland if the audit concluded that implementing the I-SaveRx program violated federal law. Holland answered yes. To add emphasis to the violation, Kasper asked if the program also violated state law, and again Holland answered firmly yes. Asked what the governor's reaction was to the conclusion of the audit, Holland reported that the governor issued a press release and expanded the program.

The final subject of Holland's testimony concerned the results of a routine audit of the Department of Central Management Services (CMS) and the so-called efficiency initiatives. As background, Holland essentially repeated the testimony he had given before the house investigating committee. He then offered an example that was sure to arouse an emotional reaction: veterans' services. The legislature had appropriated additional money for veterans' beds at the Manteno Veterans' Home, but $433,000 of that appropriation was spent on the procurement initiative without any savings being experienced by the Department of Veterans Affairs.

To clarify, Kasper asked Holland, "Why does your office believe that to be an issue or a problem?" and Holland answered that it was a problem because the General Assembly appropriates money to be spent in a certain way. The legislature is the branch of government responsible for directing how money should be spent. The Finance Act, passed by the legislature, provided for the efficiency initiatives program, but it established certain procedures for identifying efficiencies and billing from line items. CMS had abdicated its responsibility to the governor's Office of Management and Budget (OMB), which made the final decision regarding which agencies would be billed and how much they would be billed. In many instances agencies were overbilled; simply, they did not receive an equal benefit for the money. When asked the purpose of the administrative finagling between CMS and OMB, Holland was candid: "It was the intent to get a certain amount of money in place for their consultants that they would be paying" (499–502). The efficiency initiative provision was being administered like a shell game. Money was being removed from agencies and in turn was appropriated for discretionary purposes under the control of the governor's office.

The audit had also found another unusual practice: selected contractors were being allowed to participate in the development of requests for proposals (RFPs), which they would later be allowed to bid on. Participating in the development of an RFP would give an obvious advantage to a firm. Put simply, requirements of proposals could be tailored to a specific firm. Also unusual was that the governor's staff assisted agencies in drafting the RFP or sat on the selection committees that awarded the contracts. The ramifications of the handling of selection and awarding contracts did not have to be spelled out for those in the senate chamber. It seemed obvious. Selected contractors were chosen by the governor's office based not on qualifications or costs, but on connections. Holland gave the example of one firm, Illinois Property Asset Management (IPAM), which was allowed to extensively revise its proposal while consideration was being given to who would win the contract and ultimately was awarded a $25 million contract. A high-level IPAM official had dinner with a high-level CMS official shortly before the award was granted, and amazingly, IPAM was not even incorporated before the award was granted. Thus the contract was awarded to a company that did not exist. The audit also found that "there were tens of thousands of dollars of inappropriate expenditures made by IPAM and billed back to the State of Illinois" (506). Holland told the senate that CMS initially objected vehemently to the audit's conclusions that the departments under the governor had violated the Illinois Procurement Code and that the governor's office had violated the Finance Act, but eventually the agency agreed with all the findings.

As the final witness the prosecution presented to the senate, Holland had testified to factual deeds that had been uncovered, verified, and documented. His testimony was based on previous audits, conducted with transparent methodology and legal procedures. It was not based on conjecture, speculation, hypotheticals, or the possible results of future legal proceedings. The facts were clear and indisputable. The senate took a short recess for the final time, and each party caucused to formulate questions.

Questions for Holland came from both parties. The tone of the questions was supportive of Holland's remarks and punitive regarding the actions of the Blagojevich administration. All were direct reiterations of Holland's testimony or were meant to reinforce what was contained in the audit reports. In one revealing question, Senator John Jones asked, "How many millions in state agencies' efficiency payments were made in this 'money-laundering scheme' in fiscal year 2004?" Based on an audit of that year, Holland replied that "there were $137 million in efficiency payments made" (528). This amount had been billed from various agencies, and the audit identified a group of consultants who benefited from the movement of funds.

The senators were familiar with the audits, and they knew the administrative and governance implications. The audits were damning reports on the conduct and administrative abilities of Blagojevich and those around him. The CMS audit raised serious questions of wrongdoing, providing evidence of not just incompetent administration, but possible malfeasance and criminal activity. The audits had been turned over to Attorney General Lisa Madigan and provided to the general assembly (511). No investigative action had been taken by the attorney general. Jack Franks's government administration committee, with the Speaker's nod, continued to hold hearings after the audits were published. The senate Republicans responded by producing an informational handout titled "CMS Contract Abuses," which summarized the findings contained in the audit, and an editorial board briefing report, "Reforms for Sunshine and Accountability," which explained contract reform legislation offered by Republican senators. From 2005 through 2008, Christine Radogno and fellow Republicans introduced several bills that focused on contract reform, but Emil Jones controlled the progress of bills. The bills were assigned to the Senate Rules Committee, they were never considered, and they died when the general assemblies adjourned *sine die*. The response of the house Republicans was restrained. They issued a press release in May 2005 calling for an investigative task force to examine the CMS bidding process and for the attorney general to determine whether criminal statutes had been violated. The house Republican staff issued statements confirming the findings of Franks's State Government Administration Committee for the CMS audits for 2004 and 2005 but did not introduce any reform initiatives.

The Trial

For state entities, the legislature, or law enforcement agencies to investigate the governor beyond the audits remained problematic, both politically and demonstratively. Theoretically, the branches of government are assumed to work in conjunction for the common good. Any effort to openly review the governor's conduct concerning matters that could lead to criminal investigations would have meant political civil war. Any investigation by the legislature likely could not have progressed far with Emil Jones in control of the senate. An additional consideration, much on the mind of the Speaker and his staff, was that the governor was a master of public relations and political gamesmanship. He was at his best when giving a performance. It was speculated that Blagojevich would have answered any investigation with the charge that it was politically motivated, and indeed, this would have appeared to be the case if an investigation had been conducted by the office of Attorney General Lisa Madigan, who is the Speaker's daughter and was often discussed as a possible candidate for governor.

After the senate finished its questioning, Fitzgerald asked Kasper if he had any redirect questions of the witness. Kasper answered he did not. The chief justice then asked if there were any questions for the house prosecutor regarding other evidence that had been placed in the record. There were none. The house prosecutor and the senate members had nothing more to say. The prosecution had presented the justification for removal, and it was understood by the senators. Ellis rested his case. Fitzgerald noted again for the record that the governor and his counsel were not present and no defense could be made. He adjourned the senate until the next day to hear closing arguments.

But the day did not end. Immediately after the senate adjourned, a meeting was held in John Cullerton's office to discuss how and under what conditions the governor would be allowed to address the senate. Cullerton, Madiar, and Manar were joined by Senators Don Harmon and James De-Leo, along with Clayton Harris and Andrew Stolfi, attorneys on the governor's staff. Cullerton asked Madiar, "Just how they are going to do this?"[34] Allowing Blagojevich to appear before the senate, under the terms that his lawyer requested, took some mental gymnastics. Blagojevich had elected not to participate in the trial, and with the exception of closing arguments the next day, the trial was virtually complete. Chief Justice Fitzgerald had dutifully asked if the governor or his counsel was present at every segment of the proceedings where the defense could participate. SR 7, the senate trial rules, set a specific deadline for the governor to file an appearance notice, and he had failed to respond. Because his appearance would be inconsistent with the legal protocol that the trial rules established, Madiar decided that the governor could file a formal request for the senate to grant leave for him to appear, and the senate would vote on whether to grant leave.

After the discussions, Madiar sent an e-mail to Stolfi providing the formal request forms and explaining the procedures that would be followed to accommodate an appearance by the governor. He then developed a script for Chief Justice Fitzgerald to follow and e-mailed it to the Supreme Court. Harris and Stolfi went to the governor's mansion and began to write Blagojevich's speech for the next day. They had trouble getting through to the governor. When Harris called the governor's home, Patti Blagojevich told him that her husband was eating and said to call back in an hour. Even at this late stage, Harris felt that if there was any way Blagojevich could avoid removal, "he had to make a statement." When he finally did talk to the governor, he found Blagojevich uninterested in working on a speech. The governor told Harris that he was going to bed and everything would be okay. After the call, Harris and Stolfi looked at each other in amazement. "He was going to be removed from office the next day, and he was going to bed."[35]

Chapter 7

The Last Day

<hr>

On session days, when the legislature meets to consider bills, the Illinois state capitol typically takes on the air of a medieval market. It is a scene of managed chaos. Legislators and lobbyists scramble from one committee meeting to another, as crowds gather outside the doors of the senate and house chambers and hand notes or business cards to the elderly doormen to give to legislators, requesting that they come out for short meetings. Party caucuses are called, staffers rush to prepare final documents or briefings, and throngs of people descend on the legislative offices with a sense of importance and urgency, wishing to present their views regarding the thousands of bills introduced each session. As bells ring and votes are taken, the hawking, brokering, and haggling of the public policy market can be heard in the hundreds of conversations that take place where they can—in hallways, corners, or spaces temporarily claimed along the brass rail that encircles the capitol's third-floor rotunda. Policy discussions are frequently interrupted by the din of demonstrations, the chatter from visitors at informational exhibits, or the drums and horns of high school bands that blast a cacophony of unrecognizable noises from the first floor.

In contrast, on January 29, 2009, the last day of the Blagojevich trial, the capitol was quiet. People spoke in soft tones. The usual crowd of lobbyists, petitioning interest groups, and concerned citizens was absent, replaced by the pervasive presence of the media. Everyone present that day anticipated the inevitable, knowing that this would be the last day of the trial, but few talked about it. The trial prosecutors claimed that they did not know what the outcome would be, perhaps to maintain an illusion of proper protocol, but the senators and everyone else sensed the inevitable outcome. Seven weeks and three days after the arrest of Rod Blagojevich, the political drama that was gripping Illinois would end and the governor would be removed from office.

The day began relatively calmly. Arriving at their offices, many senators asked their legislative assistants to postpone any meetings; they did not want visitors. Some talked among themselves; others wanted to be alone to contemplate the day ahead. The thoughts of Republican senator Dale Righter, from Mattoon, were characteristic of the mood of the senate. While exercising at a local gym the previous evening, he had begun to think about the next day. The tall, thin, and fit practicing attorney returned to his room and started to set down his thoughts, writing the notes he would use during the final senate deliberations. Over the preceding days he had heard the evidence, and now his decision was clear. "These are *not* the words and deeds of a governor who cares or even comprehends the ideal that public office is a public trust. But these are the words spoken when he thought only his trusted co-conspirators were listening," he wrote. "Not the story of a governor who truly meant what he said about changing the way we do business or ridding state government of corruption—but rather one of an official who began, even before his election, arranging with the likes of Tony Rezko and Ali Ata to build a campaign fund through manipulation of public resources."[1]

The questions that preoccupied many that day revolved around whether the governor would appear as he had requested the day before. Many in the senate had worked with Blagojevich over the past six years. Some had been allies who now would vote to remove him, and others had political and personal conflicts, but both allies and enemies wondered and worried about what the governor would say. Would he level allegations against individuals? Would he call out his past friends? A handful of senators were not convinced that removal was justified but were aware of the overwhelming support for removal in the senate, in the media, and among the public. Conscious of the political consequences if they voted not to remove Blagojevich, they struggled with their decision.

The senate trial rules stated that the governor was allowed to be represented by counsel who could question witnesses and challenge the evidence presented against him. The rules also allowed the governor to appear as a witness under oath. Blagojevich decided not to be represented in the trial, and neither he nor his counsel ever challenged the evidence against him or played any role in the senate trial. The governor's decision perplexed former public defender John Cullerton.[2] Instead, Blagojevich hired a public relations firm and went on the national talk show circuit to make his case. He proclaimed his innocence and challenged the house impeachment, the senate trial rules, and the legislative leaders—especially John Cullerton and Speaker Michael Madigan. Until his request to appear before the senate the previous day, the governor maintained no official contact with the senate.

The questions that lingered in the minds of John Cullerton, Eric Madiar, and Andy Manar were of a procedural nature: when and how to bring the trial to a close. The governor's request to make a statement to the senate had come as a surprise, but it provided the ideal event to bring proceedings to an end. The final day would include closing arguments from the house prosecutor, the governor's statement, a rebuttal from the prosecutor, senate deliberations, and at long last, the vote. Madiar wanted the senate to be fully in charge of events.[3] He wanted to ensure that there were no procedural ambiguities. The governor's offer to appear allowed the senate to avoid the situation of a trial in absentia. Cullerton, Madiar, and Manar wanted to give the governor every opportunity to participate, and they thought it was crucial to get Blagojevich before the senate, under oath or not.

As the final day began, Madiar gave Chief Justice Thomas Fitzgerald two scripts to read at the outcome of the senate vote. He had prepared one to be read for acquittal, the other to be delivered if the governor was found guilty. Aware of potential legal challenges to the senate trial, Madiar had painstakingly scripted all procedures. Every word had to be precise. Chief Justice Fitzgerald called the senate to order at 10:00 A.M. The first order of business began with Deb Shipley, the secretary of the senate, reading the motion for leave. The senate readily agreed to allow to governor to appear, and leave was granted (551).[4] Although a motion and the granting of leave was a business-as-usual procedure for the senate, the mood quickly changed as the senators turned to the serious matter at hand. Emphasizing the gravity of the occasion, the chief justice repeated twice to the senate that he would appreciate that there be "no movement in and out of the chamber floor during closing arguments" (552). The instructions illustrated the serious nature of the proceedings and profoundly affected the senators and the spectators in the galleries. The entire chamber went silent.

Fitzgerald recognized David Ellis for closing arguments and told him that he had sixty minutes to present his case. Ellis approached the podium set up below the senate rostrum and faced the silent senators. Realizing what was at stake, he faced his task with acute focus and some trepidation. As he spoke, the spectators' eyes moved from Ellis to individual senators, attempting to gauge their reactions to the prosecutor's words. He was asking the Illinois senate to remove Blagojevich and invalidate an election—the sovereign expression of the will of the people. The trial rules prohibited any outside communication with senate members, and Ellis later stated that during his closing argument, he concentrated on his notes and his eye contact with the senators was limited. He had little indication whether his words were resonating with the audience.[5]

Several office holders were present in the galleries. State Comptroller Dan Hynes observed the proceedings closely. Representative Jack Franks, who had pressed for the governor's impeachment months before, observed the proceedings with a feeling of satisfaction and pride in the legislature and the legislative process. After months of urging the governor's removal from office, his efforts were finally about to come to fruition.[6] Representative Susana Mendoza sat in the front row of the president's gallery, her head resting on her hands. She had initially supported the efforts of Rod Blagojevich but came to realize that his words and promises were all a charade. Now she vigorously endorsed the governor's impeachment and was satisfied that she was playing a part in his removal from office.[7] Jim Durkin, the Republican spokesman on the house investigative committee, watched intently and recalled the satisfaction he had felt as a county prosecutor.[8]

In his opening statement to the senate, Ellis had informed the senators what the evidence would prove. The evidence had been presented, the witnesses had been heard, and now Ellis had one more opportunity to convince the senate that the evidence provided overwhelming cause to remove the governor. He stayed on point and recounted the evidence, incident by incident, one last time. To justify Blagojevich's removal from office,

Ellis was careful to establish both criminal charges and administrative malfeasance. His remarks were presented to the senate in two categories: criminal acts, extracted from the criminal complaint and the four supplied FBI recordings; and acts of maladministration and misadministration by Blagojevich during his six years as governor. Ellis intended to demonstrate a "pattern of abuse of power" that was motivated by the governor's personal operating criteria as described in his own words in the FBI recordings: "his legal situation, his personal situation and his political situation" (553). Ellis summarized the evidence with an air of indignation.

He started with the criminal allegations and the charge that had received the most national media attention during the prior eight weeks: the selling of the US Senate seat vacated by Barack Obama (553–55). Many of the Illinois senators, both Democrats and Republicans, had taken pride in Obama's election. Barack Obama was one of their own; most members sitting in the senate that day had served with him, and many were friends. Ellis was shrewd by leading off with the selling of the senate seat. He recognized that the scheme to trade for Obama's replacement would have a deep negative reaction among the sitting senators.

Ellis followed the senate seat sale allegation by reiterating that the governor had given instructions to inform the Tribune Company that $150 million in state assistance would depend on the firing of members of the editorial board. He reminded the senate that the *Chicago Tribune* had delivered a steady flow of criticism and had doggedly scrutinized Blagojevich, and that the newspaper had recently called for an investigation of his activities (557–59).

In May 2008 the legislature had passed an ethics bill aimed directly at stemming the governor's attempts to extort contributions in exchange for lucrative state contracts. HB 824, sponsored by Representative John Fritchey and Senator Don Harmon, prohibited state contractors who received contracts of $50,000 or more from contributing to the elected official who oversaw the contracts. After much debate and many amendments, the bill was sent to the governor on June 30, 2008.[9] Publicly, Blagojevich lauded the intentions of the bill but claimed it was flawed because it did not include all state officeholders and members of the General Assembly. Privately, he worked to kill the bill and amended it to include all state officers and the General Assembly. He sent the bill back to the legislature, confident that his amendment would not be accepted by the legislature and that there would not be enough votes to override his action, which would require a vote of three-fifths majority in the house and in the senate. A common strategy in Illinois' legislative process is to add provisions to a bill to make it so draconian that it loses support and eventually dies. Thus the governor was hoping his action would cause the bill not to be called, and it would die.

But Blagojevich received no support in the house, which, without any hesitation, overrode his amendatory veto 113 to 3 and sent the bill to the senate for action. There was some concern that the bill would not be taken up by the senate, still under the control of Blagojevich's ally Emil Jones, the senate president. If the senate did not act on the bill in a fifteen-day period, as mandated by the Illinois Constitution, the bill would die. HB 824, as sent originally to the governor, had overwhelming support of the public and among several prominent legal scholars.[10] Supporters of the bill urged presidential candidate Barack Obama to become involved because they thought he could influence Jones. Jones had often claimed to be Obama's mentor, and they knew that if Obama's home state failed to pass the ethics bill, it would reflect poorly on his candidacy. Obama called Jones and urged him to move the bill. Jones did and the senate quickly overrode the amendatory veto 55 to 0. The original HB 824 became law on January 1, 2009. Jones later said that those who urged Obama to call did not understand the Constitution and that he had plenty of time to call the bill.[11] Reportedly, Blagojevich was livid and concluded that Jones, his last ally in Springfield, had abandoned him in favor of Barack Obama.[12] Faced with the prospect of limited contributions from state contractors after January 1, Blagojevich stepped up his efforts to raise as much cash as possible in the remaining six weeks. He embarked on an ambitious fund-raising campaign to raise $2.5 million before the bill became law.

Ellis moved on to the government charges of Blagojevich's pay-to-play schemes gleaned from the wiretaps. He began with the most despicable charge: that Blagojevich had attempted to coerce Children's Memorial Hospital into making a contribution in return for the state providing pediatric care reimbursement and had contemplated breaking his commitment to the hospital if he did not receive the contribution right away (559–60). The senate sat stone-faced.

Next, Ellis reminded the senate of the tollway shakedown. In contemptuous tones that betrayed his indignation, he explained how the governor had announced a package of improvement contracts for the Illinois Tollway Authority that was contingent upon the contractors making campaign contributions. Ellis used the governor's own words from the criminal complaint:

"I could have made a larger announcement, but I wanted to see how they performed by the end of the year. If they don't perform, 'F' 'em" (560–61).

The house prosecutor moved on to the governor's scheme to extort money from an executive at Balmoral Park horse-racing track, coercing him to pay a contribution if the governor signed a bill favorable to the horse-racing industry before the end of the year. Blagojevich's former chief of staff, Lon Monk, was the lobbyist for the racetrack, and the governor used this connection to coerce Balmoral Park into raising cash in exchange for signing the bill. This charge was vividly presented to the senate, accompanied by the released government audiotapes (561–63).

During his closing arguments, Ellis again employed the recordings to supplement his narrative interpretation. Hearing the tapes along with the prosecutor's presentation of the evidence had a profound impact on the senators. Even though they had heard the tapes twice before, the senate chamber grew silent. One more time, Ellis set the scene for each of the four recordings. He emphasize that Blagojevich knew exactly what was going on. Monk and Johnston were in Springfield working to pass the bill. Ellis's choice of words in explaining the conversations to the senate served the prosecution's purpose: to divulge the governor's intent. He reminded the senators, "The Governor is saying John Johnston doesn't want to pay the contribution until he's sure the bill is actually going to reach the Governor's desk" (564), using "pay" instead of saying "make the contribution." Ellis's technique of using the recordings of the governor's voice and then interpreting what had been heard left little doubt as to Blagojevich's culpability. The senators and those in the galleries sat in silence.

In a rapid, staccato delivery, Ellis recounted numerous other pay-to-play schemes and was keen to associate Blagojevich with convicted felons. Ali Ata admitted in federal court that he had paid for a position with the Illinois Finance Authority (IFA) and that he was told to report to the now convicted Tony Rezko. Mercy Hospital received a permit for expansion only after it gave a contribution to the governor.[13] Joe Cari admitted that he told companies wishing to do business in Illinois that they needed to hire certain consultants that the governor and his administration had chosen (578–80).

Turning to Blagojevich's record of mismanagement and maladministration, Ellis reminded the senate of the role of the legislative branch regarding the separation of power. Again in rapid-fire oratorical style, his voice rising, Ellis summarized the litany of charges: The governor disregarded the verdict of the Joint Committee on Administrative Rules (JCAR) on four different occasions and instructed the Illinois Department of Healthcare and Family Services (HFS) to implement the FamilyCare program in spite of JCAR's objections. To secure jobs for selected people, often unqualified, the governor's Office of Intergovernmental Affairs directed the Illinois Department of Employment Security to manipulate job descriptions, avoid veterans' hiring preferences, and tell employees to falsify their job applications. The executive inspector general investigated and determined that the governor's office was behind these actions, which demonstrated "a complete and utter contempt for the law." The governor used the legislature's so-called efficiency initiatives to "subvert the appropriations process" and merely move funds from one agency to another, resulting in contracts to favored consultants, including one contract granted to a company that did not exist at the time. Blagojevich violated federal and state law by directing the purchase of flu vaccines from a foreign country, despite knowing that such a purchase was illegal and that the vaccines were not needed. The I-SaveRx program was "more of the same." Although the FDA told the governor—twice—that importing drugs from a foreign country was illegal, he proceeded anyway, apparently looking for "splashy press releases." Finally, Blagojevich told the Chicago Cubs baseball organization, which was seeking IFA funds, that "they better get that project done by the January meeting of the IFA" because he was "contemplating leaving office in early January 2009" (580–84).[14] To some aspiring governors sitting in the senate, those words were especially poignant.

The house prosecutor had summarized the evidence and made his case. His argument was well organized, succinct, and compelling. The recordings of the governor's voice still resonated in the senate chamber, and his culpability seemed evident to all. Now Ellis summarized the impeachment process and the governor's reaction to it. Even though Blagojevich had chosen not to participate and had instead referred to the trial as a "kangaroo court" and a "sham," claiming that "the fix is in," Ellis reminded the senate that the proceedings had been beyond reproach. He said that their actions and the actions of the house did not warrant any of the accusations leveled by Blagojevich. The senate had questioned the witnesses presented by the prosecution and had deliberated fairly. The evidence presented was overwhelming and unquestionably exhibited a pattern of abuse of power. He again interjected the names of Ali Ata and Joe Cari and their admitted corrupt activities with the Health Facilities Planning Board. Ellis ended his closing argument by declaring, "The people of this state deserve so much better. The Governor should be removed from office" (586–88).

As Ellis left the podium, the senate chamber remained hushed. The proceedings had reached the final stage, and all eyes focused on the door behind the senate rostrum. Everyone waited anxiously for the governor to appear. Following the procedure established by the senate parliamentarian, the chief justice asked, "Is the governor present?" Fitzgerald then informed the senate that he was advised that the governor was in the building and would arrive shortly. He told the senators to stay close to the chamber and to stand at ease. The chamber gave a collective sigh of relief as the senate disengaged from the spectacle before them. Some senators spoke quietly with each other, while the galleries remained silent.

John Cullerton instructed Andy Manar to find the governor and bring him to the senate floor. Madiar, Manar, and Cullerton had discussed just how to summon the governor. Andy Manar had worked with the governor on budget matters during the last session, and all three felt that Blagojevich would be more comfortable with someone he knew. As Manar left the senate floor, the pressure of working seven days a week for the last two months began to take its toll. He was anxious. Both Manar and Madiar had officially been in their jobs less than a month, but during the preceding two months, working through the Christmas and New Year holidays, they had organized the senate with new people and new committee assignments, directed swearing-in ceremonies, and prepared for the unprecedented event of a senate trial to remove the governor. The trial was being covered by national and international press, and both men felt that the world was watching. Madiar and Manar even synchronized their watches to the senate clock to ensure that the proceedings progressed in a timely fashion. Still concerned about the governor's antics—"How do you outthink crazy?"—Madiar spoke with the senate sergeant at arms, Claricel "Joe" Dominguez Jr., and asked the eight-year veteran of the US Marine Corps to stay close to the governor. Madiar and Manar were painfully aware that this had to go right.[15]

The governor had to come to the senate floor, but Manar was not convinced that Blagojevich would appear. Earlier that morning Manar had checked with the Illinois Department of Transportation to verify that the governor's plane had left Chicago for Springfield and that Blagojevich was on it. Now he had to find the governor. He left the senate floor and entered the hallway behind the senate chamber. The security staff had cleared the hallway, and the press was restricted to the senate galleries and a small roped-off area at the hallway's east end. Security staff had also closed the elevators, so Manar made his way past the press to the steel stairwell and walked down one floor to the governor's office on the capitol's second floor. He entered the backdoor of the governor's suite, where he was met with a strange silence. The office was empty—no staff and no security. Andy Manar was familiar with the governor's office; as the former policy and budget director, he had been in the office many times. He passed through several rooms and the conference room. "No one, not a single person was there," he later recalled. He went to a reception area outside the governor's office and noticed a man he did not recognize. When the person asked what he wanted, Manar said he had come to get the governor and escort him upstairs. He was told to wait in the conference room he had just walked by.

In the dark-paneled room the minutes passed, and Manar began checking his watch. Five minutes went by, then ten minutes. Suddenly the governor walked by the conference room. Blagojevich behaved as though there were nothing special about the day. He seemed to be in his usual campaign mode, walking with a spring in his step. He often would enter fund-raising events like a prizefighter enters the ring, with his staffers leading the way, their hands on each other's shoulders, chanting something unrecognizable. Now, on this final day, he seemed to have no appreciation of what was transpiring one floor above. "Hey, Andy, what are you doing here?" he asked. Manar had no time for small talk. "Governor, we need to go upstairs," he said. Blagojevich looked puzzled. "Why do I have to go upstairs?" he asked. After an awkward moment, Blagojevich seemed to regain himself and acknowledged what was happening. They went into the governor's office, where moments later they were joined by a group of people. Deputy Governor Louanner Peters was among them, but the rest were strangers to Manar. The group began to joke and engage in small talk. Manar was cognizant of the time and the people waiting upstairs. "Governor, it's time to leave," he said. Rod Blagojevich seemed to acknowledge the moment. He went into the washroom just off the governor's office, and after several minutes the door flew open. The several minutes in the washroom seemed to rejuvenate Blagojevich. If he had been hesitant before, he was running now, toward the back stairs, with his entourage running behind. Andy Manar struggled to catch up.

On the landing before the third floor, he finally caught up with the governor and stopped him. A few feet above, the press waited in the hallway behind the roped-off area. Stopped on a narrow stairway landing, the small entourage was isolated from the crowd of reporters that waited a few feet away. Their voices were amplified in the cavernous stairwell and resonated between the capitol floors. Manar began telling the governor what to expect when they arrived in the hallway behind the senate. The crush of reporters would be on the left behind a rope, he explained, and they would proceed directly to the senate floor, through the door from the back hallway. He informed Blagojevich that no one else would be allowed on the senate floor. Blagojevich insisted that a woman with the group be allowed to accompany him to the senate floor. "This is personal," he said. Aware of the time passing, Manar relented after some discussion, even though he did not know who the woman was. Upon reaching the third floor, he discovered that the woman had a press badge. Manar told the governor that no members of the press were allowed on the senate floor and that the woman would not be allowed to accompany him. After further, somewhat intense discussion, the governor finally relented.

Andy Manar and Rod Blagojevich entered the senate hallway and walked quickly past the suddenly animated reporters shouting out questions. The woman and the rest of the entourage proceeded up one more flight of stairs to the senate gallery. From the senate hallway, a small wood-paneled corridor leads into the senate chamber. The corridor has a door to the hallway and, at the opposite end, a door leading to the senate chamber. Manar and Blagojevich entered the corridor, and Manar closed the hallway door behind them. Alone with the governor, Andy Manar was "struck by the strange silence." The audio system was on, all the senators were in their seats, the galleries were full, but the chamber was deafeningly silent. Blagojevich had stood at the senate rostrum when swearing in the senate a few days before, but now Chief Justice Fitzgerald was at the rostrum, presiding over the impeachment trial. Manar wanted to make sure that the governor knew where to go; he did not want an awkward moment. He explained to Blagojevich, "I'm going to open the door, Governor, and when you walk in, turn to the right and a podium is set up for you to speak from. There's a pencil and paper on the podium for you to use." With those words, Andy Manar reached for the door to the senate. Before he could open the door, however, the governor reached over and put his hand on Manar's forearm. Looking straight at Manar, Blagojevich said, "Andy, I didn't do anything wrong." "Governor, you don't have to convince me," Manar replied, pointing to himself. "You have to convince those fifty-nine people out there." He opened the door, and Rod Blagojevich walked onto the senate floor.[16]

When Chief Justice Fitzgerald noticed the governor, he called for the sergeant at arms, Joe Dominguez, to escort the governor into the chamber. Fitzgerald welcomed the governor and informed him that the podium was the same one used by the house prosecutor and that it would be permissible to move a "step or two away" if he needed to (590). Blagojevich, dressed in a finely tailored dark suit with a solid-colored tie, set his notes on the podium. The governor had not taken part in the preceding days of the senate trial and had chosen not to be represented by counsel, but he had lawyers observing from the senate gallery.[17] He had been briefed on the events of the past days and knew what had been said.

He began his statement by telling the senate that in the past weeks he had been talking "to as many people as [he] possibly could" about his desire to appear before the senate to "tell the whole story" and show that he had "done absolutely nothing wrong." Blagojevich had appeared on radio and television entertainment talk shows, pleading to be allowed to call witnesses who could attest to his innocence. The witnesses Blagojevich was presumably referring to during his public-relations campaign, and now before the senate, would address the criminal charges brought by the US attorney, which would be the subject of a trial in federal court several months or perhaps years later. The senate had limited access to the evidence concerning the criminal charges, as only four recordings had been provided by the US attorney. Although the first eight articles of the house impeachment resolution addressed criminal charges, only the evidence concerning the governor's attempt to coerce a campaign contribution for signing the horse-racing bill was made available to the Ellis and presented to the senate.

The governor's defense strategy was to claim his innocence and demand that witnesses be subpoenaed and allowed to be cross-examined during the impeachment trial. Blagojevich argued that if the government released all the tapes and he was allowed to call and question witnesses, he could prove his innocence. The house prosecutor had previously addressed this strategy. During both the house investigation and the senate trial, Ellis had often reminded the bodies that they were not a court of law. The proceedings were not intended to determine whether the governor had committed the crimes he was charged with by the US attorney, but to decide whether justifiable cause existed to remove him from office.

Blagojevich told the senate he wished to bring in Rahm Emanuel, President Obama's chief of staff, and US senators Richard Durbin, Harry Reid, and Robert Menendez, all presumably related to the charge of trading

Barack Obama's Senate seat. Repeatedly, he emphasized how his inability to bring in witnesses was unfair: "fundamental fairness, fundamental justice, natural law and constitutional rights suggest I should be able to bring witnesses in to say I didn't do the things they said I did." He asked the senate to put themselves in his shoes and repeatedly proclaimed that he had not done anything wrong (591–94).

Blagojevich acknowledged that the impeachment resolution was divided into "basically two portions": allegations that he referred to as an abuse of "executive discretion" and allegations of criminal activity. The only evidence presented to the senate, he rightly said, were the four recordings that dealt with the allegation of coercing a campaign contribution related to the horse-racing bill. Justifying his remarks in those recordings, and speaking familiarly to the senators, he said, "You guys are in politics. You know what we have to do to go out and run—run elections. There was no criminal activity on those four tapes." He reminded the senate that "those are conversations relating to the things all of us in politics do in order to run campaigns and try to win elections" (596–97). The senators were stunned by the remarks. They sat motionless, their faces radiating disdain. The spectators in the galleries were amazed, some mildly amused. Several spectators began to shake their heads in disbelief, while others smiled. The governor was telling the senate that extortion and coercion were business as usual in public service, in politics. He was telling the senators that they all did it. With that one remark, it seemed to many that Blagojevich sealed his fate.

The governor then returned to the issue of witnesses and complained that it was unfair that he could not call people who could challenge the allegations. He argued that the house prosecutor had not proven criminal activity and asked the senate, "How can you throw a governor out of office who is clamoring and begging and pleading with you to give him a chance to bring witnesses in to prove his innocence?" Over and over he repeated his mantra: let me call in witnesses; give me a chance (597–99).

Blagojevich had prepared notes, but he rarely consulted them. His remarks were in the form of a campaign speech: establish some talking points, engage in small talk, and try to connect with the crowd. Several times he veered off the topic, and in an attempt to bond with the senate, he told stories. He told of serving on a congressional committee and being in the same room with US senators Ted Kennedy, John Glenn, John McCain, and John Warner. Warner, he pointed out to the senate, had been married to Elizabeth Taylor, and he told of the time Senator Warner thought he was a young staffer and told him to fetch him a cup of coffee (600–601). Although this was a favorite story on the campaign trail, here the tale felt lame, inappropriate, and overtly manipulative to the senate and spectators.

The instincts of a seasoned politician were apparent. Blagojevich used the familiar Warner story as a lead to defending his actions with the Joint Committee on Administrative Rules. Some senators served on JCAR, and Blagojevich attempted to establish a parity with them by noting his having served on a US congressional committee. "I know how important it is for those of you who are appointed to a committee like that, but let me respectfully suggest a couple of things," he said. He maintained that JCAR was only an advisory committee and could not dictate policy to the executive branch, saying, "12 lawmakers picked by . . . legislative leaders cannot constitutionally thwart the executive branch." He reminded the Democrats that he had worked with senate leader Emil Jones and, recalling the past animosities between Jones and Speaker Michael Madigan, stated that the house had blocked his and Jones's efforts to fund an expansion of health care. He appealed to his purpose—to help poor families obtain health care. "Now, how is it an impeachable offense to protect low-income parents from losing their healthcare?" he implored. The governor said that he had received the advice of lawyers and, attempting to appeal to the Democratic members of the senate, that his actions were in concert with the senate Democratic leadership. Besides, he continued, the issue of JCAR's authority had not been settled and was still the subject of litigation (601–5).

He turned to the procurement of the flu vaccines and told of warnings by the US Centers for Disease Control that the flu season of 2005–6 would be "one of the worst flu seasons in recent American history." A portion of Illinois' normal supply of flu vaccine was contaminated, and it had been determined that a shortage existed. His decision to obtain the vaccine from Canada "was a no-brainer" and was for a straightforward reason: "because I was foreseeing the possibility that our elderly and infants might be vulnerable to flus that could conceivably take their lives." In a self-righteous tone he added, "And by the way, if I get criticized for it, that ain't the first time." He claimed that officials in other states contemplated the idea until the FDA became involved and blocked the delivery of the flu vaccine to Illinois. He said the state had not lost $2.5 million because the case was not settled and was still before the Illinois Court of Claims, and Illinois' attorney general had argued that the state's taxpayers should not pay the bill. Again he argued, "How can you throw a governor out of office who was acting to protect the lives of senior citizens and infants and trying to find ways to be able to help families?" (605–8).

Blagojevich turned next to an arguable point: the charge related to the flu vaccine had taken place during his first term, but the house did not pass or even consider an impeachment resolution in 2005. He had stood for reelection and the people had again elected him, presumably with the full knowledge and approval of his actions (609). This valid and problematic argument had worried the house prosecutor and the senate chief legal counsel, Eric Madiar. Should the Illinois senate invalidate the sovereign will of the electorate expressed through the reelection of Rod Blagojevich?

The governor moved next to the I-SaveRx program, his effort to provide lower-cost drugs from Canada. "I can't wait to talk about this one," he said. Blagojevich told the senate that the idea was given to him by Rahm Emanuel, and again attempting a personal connection, reminded the senate that Emanuel was his congressman and also Senator Cullerton's congressman at the time. "Think about the morality of this," he posed to the senate. He had thought about helping senior citizens and families, he said, "and I loved the idea, and we did it." He claimed to have worked with Senators Ted Kennedy and John McCain on the issue of importation of prescription drugs and said that if what he had done was so wrong, then "let's demand that President Obama fire Rahm Emanuel." Again he reminded the senate that the I-SaveRx incident had also occurred during his first term, pointing out, "The people of Illinois elected me a second time knowing what I did with regard to prescription drugs for our senior citizens" (609–12).

The governor then attempted to refute charges related to the efficiency initiatives, that funds had been removed from one agency to another without legislative approval. Many considered the efficiency initiatives a simple shell game with little or no accountability. The governor began by extolling the many accomplishments of his administration and reminded the senators that in many past instances they had been his allies and that he could not have accomplished the "big achievements" without the senate's support. He justified and obfuscated the alleged manipulations by stating that the expansion of health care to 750,000 families and an increase of $8.4 billion in education funding was not accomplished "on the backs of the middle class by raising their taxes," but through "efficiency, consolidating functions," and streamlining operations. He claimed that Central Management Services (CMS) found ways to save money and had saved over $500 million for taxpayers and "wanted to . . . allow us to be able to use that money in the General Revenue Fund to invest in healthcare and education and other general revenue items, but then the Auditor General got involved and said, stop, don't do it." Minimizing the situation as merely an administrative disagreement, Blagojevich likened the discussions between Auditor General Bill Holland and the head of CMS as "a couple of accountants kind of scrapping over the issue of whether or not the money should be spent in a certain way." Blagojevich noted that CMS had stopped the practice and that this was another issue that had occurred during the first term (613–15).

The last article in the impeachment resolution concerned abuses in hiring and firing state employees. The allegations were uncovered through an investigation of the hiring practices of the Blagojevich administration conducted by the Illinois inspector general. The house investigative committee reiterated the findings of the inspector general: that the governor's Office of Intergovernmental Affairs directed the Illinois Department of Employment Security to bypass hiring protocol and violate the *Rutan* hiring mandate and veteran hiring preference.[18] The governor said little about the charge except that he had supported the legislation that created the position of inspector general and that the allegations were not yet proven. He did not deny the allegation, but he claimed that the inspector general had not presented any evidence that the governor knew about the activity or was involved. He also reminded the senate that the allegations of employment abuse, like the other maladministration charges, had occurred during his first term in office. He dismissed the allegations as administrative disagreements that came about through his desire to help people (616–19). His message was clear: if he only had the chance to bring in witnesses, they would exonerate him.

The governor had covered all the charges contained in the impeachment resolution and offered nothing more of substance. But he was not finished. Blagojevich now shifted from the role of the accused answering specific charges to a role where he was at his best—Rod Blagojevich on the campaign stump. His campaign speeches were structured with phrases and stories designed to stir audiences. Common content in his political speeches included expressions of humility, attempts to identify with the audience, displays of concern for the disadvantaged and downtrodden, tales of his focus on economic growth using unsubstantiated job projections, heartrending stories that the audience easily accepted and no one could challenge, acknowledgements of connections with famous people or with familiar people in the audience, and a self-narrative of Rod Blagojevich, the family man.[19] While addressing the specific charges in the impeachment resolution, Blagojevich had occasionally referred to his notes. Now he did not need notes. His campaign-style remarks were guided by the instincts that the seasoned politician had acquired through years of campaign performances. He used all the hackneyed phrases and allusions commonly employed in campaign speeches, but he was addressing an audience of politicians who received his remarks with an air of incredulity and cynicism.

Over and over, in dolorous tones, he implored the senate to give him a chance to bring in witnesses who could prove his innocence. Justifying his administrative actions, he claimed legal means with moral motivations. He was just trying to help poor people keep their health care and had "found a way that [he could] actually do something and help them be able to have a better quality of life, not ration their medicine, maybe extend their lives, [and] the means are legal." In an effort to associate himself with other prominent public figures, he continued; "because if they're not, then the governor of Wisconsin, the governor of Kansas, and Ted Kennedy and Rahm Emanuel and John McCain and others ought to be co-conspirators with me." He again attempted to establish commonality and kinship with the Illinois senate and talked of the things they had accomplished together. To display humility and solicit compassion, he solemnly admitted, "I know sometimes I probably push too much and prod too hard. I know you guys have this impression that sometimes, you know, I go outside of you and say certain things" (620–21).

He then launched into his familiar autobiography, painting a picture of Rod Blagojevich as the embodiment of the American dream—the poor boy who makes good. He told the Illinois senate that he was the product of humble beginnings and through hard work had risen to become the governor of Illinois. But he remained a man of the people, always looking out for the little guy, the poor, seniors, the sick, and minorities—always fighting those in power who sought to curtail him. Now he was the victim, the object of the wrath of entrenched power. Rod Blagojevich, champion of the underdog, was fighting again, this time to prove his innocence and his mettle. His good works would triumph over evil if only given a fair chance.

He stated that his father had been "a Republican cold warrior [who] spent four years in a Nazi prisoner of war camp." He told of how his father immigrated to the United States and "was a factory worker, a steel worker, and worked all the time, 50, 60, 70 hours a week." Attempting to draw a connection with individual senators and prompt them to identify with his story, he said, "He got to a point in his life, and you know this probably from your parents, when you realize it ain't there for you, so I'm going to do everything I can to create opportunities for my kids." His father had to "scratch and claw and sacrifice" for the betterment of his children. His mother worked as a ticket agent for the Chicago Transit Authority, and "everything they did was to work and sacrifice for their kids and give us a chance at a better life that wasn't there for them. And then one day their youngest son grows up, and he becomes governor of the fifth largest state." He remarked how proud he was to reach the governor's office, how he had "hit a pinnacle." He tried to connect with Cullerton, saying that he suspected the senator had felt the same pride when he became senate president that Blagojevich felt when he became governor. He recognized Senator Willie Delgado as coming from the same type of neighborhood and Senator James DeLeo as having had similar life experiences (621–24).

Blagojevich told the senators the story of a hardworking woman raised by an immigrant Mexican mother who could benefit from the expanded FamilyCare program. In graphic terms, he explained how she was a working woman who struggled each day: "She's up before dawn. Her kids are still in bed. She sits down. Mom comes up, her mom, has a cup of coffee with her. They talk about the things of the day, and then she's ready to go work. It's still dark outside if it's winter. She tippy-toes into the bedroom and kisses her boys goodbye and leaves them to their grandmother." The heartrending story was carefully constructed. The woman was the daughter of Mexican immigrants and, importantly, a working woman. She has quiet, soft, reflective moments as she wakes in the early dawn, speaking intimately with her mother "about the things of the day" (625–28). Listeners could visualize the darkness outside, feel the cold associated with winter, and sense compassion as the woman quietly kissed her children before she had to leave them to someone else. On the campaign trail, it would have been a good story. To the senate, it was recognized as pure fabrication.

In penitent tones, Blagojevich confessed that he became impatient and frustrated with legislative gridlock. Yes, his methods were sometimes harsh, but his policies came from his desire to do good and had always been about helping families like the woman in the story. "I confess maybe I fight maybe too much, but I ask you to remember it ain't about me," he said. "Charge it to my heart. Charge it to my desire to help families I came from and life stories I've heard along the way in my life and as governor" (628–29).

He drew attention to the common experiences he shared with senate members and talked about his two daughters. Blagojevich pleaded with the senate, "I didn't let you down, give me a chance to show you. It's painful, and it's lonely." He concluded his defense by asking each senator to "think about the dangerous precedent" they would set if they removed him "without proving any wrongdoing." And finally, "Think about all the good things we've been able to do for people. Give me a chance to stay here so we can roll up our sleeves and continue to do good things for the people" (634–36).

Blagojevich was at his campaign best, but his concluding remarks failed to sway the senate or the spectators. He was speaking to an audience of seasoned politicians and political observers who had heard it all before. They could not reconcile Blagojevich's self-defined image of the pious, sincere street kid from Chicago who only wanted to help people and was wrongfully accused with the vulgar, plotting, scheming voice revealed on the FBI recordings or the experiences of many who had attempted to work with the governor for the previous six years. The stony stares on the faces of the senate members betrayed their reactions. There was an awkward silence as senators and spectators digested the governor's speech. His closing remarks were the insincere ramblings of leftover campaign rhetoric, and his motives were transparent. In the galleries, there was noticeable shifting. Some were amused at his audacity, but most were amazed. In Springfield's medieval market fair, the governor had become the jester. He had lost any semblance of substance or trust and could offer only a woefully inadequate performance.

The silence was quickly interrupted by the procedurally efficient Chief Justice Fitzgerald, who informed the governor that since he had filed to appear before the senate to represent himself, he was welcome to remain. The governor thanked the chief justice and replied that the senate was "welcome to deliberate whatever they think is right," and indicated that he would leave (636). As Blagojevich was exiting the building, he quipped to Deputy Governor Louanner Peters, "Well, baby, we're out of here," and departed through the capitol's basement entrance.[20] Cullerton and Radogno each asked for a one-hour caucus, and the senate recessed.

Senator Don Harmon, a Democrat from Oak Park, commented to those sitting around him, "When the cameras are on, you see one person, and when they are off, you see another."[21] Senator Matt Murphy, a Republican from Palatine, who had worked on the senate impeachment rules, was "fuming" at the impudence and patronizing tone of the speech and worried that the general public would again be fooled by his performance.[22] Senator Dave Luechtefeld, a Republican from Okawville, looked at Senator

Dale Righter, shook his head, and said, "It doesn't get any better than that." Luechtefeld was "absolutely amazed" at the audacity of the performance he had just witnessed.[23] And there was reaction from the national press. A native of Illinois, the *Washington Post*'s David Broder wrote, "Blagojevich has tried to duck responsibility for his foul words and deeds while cloaking himself in phony martyrdom." Taking his journalist colleagues to task for the cavalier reporting of Blagojevich's recent media appearances, Broder sincerely wrote, "That's a joke to some people, but not to a state I love."[24]

Heather Wier Vaught, Mike Kasper, and Cindy Grant returned to Ellis's capitol office. They had not eaten and Weir had ordered Jimmy John's sandwiches. As the prosecution team sat eating lunch, Ellis banged on the desk and said a few choice words about the governor. He could not believe what he had just heard. When contemplating the governor's appearance, he had assumed that Blagojevich would attempt to address the charges against him. The prosecution team had worked in the house chambers past midnight the previous night, preparing a rebuttal for what Ellis thought Blagojevich might say. Then Ellis had returned to his hotel room and continued to work through the final version. But in court today, rather than addressing the charges, the governor had merely given a political speech. Ellis was angry and expressed his frustrations to the rest of the prosecution team in a somewhat animated fashion. "That's what you have to do," Cindy Grant said, her index finger pointing directly at Ellis. "Get mad. Talk right back at him."[25] Vaught and Kasper agreed. Kasper, who had been standing close to Harmon when he made his remarks concerning cameras and Blagojevich's speech, repeated them to the group: When the cameras are on, you hear one version of Blagojevich; when they are off, you hear another. "Tell the senate what he did not say," Kasper advised Ellis. "Tell them he did not address the charges and offer any defense. Instead, he came to the senate and gave a political speech."[26] Ellis agreed. He did not need to prepare notes. The prosecutor's remarks would not be a rebuttal of Blagojevich's defense, as he had offered no defense, but rather a denunciation of the governor's audacity to come before the senate on such a grave occasion and deliver a political speech to fifty-nine politicians. Ellis took a bite of his sandwich.

When the senators returned to the floor after their caucus, Chief Justice Fitzgerald called the senate to order and recognized the house prosecutor, David Ellis. The chief justice allotted the prosecutor thirty minutes for his closing rebuttal, but a confident Ellis said he would not need that much time. Indeed, Ellis's remarks were surprisingly brief. He did not use a script.

His anger now keenly focused, he remarked on what the governor had not said or done. Echoing Senator Don Harmon's observations at the end of Blagojevich's speech, and following Kasper's suggestion, Ellis opened by telling the senate, "When the cameras are on and he thinks people are listening, the Governor can give a pretty good speech, but I want to talk about the Rod Blagojevich when he's off camera when he doesn't know people are listening" (638). The house prosecutor sensed that behind him were millions of Illinois residents, and "they demand better and they deserve better" than what Blagojevich had just given them, he later recalled. For the normally controlled Ellis, it was an emotional moment.[27]

Ellis reminded the senate of the governor's remarks on the FBI recordings about the tollway and children's hospital shakedowns. When the camera was on, he wanted to create jobs and provide health care for children, but in the recorded conversations, Blagojevich spoke of coercing contributions in exchange for funding. The house prosecutor then drew a distinction between the governor's public professions to be "for the little guy" and his private proclamation recorded by the FBI stating his selfish motivations: "legal, personal, political" (638–40).

The witnesses the governor had claimed would exonerate him could not be called, Ellis said, and further, the case was built not on what others did or did not do, but on the governor's own words. He questioned why the governor chose not to testify under oath, why he said the words that were caught on tape, and why he did not at least provide the context of the recorded conversations. Instead of participating in the trial, Ellis pointed out, the governor went on national television to proclaim his innocence. Blagojevich did not say a word to the senate about selling the vacant US Senate seat, the Tribune Company, or the pay-to-play allegations. Instead, "he comes in and says there's no evidence and gets off the stage." Ellis emphasized that there were sixty recorded conversations confirmed by a federal agent. Referring to the governor's appeal that the senate "walk a mile in his shoes," Ellis said, "if I were innocent and I were in his shoes, I would have taken that witness stand and I would have testified and I would have told you why I was innocent" (640–42).

Ellis concluded the prosecution's rebuttal by addressing the mismanagement of the Blagojevich administration. Impeachment was warranted, he said, because the citizens of Illinois had to be protected. He mentioned the state's falling bond rating, which would cost the taxpayers more money, and the fact that Illinois was the only state whose governor did not "have access to security information from the federal government," because the governor's security clearance had been withdrawn at the time of his arrest. "Every constitutional officer" and the president of the United States had asked the governor to resign. Although Rod Blagojevich had "a constitutional right" to "a fair trial and proof beyond a reasonable doubt" in court before being put in jail, "he does not have a constitutional right to be Governor," Ellis declared. "Being Governor is not a right, it is a privilege, and he has forfeited that privilege." Ellis said that "the people of this state have had enough," and they wanted to know if the state was going to begin "a new era." He asked rhetorically, "The people want to know are we finally going to turn the page?" (643–44).

After Ellis concluded his rebuttal, John Cullerton and Christine Radogno each requested an additional party caucus for one hour. The requests did not surprise the senators, but the observers in the galleries were intrigued by the request for an additional caucus. There was speculation that the senate did not want to deliberate and vote to remove Blagojevich until they were assured that the state plane had left Springfield and was on its way back to Chicago. Once Blagojevich was removed from office, he would no longer have access to the state plane, and getting back to Chicago could have been a problem for him.

When the senate returned from caucus, Justice Fitzgerald called the body to order and recognized Senator Rickey Hendon. Regardless of the illegality and consequences, Hendon had supported the governor's efforts to expand health care, the purchase of flu vaccines, and the prescription drug program for senior citizens. Hendon asked the chief justice to divide the articles of impeachment and allow a vote on the articles referring to these three programs on separate roll calls. "If you allow us this, your Honor, I think it will be in the best interest of justice," he said. Chief Justice Fitzgerald responded that the articles of impeachment had been drafted and passed by the Illinois house of representatives, and only that body "pursuant to their authority" under the Illinois Constitution could change them. Further, the senate trial rules prohibited the division of the question before the senate. Fitzgerald therefore denied Hendon's request. The chief justice then declared that "the time has come for the final action of this impeachment tribunal": the senate would deliberate before voting to remove the governor. He recognized senate president John Cullerton to preside over the final debate and called for David Ellis to accompany him out of the senate chamber (646–48).

The Last Day

Cullerton was acutely aware of the importance of the final debate. The entire trial would be judged by what took place as the senate deliberated. The senate trial rules committee had discussed whether the debate should be accomplished while the senate was sequestered, as in a normal jury procedure, or in an open forum. There were mixed opinions, but transparency won out, and the committee decided on an open forum. The Illinois Senate had never before removed an office holder, and both parties were conscious that the senate trial must be fair, nonpartisan, dignified, and above all, transparent. Both party caucuses also discussed what decorum and attitude they wanted to project during the debate. The tone of the discussion and the integrity of the trial were of paramount importance, but neither Democratic nor Republican leaders could predict what individual senators would say on the senate floor. Debates in the Illinois senate are not usually regarded as theaters of compelling rhetoric, but on this subject, thirty-seven senators—eighteen Republicans and nineteen Democrats— offered comments. Not one senator spoke in favor of Blagojevich.

The initial speaker is important in legislative debates, setting the guidelines and direction of the discussion. In routine legislative procedures, the sponsor of a particular initiative explains why the proposal is being presented and advocates for its passage. But this debate to decide the fate of a governor was anything but routine, and the initiative was not sponsored by any member of the senate but brought about through Illinois' constitutional provision that allows the house of representatives to bring impeachment proceedings for cause. It was the senate's role to hear the house prosecutor's arguments and make a judgment based on the evidence. Aware that the senate was approaching a highly emotionally charged issue, Cullerton wanted the lead speaker to provide the standard for debate, focus on the evidence, and recapitulate the presentations by the house prosecutor and the governor's response.

Cullerton recognized Senator William Haine. A Democrat from Alton, Haine was an ideal choice to establish the tone of the discussion. He had been a member of the committee that drafted the senate trial rules and had served in the Illinois senate since 2002. Before that he had served as Madison County's state's attorney for fourteen years. The gray-haired, bespectacled, modest grandfather represented the industrial southwestern area of the state, but he exuded the air of a genteel country lawyer. Always courteous in debate, he was respected in the Illinois senate for his integrity, honesty, and legal acumen. Now his remarks were to the point: the governor's statement before the senate offered no evidence contradictory to the charges presented in the impeachment articles. He pointed out that Blagojevich's failure to offer any opposing evidence was consistent with a "pattern of abuse . . . based upon an arrogant assumption of power." Haine characterized the governor's media appearances of the last month as "a dishonest effort to mischaracterize the proceeding here today and this past week." He urged the senate to disregard the governor's "presentation": "It is dishonest, and it should be rejected by the members of this Senate" (648–51).

Senator Dale Righter, also a member of the senate trial rules drafting committee, was the first Republican to speak. He recalled his thoughts and notes from the night before, stating that "representing the public is a public trust." Echoing Luechtefeld's earlier remarks concerning Blagojevich's performance, he said, "We heard a spell-binding performance today." He remarked on Blagojevich's ability to charm an audience and the empathetic, sometimes inspiring rhetoric that carried Blagojevich to the highest office in Illinois (651–52). He knew that the governor's public performances could be compelling and later found out that his district office in Mattoon received e-mails immediately after the governor's closing remarks, urging him to vote to acquit. But the former drug prosecutor looked at the evidence presented during the last four days and focused on the governor's words spoken on the FBI recordings. Appointed by Christine Radogno as the Republican deputy leader, Righter had long been known as a spokesman for senate Republicans. With extraordinary knowledge of legislation and the legislative process, his party could rely on him to present a probing challenge to the Democrats' legislative initiatives. This day, however, he spoke for a united senate. Both Democrats and Republicans shared a common revulsion toward what they had heard on the FBI recordings. For the lawyer who had chosen to study law at St Louis University because of "religious instruction as a component of the education of law," it was not a partisan issue, it was a moral issue of betrayed trust.[28] The governor's words exposed "a devious, cynical, crass and corrupt politician" (654).

Republican senator Matt Murphy was the next to speak. He was incensed by the governor's performance. Like Dale Righter, Murphy recognized Blagojevich's ability to distort and deceive: "He reminded us today in real detail that he is an unusually good liar." An experienced lawyer in private practice, Murphy had also served on the committee to draft the senate trial rules and had acted as a spokesman, defending the rules before the Chicago-based media. The practicing attorney took the governor's words

183

before the senate as a personal affront. "He lied about the process, that the rules that we put in place, that we adopted for this solemn occasion were unfair to him," he said. Murphy stressed that the rules of the trial were developed in a "nonpartisan" way and that the committee "bent over backwards to make this process fair for this governor." The governor's decision not to appear before the senate to refute the charges showed disrespect for the people of Illinois and for the Illinois Constitution, he said. His decision to "go on a media circus" was a choice that he would have to live with, but it was "disingenuous" for the governor to equate the decision not to appear with the fairness of the trail. As were most members of the senate, Murphy was especially repulsed by the attempted effort "to extort [money] from the caregivers of sick children." Murphy mentioned the rebuttal comments by David Ellis about Blagojevich on camera versus off camera. "He showed us the true test of his character on those tapes," Murphy said. He contended that the governor was "beneath the dignity of the State of Illinois" and was "no longer worthy to be our Governor" (661–64).

Several other senators shared similar thoughts, all agreeing that the governor should be impeached. Then Senator David Luechtefeld was recognized to speak. Luechtefeld had been a high school teacher coach when Frank Watson approached him to run for the senate. Reluctant at first, he eventually consented and was elected. An imposing figure with a gentle manner, he was universally respected by his colleagues. His remarks were influenced by his sense of propriety but also by his personal experiences with Blagojevich. He had dealt with the governor in the past and characterized his behavior on occasions as childlike and bizarre.[29] Luechtefeld recalled the conviction and sentencing of George Ryan, Illinois' previous governor. He remembered saying to his wife, "If this doesn't change anything in this state, then it's really not been worth it." Now Illinois was "faced with the same situation," he said, "and if this doesn't change the state and the culture of corruption that we obviously have had over the years, then it really hasn't been worth it." The governor had asked if he "deserved to be convicted and impeached" and argued that many of the charges against him had occurred during his first term. Luechtefeld reminded the senate that "an awful lot of people helped him win that last election . . . and sometimes people get what they deserve." He appealed to the senators, "Let's decide to make this a better state" (685–86).

Senator James Meeks, a Democrat from Chicago, was well known for his senate oratory. Meeks was an ordained minister, a community activist, and the pastor of the Salem Baptist Church, a predominantly black megachurch on Chicago's Far South Side. His colleagues in the legislature, statehouse staff, and lobbyists all called him Reverend Meeks. After taking office, the governor would on occasion, with much publicity, attend services at the Salem Baptist Church. The Sunday evening news would sometimes cover the governor sitting in the church, listening attentively to Reverend Meeks's sermon. At times Meeks led demonstrations in Chicago and the surrounding suburbs, and he had gained notoriety with the Chicago media. He was especially adamant about increased funding for Chicago schools and sought increased state support. He hesitated to back Blagojevich for a second term and threatened to run for governor himself to leverage his demands for increased money for Chicago schools. Meeks had the ability to attract a large number of black voters, and losing black votes was problematic for Rod Blagojevich, so he met with Meeks and assured him of a funding increase for the Chicago schools. Meeks did not run for governor and Blagojevich was reelected. The increased funding never came.

Now, to the senate, Meeks exclaimed with the resonating, stentorious voice of a preacher in the pulpit, "This is not a sad day for me; this is a great day." Speaking of the impeachment process, he explained that the state was "not ruled by angels" but "by human beings just like the rest of us," and that when those leaders step over the line "into criminal activity or abuse of power," "what a joy we have a process" to remove them. Meeks said that he was happy to participate in the impeachment process. "I say we have this thing called impeachment, and it's bleeping golden, and we've used it the right way" (728–29). Many in the galleries smiled at Meeks's paraphrase of Blagojevich's words on the FBI recordings.

Several others spoke. One of the last was Senator Frank Watson. The attention of the audience was amplified. Watson, who had served as the Republican minority leader for the past six years, had suffered a stroke in October 2008 and was undergoing rehabilitation when the governor was arrested. His recovery progressed such that he was able to return to the senate, but he knew his limitations. When the stroke occurred, he resigned as minority leader and endorsed the deputy leader, Christine Radogno, who was subsequently elected minority leader.

When Watson rose to speak, his personal and political burdens of the last six years and the weight of his recent affliction influenced his words. He struggled with the effects of his stroke—awkward balance, spontaneous emotions, and difficulty pronouncing words. Nevertheless, he tried to say it all and his thoughts flowed out, unrestrained by the decorum of the circumstance. The comic opera of the last six years was finally over. Watson spoke of his own failings to "work well" with Emil Jones and the need for cooperation between the two parties. Overcome by emotion as he congratulated the Republican staff and Auditor General Bill Holland for their work during the trial, he asked the senate's understanding. The task was difficult. He said that he "went toe to toe" with the governor and was proud of his caucus. Blagojevich had not looked at Frank Watson during his closing arguments, but Watson felt that the governor's words concerning the I-SaveRx program were directed at him. The governor called the program "helping kids," but Watson, the pharmacist, called it "counterfeit drugs from Canada."[30] He acknowledged that things "could have been different" and challenged John Cullerton to "continue to work together" with Christine Radogno (742–43). Compromised by his physical condition, the former Republican leader's talk was short. He did not need an extensive discourse. Everyone in the senate chamber knew Frank Watson, and they knew of his political and personal struggles. In sharp contrast to Blagojevich's failure to stir the senate and the spectators, Watson's short speech created a palpable air of compassion. Many wondered if the animosities and battles of the last six years had finally ended.

At the conclusion of an important debate, it is customary for the senate minority leader to make a final argument, followed by the senate president. Although little remained to be said, the quiet, conscientious, and capable Radogno expressed her pride in the way the senate had conducted the trial and her gratitude to the senate staff and Chief Justice Fitzgerald. Without hyperbole, her remarks addressed the evidence presented and emphasized that the house and senate processes had been "fair and open and thorough." She posited that the evidence made it clear that "Governor Blagojevich has abused his power repeatedly and over a long period of time. . . . We can all vote with a clear conscience to remove Governor Blagojevich from office" (745).

Rather than leave the rostrum and deliver the final remarks, Cullerton designated the senate majority leader, Democratic senator James Clayborne from Belleville, an experienced prosecutor who had served in the senate since 1995, to end the debate. Cullerton had purposely not played a public role in the impeachment trial.[31] He was conscious of the need to conduct the trial in a fair and open manner and was determined to avoid any appearance of political impropriety.

Clayborne's remarks, like Radogno's and Watson's, were brief. He was speaking more out of the requirements of senate protocol than out of necessity. Everyone wanted the proceedings to end. He made the point that the only testimony and documents presented to the senate were from the prosecution or the prosecution's witnesses, "and that's the only thing that we can base whether the Governor abused his power or whether or not he was involved in some criminal activities." To accentuate Blagojevich's failure to address the evidence against him, Clayborne spoke to an absent governor, asking why Blagojevich had not called his brother, Robert, to refute what FBI special agent Cain had said that the governor had "implied on the wiretap." Raising his voice, Clayborne confirmed, "You didn't refute it." Clayborne went through the litany of charges and asked why the governor had chosen not to answer any accusation. "You chose not to put on any evidence at all," he said, concluding, "I believe that, Governor, you are unfit." Clayborne ended his short remarks by referring to a lesson he taught his four sons: "I have sons, and I constantly remind them that you will be held accountable for your actions or your inactions, and in this case, Governor, you will be held accountable for your actions and your lack of actions" (746–50).

For a moment after Clayborne's remarks, an awkward silence overtook the chamber. The senate members sat quietly and the galleries remained still, as all those in attendance anticipated the final action. Many veteran observers in the galleries had witnessed hundreds of senate votes, but this moment was different. The highest official in Illinois government, elected by the sovereign will of the people, was about to be cast out of office.

Then Cullerton declared the debate concluded and told the senate sergeant at arms to inform the house prosecutor and the chief justice to return to the senate chamber. He relinquished the senate chair to Chief Justice Fitzgerald. The chief justice, in his usual prompt manner, proceeded to explain that under the senate impeachment rules adopted by SR 6, the senate would first vote to sustain the articles of impeachment. If the two-thirds majority vote required for the governor to be removed from office was not obtained, then a judgment of acquittal would be entered in the senate journal. If it was obtained, then the chief justice would announce a judgment of conviction, which would be entered in the senate journal, and the governor would be removed from office. Additionally, if a two-thirds vote to convict was obtained, the senate would take a second vote to disqualify Rod Blagojevich from holding future public office in the state, which would also require a two-thirds majority. Each senator would rise as his or her name was called and answer yes to convict or no to acquit, while simultaneously registering an electronic vote (750–52).

The chief justice instructed Deb Shipley, the secretary of the senate, to call the names of the senators and record their responses. As the names were called in alphabetical order, each proceeded to vote yes for conviction. When the secretary called the name of the senate president, the last to vote according to senate protocol, Cullerton rose and voted yes, making the vote unanimous. As soon as Cullerton said yes, Chief Justice Fitzgerald uttered the words that would render the senate's action official: "take the record." Whenever a recorded vote is taken, the presiding officer of the senate instructs the secretary to "take the record." The secretary records the vote upon hearing the pronouncement of the letter *d* in the word *record*. Cullerton had been intently focused on the vote tally board as he said yes, and the chief justice pronounced "take the record" before the senate president had a chance to press his electronic switch and confirm his voice vote. The electronic result was fifty-eight senators voting yes, as the senate president's vote was not recorded.

Some confusion and discussion followed, and Fitzgerald informed the secretary that the senate would redo the roll call. He then read the question a second time, asking the senate if they sustained the articles of impeachment. The vote the second time did not require each senator to rise and state his or her decision but was accomplished electronically. This time the vote was fifty-nine in favor of the question. The chief justice then uttered the words announcing the impeachment of an officeholder for the first time in the history of Illinois: "I now pronounce the judgment of conviction against Rod R. Blagojevich, thereby removing him from the Office of Governor effective immediately" (758).

The gravity of the situation was suspended momentarily when Fitzgerald immediately asked if there was a motion to disqualify the governor from holding future office in Illinois. Senator Michael Frerichs, a Democrat from Champaign, rose and made the motion. The secretary called the roll, and each senator responded in the same manner as in the first vote, both verbally and electronically. The vote was again unanimous: all fifty-nine senators voted yes.

The chief justice then said, "I now pronounce judgment of disqualification against Rod R. Blagojevich, thereby disqualifying him from holding any future public office of this state effective immediately," and announced that he was signing an order reporting the senate's judgment. He instructed the secretary of the senate to file the order with the secretary of state and officially notify the house of the senate's action (766).

The impeachment trial had come to an end, but the senate's procedural commitments postponed the chance for measured reflection, for a while at least. Fitzgerald thanked the senate for approaching the proceedings of the last four days with seriousness and said he was proud of their conduct. In the galleries, the spectators withdrew from their intense postures and seemed to relax. Cullerton and Radogno offered a resolution congratulating the chief justice for his efforts, and it was adopted. John Cullerton then moved that the senate arise from "sitting as an impeachment tribunal," and Fitzgerald declared that all matters of the impeachment had concluded (767–71).

Epilogue

As the state plane took off from the Illinois Aeronautics Terminal, on the north end of Abraham Lincoln Capital Airport in Springfield, it banked and flew northeast toward Chicago. Below, the corn and bean fields, barren in winter, stretched endlessly. Blagojevich was taking his last ride as governor. The phone rang but, according to the *New York Times* reporter on board, the governor instructed his aides not to answer it.[1] When the plane landed at Chicago Midway International Airport, it taxied to the west side. Not knowing whether the senate action had been completed, his state police bodyguards took him home for the last time.[2]

Outside Blagojevich's Northwest Side home, a small crowd had gathered and offered cheering support. The media covered all aspects of the governor's movements—at the airport, along the route, and at his home. With his wife by his side, Blagojevich offered a few brief statements to the press and the crowd. Then he entered the house, the door closed, and six years of political turmoil and kleptocratic administration in Illinois had come to an end. The senate had voted, and Rod Blagojevich was governor no longer.

The legislature had accomplished the unprecedented. It had exercised its prerogative and used its discretion to determine cause and remove Rod Blagojevich from office. It was a political act, but not an act of a passionate partisan majority, something the founders had feared. It is difficult to generalize why the vast majority of Democrats and Republicans overwhelmingly supported removal. Each legislator had personal reasons that prompted his or her decision to remove the governor. Blagojevich's methods of administration, disregard of the legislature, and bizarre behavior during his past six years as governor had alienated many. He had few supporters and several enemies. While some legislators felt that their past expressions of opposition toward Blagojevich were at last vindicated, few felt that they needed to settle a vendetta. The evidence for cause was overwhelming, and Blagojevich's arrest, expected indictment, and subsequent trial made his continued term as governor impossible. The few who were allied with Blagojevich sought political cover and voted with the majority to remove him. The action taken by the senate was unanimous, and in the house only the governor's sister-in-law had stood by him.

The rule of law is a central component to any theory of liberal constitutionalism, and it is a sacred component of the American system of government. But the actions of the Illinois legislature were not bound by the prescribed rule of law. The prerogative of impeachment and removal was granted to the legislature by the 1970 Illinois Constitution. The convention delegates provided only the tacit assumption that reasonable judgments would be made by virtuous people. The action of the legislature to impeach and remove was deemed by the constitutional convention to be discretionary.

Although the house hearings and the senate trial were not bound by the constraints of courtroom procedure, the legislative leaders did their best to follow the practice and precedent of the written law. During the house hearings, the governor was invited to appear, and the defense was allowed to submit witnesses and ask clarifying questions of the witnesses summoned by the house. The governor was also invited to participate in the trial and offer a defense, but he chose not to. The individuals who participated in the hearings and the trial were conscious of the sanctity of the rule of law. They did their best to adhere to the principle of due process and the written law while confronting extraordinary circumstances and exercising the constitutional prerogative to be outside the law.

Prerogative, it has been argued, is an extralegal means of serving the natural law. As Clement Fatovic said in *Outside the Law*, it is "not a substitute for law, but a supplement to law."[3] Prerogative is a means of meeting contingencies not addressed by the written law. "It was one thing to accept a certain level of necessary legality," wrote Fatovic; "it was an entirely different thing to tolerate any degree of calculated immorality."[4] Many of the Blagojevich administration's actions were characterized by gross incompetence and malfeasance. Moreover, the administration operated as a criminal enterprise, later substantiated by the convictions of the governor and his associates, with the governor receiving a sentence of fourteen years in prison. The action of the legislature was guided by the common-law maxim *salus populi suprema lex est*, "the welfare of the people is the supreme law."[5]

The impeachment and removal of Rod Blagojevich tested the Illinois Constitution, as well as the women and men of the Illinois legislature. By conferring the prerogative to impeach for cause, the delegates to the 1970 Constitutional Convention accepted that impeachment was "a political thing," but they had tacit faith that legislators would make "good political judgments."[6] Whether motivated by political circumstances or institutional constraints, the Illinois legislature has been remarkably restrained over the years. The leadership of both parties in the house and the senate understood the implications of removing the governor and the precedent it could set for themselves and for future office holders. Individual members of the legislature were deeply saddened, embarrassed, and angry.[7] For the legislative leaders, impeachment and removal remained the final option, and they acted quickly and decisively after the governor's arrest.

The impeachment and removal of Rod Blagojevich did not result from a movement or spirit and did not inaugurate a new chapter in Illinois' political process. There was no sustained public demand for a change in Illinois' political culture. Rather, removal was a rational, pragmatic response to a contingency. Blagojevich had exceeded the limits of realpolitik. He had allowed his administration, from the beginning, to operate as a criminal enterprise.

Notes
Index

Notes

Prologue

1. Rod Blagojevich, governor of Illinois, Executive Order No. 10, 2003, "Executive Order to Consolidate Facilities Management, Internal Auditing, and Staff Legal Functions," April 9, 2003.
2. Jeff Coen and John Chase, *Golden: How Rod Blagojevich Talked Himself out of Office and into Prison* (Chicago: Chicago Review Press, 2012), 163–72.
3. Ill. Const., art. 4, sec. 5.
4. John Fritchey, taped interview by the author, March 18, 2014.
5. Ill. Const., art. 4, sec. 14.
6. Ron Smith, interview by the author, May 15, 2014; Ann Lousin, interview by the author, May 15, 2014.
7. *Debates of the Constitutional Convention State of Illinois, 1870*, Springfield; Arthur Charles Cole, comp., *The Constitutional Debates of 1847*, 2 vols. (Urbana: University of Illinois Press, 1919). Cole used period newspapers as the basis for his synthesis. The debates of the 1862 convention were not collected in book form because the resulting constitution failed to be ratified. These debates can be found in issues of the Springfield newspapers the *State Journal* and the *State Register* published during the convention, both of which carried word-for-word coverage.
8. Cass R. Sunstein, *Designing Democracy: What Constitutions Do* (New York: Oxford University Press, 2001); Richard A. Posner, *An Affair of State: The Investigation, Impeachment, and Trial of President Clinton* (Cambridge,

MA: Harvard University Press, 1999); Roger Foster, *Commentaries on the Constitution of the United States: Historical and Judicial* (Boston: Boston Book Company, 1895).

9. Bernard H. Sieracki, *Order and Opportunity: The Development of the Illinois Railroad and Warehouse Commission* (Ann Arbor: ProQuest, 2008).

10. "Records of the Senate as a Court of Impeachment in the Trial of the Hon. Theophilus W. Smith," in *Journal of the Senate* (Vandalia, IL: Grelner and Sherman, 1833); Usher Linder, *Reminiscences of the Bench and Bar of Illinois* (Chicago: Chicago Legal News Company, 1879); John Palmer, *The Bench and Bar of Illinois* (Chicago: Lewis Publishing Company, 1899); Thomas Ford, *A History of Illinois: From Its Commencement as a State in 1818 to 1847* (1854; repr., Urbana: University of Illinois Press, 1995); Sieracki, *Order and Opportunity*.

1. The Crisis Erupts

1. Paul Meincke, taped interview by the author, August 14, 2013.
2. Andrew Porte, e-mail message to Paul Meincke, July 31, 2013.
3. Chuck Goudie, e-mail message to Paul Meincke, July 31, 2013.
4. Julie Unruh, telephone interview by the author, June 26, 2014.
5. Jim Durkin, taped interview by the author, January 15, 2013.
6. Ibid.
7. Jack Franks, taped interview by the author, February 6, 2013.
8. Fritchey, interview.
9. Ibid.
10. Andy Manar, taped interview by the author, January 24, 2012.
11. Clayton Harris, taped interview by the author, July 25, 2014.
12. Ibid.
13. Ibid.
14. Michael Madigan, taped interview by the author, November 16, 2013.
15. Ibid.; Larry Bomke, taped interview by the author, June 6, 2013.
16. Ill. Const., art. 5, sec. 6
17. David Ellis, taped interview by the author, October 15, 2012; Madigan, interview.
18. Ellis, interview.
19. Madigan, interview.
20. John Cullerton, taped interview by the author, July 14, 2014.
21. Madigan, interview.
22. Emil Jones, taped interview by the author, March 5, 2013.
23. Frank Watson, taped interview by the author, May 8, 2013.

24. Ibid.

25. Harris, interview.

26. Senator Michael Jacobs, taped interview by the author, February 13, 2013.

27. Watson, interview; Senator William Haine, taped interview by the author, February 26, 2014; Senator Dave Luechtefeld, taped interview by the author, April 18, 2013.

2. Cause for Impeachment

1. Ellis, interview; Madigan, interview.

2. Ill. Const., art. 4, sec. 14.

3. House rules established that all legislative initiatives are sent to the Rules Committee for assignment to committees and resolutions are sent to the full house for further consideration. The Rules Committee is controlled by the majority party. If an initiative is not voted out of the Rules Committee, it receives no further consideration.

4. Illinois House of Representatives, 95th General Assembly, Transcription Debate, December 15, 2008, http://www.ilga.gov/house/transcripts /htrans95/09500295.pdf.

5. Barbara Currie, taped interview by the author, December 17, 2012.

6. Madigan, interview; Ellis, interview.

7. Illinois Office of the Auditor General, *Management Audit of the Flu Vaccine Procurement and the I-SaveRx Program* (Springfield: Illinois Office of the Auditor General, 2006), 24(hereafter cited as *Management Audit*).

8. Ibid.; Illinois House of Representatives, Proposed Report of the Special Investigative Committee, 95th General Assembly, 2009, 35(hereafter cited as Proposed Report of the SIC).

9. Proposed Report of the SIC, 37.

10. *Management Audit*, 33, 36.

11. Proposed Report of the SIC, 38; *Management Audit*, 26.

12. *Management Audit*, 48.

13. Proposed Report of the SIC, 40.

14. Franks, interview.

15. Illinois HR Res. 394, 94th General Assembly (2005); Illinois HJ Res. 040, 94th General Assembly (2005).

16. Bill Holland, taped interview by the author, June 25, 2013.

17. Ibid.

18. *Management Audit*, Synopsis I.

19. Jack Franks declined to name the individual who contacted him. Franks, interview.

20. Illinois Office of the Auditor General, Department of Central Management Services Compliance Examination, April 1, 2005 (hereafter cited as Compliance Examination).

21. Proposed Report of the SIC, 44.

22. Compliance Examination, 12.

23. Franks, interview; Illinois House of Representatives, 95th General Assembly, House Impeachment Committee Transcript, December 18, 2008, 424, http://www.ilga.gov/senate/house%20impeachment%20records /Committee%20transcripts/Transcript%2012-18-08.pdf.

24. Compliance Examination, 16–17.

25. IPAM was contracted to catalog the state's assets. The principle owner of the company was the Chicago-based Mesirow Stein Development Services.

26. 30 ILCS 500/20–80(b).

27. Compliance Examination, 34.

28. Holland, interview.

29. Ibid.

30. Vicki Thomas, testimony, House Impeachment Committee Transcript, December 18, 2008.

31. Andrew Morriss and Robert Rich, testimony, House Impeachment Committee Transcript, December 18, 2008, 199–210.

32. An emergency rule is a procedure that is reserved for emergency situations and allows an agency to implement rules without immediate review by JCAR. The emergency rule is ultimately reviewed by JCAR and follows normal review.

33. Robert Rich, interview by the author, July 25, 2013.

34. Ibid.

35. Matt Brown, testimony, Illinois House of Representatives, 95th General Assembly, House Impeachment Committee Transcript, December 22, 2008, 603, http://www.ilga.gov/senate/house%20impeachment%20records /Committee%20transcripts/Transcript%2012-22-08.pdf.

36. Matt Brown, interview by the author, July 31, 2013.

37. Brown, interview.

38. Ibid.

3. The House Investigation

1. Jil Tracy, interview by the author, July 20, 2013.

2. Illinois House of Representatives, 95th General Assembly, House Impeachment Committee Transcript, December 16, 2008, 5–9, http://www

.ilga.govsenate/house%20impeachment%20records/Committee%20
transcripts/Transcript%2012-16-08.pdf.

3. Ibid., 10–11.
4. Edward Genson, taped interview by the author, May 6, 2013.
5. Illinois House of Representatives, 95th General Assembly, House Impeachment Committee Transcript, December 17, 2008, http://www.ilga.gov/
   senate/house%20impeachment%20records/Committee%20transcripts/
   Transcript%2012-17-08.pdf. This and subsequent page numbers in parentheses in this section are from this source.
6. Durkin, interview.
7. Madigan, interview.
8. Illinois House of Representatives, Committee Rules of the Special Investigative Committee of the 95th General Assembly, December 17, 2008, http://
   www.ilga.gov/house/committees/95Documents/Committee%20Rules%20
   of%20the%20Special%20Investigative%20Committee%20of%20the%20
   95th%20General%20Assembly.pdf.
9. Ali Ata pleaded guilty to tax fraud and making false statements to the FBI.
   He testified at the trial of Tony Rezko that he had made campaign donations to Blagojevich in direct exchange for an appointment as executive
   director of the Illinois Finance Authority and that he was cooperating with
   the federal prosecutors. Joe Cari was a former Democratic National Committee finance chairman and a director of Health Point, a private equity
   fund that received $35 million in investment contracts from the Illinois
   retirement system. In 2003, Cari pleaded guilty of attempting to extort
   money from JER, a real estate investment firm seeking an investment
   contract with the Illinois Teachers Retirement System. Cari also testified
   to scheming with Rod Blagojevich, Chris Kelly, and Rezko to develop an
   extortion plan to require individuals who received state contracts to make
   political contributions.
10. *United States of America v. Rod R. Blagojevich and John Harris*, US Dist.
    Ct., N. Dist. Ill., East. Div. (2008). Legislators used the words *criminal
    complaint* and *affidavit* interchangeably to refer to the court documents.
11. Illinois HB 824, 95th General Assembly (2008). HB 824 was passed by the
    Illinois legislature in 2008 and subsequently amended by the governor to
    include all members of the General Assembly. The legislature overrode the
    governor's amendatory veto, and HB 824 became law on January 1, 2009.
12. *US v. Blagojevich*. The Illinois Finance Authority (IFA) was created to "ac-
    complish and carry out policies of the State which are in the interest of the

State and of its taxpayers and residents." The IFA is authorized to accept state and federal funds for use in connection with the IFA's purposes.

13. Samuel P. Huntington, *American Politics: The Promise of Disharmony* (Cambridge, MA: Harvard University Press, 1981).

14. Alonzo "Lon" Monk initially declined to cooperate with federal prosecutors but later reconsidered. He pleaded guilty to wire fraud and testified against Rod Blagojevich in exchange for a recommended sentence of two years. In April 2012 he was sentenced to two years in prison. "Ex Blago Aide Lon Monk Sentenced to Two Years in Prison," *Chicago Sun-Times*, April 3, 2012.

15. Antoin "Tony" Rezko was a private businessman who became associated with Blagojevich prior to his election as governor. Rezko is credited with helping set up the Blagojevich administration. Tony Rezko never held an official position in state government, but he chose who served on state boards and was one of the most influential advisors in the governor's inner circle. He was charged in the federal fraud investigation known as Operation Board Games with twenty-four counts of wire fraud, bribery, money laundering, and attempted extortion. It was claimed that Rezko extorted millions of dollars from firms seeking to do business with the state. In 2008 he was found guilty of sixteen of the twenty-four charges, and in 2011 he was sentenced to ten and a half years in prison.

16. *US v Blagojevich,* 9, 16.

17. Ibid., 13–16.

18. Tracy, interview.

19. Illinois House of Representatives, 95th General Assembly, House Impeachment Committee Transcript, December 18, 2008, http://www.ilga.gov/senate/house%20impeachment%20records/Committee%20transcripts/Transcript%2012-18-08.pdf. These and subsequent page numbers in parentheses in this section are from this source.

20. Vicki Thomas, taped interview by the author, August 29, 2013.

21. Barry Maram said that he preferred not to discuss the impeachment hearings in a telephone conversation with the author, September 10, 2013.

22. Genson, interview. After agreeing to represent Blagojevich, Genson contacted Sam Adam Jr. and invited him to join the case. Genson had been a friend of Adam's father, Sam Adam Sr., and knew both men well. When Adam Jr. asked to include his father in the case, Genson refused at first but later consented. A rift over defense tactics developed quickly between Genson and the Adam father-and-son team, and as a result, Genson resigned from the case the following month.

23. Durkin, interview.

24. Illinois House of Representatives, 95th General Assembly, House Impeachment Committee Transcript, December 22, 2008, http://www.ilga.gov/senate/house%20impeachment%20records/Committee%20transcripts/Transcript%2012-22-08.pdf. These and subsequent page numbers in parentheses in this section are from this source.
25. David Ellis, taped interview by the author, January 28, 2014.
26. Durkin, interview. The person making the calls was never indicted, and Durkin chose not to reveal the person's name.
27. The criminal complaint referred to these people only by code names, such as Candidate A or B, and they had not been officially identified by the government, but the Chicago media speculated that Valerie Jarrett and Jesse Jackson Jr. were among the senate candidates discussed and that Nils Larsen was the Tribune Company executive.
28. Illinois House of Representatives, 95th General Assembly, House Impeachment Committee Transcript, December 29, 2008, http://www.ilga.gov/senate/house%20impeachment%20records/Committee%20transcripts/Transcript%2012-29-08.pdf. These and subsequent page numbers in parentheses in this section are from this source.
29. Genson, interview.
30. Durkin, interview.
31. Lou Lang, taped interview by the author, January 21, 2014.
32. Before he attempted to expand FamilyCare by executive edict, Blagojevich had tried to pass a gross receipts tax on all service transactions, intending to use the revenue from this tax to finance the FamilyCare expansion. The tax failed to garner a single vote in the house. The loss of the gross receipts tax was a major embarrassment for Blagojevich.
33. Coen and Chase, *Golden*.
34. Ibid., 202.
35. Illinois House of Representatives, 95th General Assembly, House Impeachment Committee Transcript, January 7, 2009, 890.
36. Ibid., 891.
37. Ill. Const., art. 5, sec. 6.
38. Coen and Chase, *Golden*, 307.
39. Genson, interview.
40. Durkin, interview.
41. Ibid.; Illinois House of Representatives, 95th General Assembly, House Impeachment Committee Transcript, January 8, 2009, 961–62, http://www.ilga.gov/house/committees/95Documents/January%208,%202009%20Transcript%20of%20Testimony%20from%20Roland%20Burris.pdf.

42. Durkin, interview.
43. House Impeachment Committee Transcript, January 8, 2009, 946–48.
44. Ibid., 966.
45. Ibid., 985.
46. Genson, interview.
47. Coen and Chase, *Golden*, 308.
48. Illinois Governor Impeachment Panel Vote, January 8, 2009, 1014.

4. The Impeachment Resolution

1. Illinois HR Res. 1671, 95th General Assembly (2009).
2. State of Illinois, 95th General Assembly, House of Representatives Debate Transcript, January 9, 2009, http://www.ilga.gov/house/transcripts/htrans95/09500300.pdf. This and subsequent page numbers in parentheses in this chapter are from this source.
3. Susana Mendoza, taped interview by the author, April 30, 2013.
4. David Miller, telephone conversation with the author, January 10, 2013.
5. Ibid.
6. For a discussion of the criteria for federal impeachment, see Sunstein, *Designing Democracy*.
7. Ellis, interview (2014).
8. Heather Wier Vaught, chief counsel to the Illinois house Speaker, interview by the author, December 27, 2013.

5. Senate Preparations

1. Cullerton, interview; Christine Radogno, interview by the author, December 5, 2012.
2. Radogno, interview.
3. Cullerton, interview.
4. Illinois S. Res. 966, 95th General Assembly (2008).
5. Cullerton, interview.
6. Eric Madiar, interview by the author, June 11, 2014.
7. Ibid.
8. House Resolutions 1, 2, and 3 dealt with house organizational matters.
9. Madiar, interview.
10. State of Illinois, 96th General Assembly, Senate Transcript, January 14, 2009, 20–21.
11. Ibid., 27.
12. The Illinois Senate has fifty-nine members, but Senator Frank Watson, the former Republican leader, was absent because of a recent illness.

13. Pam Althoff, interview by the author, May 29, 2014.

14. State of Illinois, 96th General Assembly, Senate Transcript, January 14, 2009, 48.

6. The Trial

1. Ellis, interview (2014).

2. Manar, interview.

3. Vaught, interview.

4. State of Illinois, 96th General Assembly, Senate Impeachment Tribunal Transcript, January 26, 2009, http://ediillinois.org/ppa/docs/00/00/00/01/51/44/20090209191257_1-26-2009Transcript-Approved.pdf. This and subsequent page numbers in parentheses in this section are from this source.

5. Coen and Chase, *Golden*.

6. See Gordon S. Wood, *Empire of Liberty* (New York, Oxford University Press, 2009), 422–24. Chase was impeached by the US House of Representatives in 1804 and tried in the US Senate in 1805. An outspoken Federalist, he was accused of criminal behavior and mistakes in procedure during one of his trials. He was charged with eight articles of impeachment. The Republican-controlled Senate managed to get a simple majority conviction on three of the articles, but could not reach the two-thirds necessary for conviction.

7. Althoff, interview.

8. *US v. Blagojevich*, para. 2.

9. State of Illinois, 96th General Assembly, Senate Impeachment Tribunal Transcript, January 27, 2009, http://ediillinois.org/ppa/docs/00/00/00/01/51/45/20090209191331_1-27-2009Transcript-Approved.pdf. This and subsequent page numbers in parentheses in this section are from this source; paragraph numbers are from *US v. Blagojevich*.

10. Coen and Chase, *Golden*, 395.

11. Coen and Chase, *Golden*.

12. Press release, Patrick Fitzgerald, "Businessman and Political Fundraiser Antoin Rezko Indicted in Two Fraud Cases . . . ," US Department of Justice, October 11, 2006.

13. Mathew A. Crenson, *The Federal Machine: Beginning of Bureaucracy in Jacksonian America* (Baltimore: Johns Hopkins University Press, 1975).

14. Coen and Chase, *Golden*.

15. Ibid., 163–64.

16. Levine was sentenced in July 2012 to sixty-seven months in prison. "Stuart Levine, a Key Figure in Blagojevich Case, Gets 67 Months in Prison," *Chicago Sun-Times*, July 19, 2012.

17. Coen and Chase, *Golden*, 181–82.

18. Steve Loren cooperated with the federal authorities and was sentenced to two years' probation for his role in the Mercy Hospital incident. Jacob Kiferbaum also cooperated with the federal authorities and was sentenced to twenty-seven months in prison. "Corrupt Attorney Who Cooperated in Blagojevich Probe Gets Probation," *Chicago Tribune*, September 19, 2012; "Final Board Games Defendant Faces Sentencing," *Chicago Tribune*, July 30, 2013.

19. Krozel subsequently testified at Blagojevich's criminal trial. Coen and Chase, *Golden*.

20. See also ibid., 239.

21. Ibid., 242.

22. Ibid., 205.

23. Lon Monk was representative of a type of lobbyist that has descended on Springfield in recent decades. Lobbyists are traditionally advocates of their clients' causes and represent their clients' points of view in the public debate. Traditional lobbyists are retained based on their understanding of the client's interests, knowledge of the legislative process, and ability to negotiate within the policy dialog. But during the last decade, Springfield has been inundated with individuals who sell their connections with powerful office holders. Such lobbyists usually have past relationships with the office holders. In some cases, the powerful office holder refers the lobbyist to potential clients, sometimes subtly but often overtly. The potential client, conscious of his own interests and issues, hires the lobbyist recommended by the office holder. The lobbyist provides the client with clout and direct access to decision makers. The arrangement with the office holder is ongoing. The office holder expects continued support from the lobbyist, and support usually comes in the form of campaign contributions from the clients. For the lobbyist and the office holder, this results in a plus-sum game. The office holder wins by ensuring a source of campaign money, and the lobbyist wins by attracting a list of high-paying clients. When Blagojevich took office in 2003, several people with no prior Illinois legislative experience suddenly appeared as lobbyists and had large lists of clients. After working in the Blagojevich administration, Monk became a lobbyist.

24. The conclusion in *US v. Blagojevich*, sec. 3, para. 117 reads:

> Based upon the facts set forth in this affidavit, I believe that there is probable cause to believe that: (a) Rod Blagojevich and John Harris, and others have conspired with each other and with others to commit

offenses against the United States, namely to devise and participate in a scheme to defraud the State of Illinois and the people of the State of Illinois of the honest services of Rod Blagojevich and John Harris, in furtherance of which the mails and interstate wire communications would be used, in violation of Title 18, United States Code, Sections 1341, 1343 and 1346; all in violation of Title 18, United States Code, Section 1349; and (b) Rod Blagojevich and John Harris, being agents of the State of Illinois, a State government which during a one-year period, beginning January 1, 2008 and continuing to the present, received federal benefits in excess of $10,000, corruptly solicited and demanded a thing of value, namely, the firing of certain Chicago Tribune editorial members responsible for widely-circulated editorials critical of Rod Blagojevich intending to be influenced and rewarded in connection with business and transactions of the State of Illinois involving a thing of value of $5,000 or more, namely, the provision of millions of dollars in financial assistance by the State of Illinois, including through the Illinois Finance Authority, to the Tribune Company involving the Wrigley Field baseball stadium; in violation of Title 18, United States Code, Sections 666 (a) (1) (b) and 2. Accordingly, it is requested that arrest warrants be issued as detailed in this affidavit.

25. Michael Kasper, taped interview by the author, February 10, 2014.
26. Madiar, interview.
27. Althoff, interview.
28. State of Illinois, 96th General Assembly, Senate Impeachment Tribunal Transcript, January 28, 2009, http://ediillinois.org/ppa/docs/00/00/00/01 /51/47/20090209191423_1-28-2009Transcript-Approved.pdf. This and subsequent page numbers in parentheses in this section are from this source.
29. Althoff, interview.
30. Harris, interview. Harris felt that Blagojevich took Cullerton's appearance before the press as a personal challenge. Blagojevich was someone who had to be the center of attention and considered himself always correct and always in charge, he said. When Cullerton implied that the governor's reluctance to come before the senate and instead go on national television was cowardly, Blagojevich, who looked at politics as individual combat, could not resist the challenge.
31. Ibid.
32. Cullerton's press secretary Rikeesha Phelon, interview by the author, July 1, 2014.

33. Dale Righter, taped interview by the author, February 13, 2013.
34. Madiar, interview.
35. Harris, interview.

7. The Last Day

1. Dale Righter, notes, January 28, 2009; Righter, interview.
2. Cullerton, interview.
3. Madiar, interview.
4. State of Illinois, 96th General Assembly, Senate Impeachment Tribunal Transcript, January 29, 2009, http://ediillinois.org/ppa/docs/00/00/00/01/51/48/20090209191510_1-29-09DRAFTTranscript-PendingApproval.pdf. This and subsequent page numbers in parentheses in this chapter are from this source.
5. Ellis, interview (2014).
6. Franks, interview.
7. Mendoza, interview.
8. Durkin, interview.
9. The Illinois Constitution provides that a governor can sign a bill, veto it, or make changes through an amendatory veto and send it back to the legislature.
10. Dawn Clark Netsch, telephone conversation with the author, November 16, 2012.
11. Jones, interview.
12. Coen and Chase, *Golden*.
13. The charge of a contribution for receiving the permit was corroborated by independent witnesses during the Rezko trial and later admitted by Tony Rezko.
14. Blagojevich confessed that he no longer wished to be governor and expressed frustration at being "stuck as governor."
15. Manar, interview.
16. Ibid.
17. Vaught, interview.
18. Illinois House of Representatives, Final Report of the Special Investigative Committee, 96th General Assembly, January 8, 2009, 54. *Rutan* prohibits the hiring, firing, promotion, transfer, or recall of a lower-level public employee on the basis of his or her party affiliation.
19. Blagojevich was a master on the campaign stump. A favorite story told of the time President Bill Clinton asked Blagojevich to travel with him on Air Force One. The first thing Rod Blagojevich, the kid from a Chicago

working-class neighborhood, did after boarding the president's plane was to call his mother. The symbols contained in the narrative served the desired image. The story associated Blagojevich with the prestige of the presidency and Air Force One. He was asked to fly with the president, which associated him with the popularity of Bill Clinton, and what was the first thing this kid from Chicago did when presented with the honor of flying with the president of the United States? He called his mother. Elderly women would smile. It worked with campaign audiences.

20. Monica Davey, "Blagojevich Has His Final Say, Making a Day of It," *New York Times*, January 30, 2009, 1.
21. Don Harmon, taped interview by the author, March 1, 2013.
22. Matt Murphy, interview by the author, April 10, 2013.
23. Luechtefeld, interview.
24. David S. Broder, "The Blagojevich Show: It's No Joke to Illinois," Opinions, *Washington Post*, January 29, 2009.
25. Cindy Grant, taped interview by the author, January 31, 2014.
26. Mike Kasper, taped interview by the author, February 10, 2014.
27. Ellis, interview (2014).
28. Righter, interview.
29. Luechtefeld, interview. One occasion that left a lasting impression was the day Luechtefeld met the governor by chance as they were leaving the capitol building after a legislative session. "Hey, coach," Blagojevich called out, using the moniker familiar to Luechtefeld's statehouse friends. In patronizing tones, the governor asked if there was anything he could do for him. The veteran senator was surprised and amused by the obvious insincerity. "Why in the world was he saying he wanted to do something for me?" Luechtefeld thought. Then, in a boisterous tone, the governor said there was someone he wanted the senator to meet. He took Luechtefeld over to introduce him to a member of the capitol security force. "This man is going somewhere in his life," the governor proclaimed. "Oh, really?" Luechtefeld said with an inquisitive inflection. To Luechtefeld's surprise, the governor asked the man to pull up his pant leg, revealing that his leg was tattooed with the name Elvis. Luechtefeld was bewildered and astonished, and he thought how inappropriate the scene was and how childish Blagojevich's behavior was. This was the governor of Illinois! Blagojevich was fascinated with the entertainer Elvis Presley and surrounded himself with Elvis memorabilia. In meetings with legislators he often quoted lines from Elvis Presley movies that were completely unrelated to anything being discussed.

30. Watson, interview.
31. The governor lived in Cullerton's district but had become a frequent critic of the new senate president. Despite the residential proximity and similar Chicago political experiences, the two men were vastly different and their relationship was strained. Cullerton was not a member of Emil Jones's leadership team and had no association with the past alliance between Jones and the governor.

Epilogue

1. The governor had invited a reporter and a photographer from the *New York Times* to accompany him on his last day. The *New York Times* personnel paid their own expenses. *New York Times*, January 30, 2009.
2. Ibid.
3. Clement Fatovic, *Outside the Law: Emergency and Executive Power* (Baltimore: Johns Hopkins University Press, 2009), 41.
4. Ibid., 19. Fatovic was addressing executive power and emergency contingencies, but his premise is applicable to actions by the Illinois legislature in regard to Blagojevich.
5. Robert Novak, *The People's Welfare* (Chapel Hill: University of North Carolina Press, 1996), 9–10.
6. Smith, interview.
7. Althoff, interview.

Index

Page numbers in italics denote images.

Index

Index

Index

Index

Index

Bernard H. Sieracki teaches public administration at the University of Illinois at Chicago. He also teaches at the Stuart School of Business, Illinois Institute of Technology, Chicago. Prior to teaching, Sieracki was an Illinois lobbyist for nearly four decades. He received his PhD from the University of Illinois at Chicago.